D0343425

DISTRICT CLERK
300 N. GRANT ST.   ROOM 301
ODESSA, TEXAS 79761- 5158

PLACE
STAMP
HERE

JUROR'S RIGHTS AND RESPONSIBILITIES   NOVEMBER 1, 2010

Right to Reemployment: A private employer may not terminate the employment of a permanent employee because the employee serves as a juror. An employee whose employment is terminated in violation of this section is entitled to return to the same employment that the employee held when summoned for jury service if the employee, as soon as practical after release from jury service, gives the employer actual notice that the employee intends to return. (Civil Practice and Remedies Code, Section 122.001).

Failure to Answer Summons and Penalties: A person who fails to comply with this summons is subject to a contempt action punishable by a fine of not less than $100 nor more than $1,000. (Government Code, Section 62.0141). Additionally, a person shall be fined not less than $10 nor more than $100 if the person: (1) fails to attend court in obedience to the notice without reasonable excuse; or (2) files a false claim of exemption from jury service. (Government Code, Section 62.111).

Proper Clothing Required: All persons entering the courtroom should be dressed in clothing reasonably befitting the dignity and solemnity of the court proceedings.

Exempt or Disqualified: You do not need to appear in person if you are exempt or not qualified for jury service. To claim an exemption or report your disqualification you must complete the "Exemptions From Jury Service" form, sign it and mail or personally bring it immediately to the address printed on the back of the return card.

GENERAL QUALIFICATIONS FOR JURY SERVICE (Government Code, Section 62.102)	EXEMPTIONS FROM JURY SERVICE * (Government Code, Section 62.106)
To serve as a juror you *must* meet qualifications: you must 1. be at least 18 years of age; 2. be a citizen of this state and a resident of the county in which you are to serve as a juror; 3. be qualified under the Constitution and laws to vote in the county in which you are to serve as a juror *(Note: you DO NOT have to be registered to vote to be qualified to vote)*; 4. be of sound mind and good moral character; 5. be able to read and write; 6. not have served as a juror for six days during the preceding three months in the county court or during the preceding six months in the district court; 7. not have been convicted of theft or any felony; and 8. not be under indictment or other legal accusation of a misdemeanor theft, felony theft or any other felony charge.	You *may* be excused from jury service if: 1. you are over 70 years of age; 2. you have legal custody of a child or children younger than 10 years of age and service on the jury would require leaving the child or children without adequate supervision; 3. you are a student at a public or private high school; 4. you are enrolled and attend college; 5. you are an officer or an employee of the Senate, the House of Representatives, or any department, commission, board, office, or any other agency in the legislative branch of state government; 6. you are the primary caretaker of a person who is an invalid unable to care for himself or herself. (This exemption does not apply to health care workers.) * You are not required to claim an exemption. It is your choice.

I DO HEREBY CERTIFY UNDER PENALTY OF PERJURY THAT I AM

☐ DISQUALIFIED because of the reason circled above   ☐ EXEMPT because of the reason circled above

Date: _____

Summons Number

658

02 1M
000 4275654
OCT 21 2010

60.02

Please sign here:

"Those adults blessed with the privilege of programming our next generation of leaders should read this book right now! Dr. Tim Elmore's research into the iY phenomenon provides insightful information why many young adults are struggling with their transition to adulthood as well as offers strategies to help them acquire the necessary tools for success."

JOSEPH R. CASTIGLIONE · *Vice President for Intercollegiate Athletics, University of Oklahoma*

"In my experience as a mother and senior corporate executive, I know the importance of bringing along the next generation of leaders. Dr. Tim Elmore outlines a solid plan of action. To date I have not found another book that equips a parent, employer, or educator to accomplish this task. This one gets it done! A must read for anyone in the position of growing future leaders."

TAMI HEIM · *Mother of a 23-year-old daughter,*
Former president, Borders Inc.
Partner, The A Group Brand Development

"I have admired the work of Tim Elmore and his passion to train future leaders. He has incredible insights into the unique challenges of the iY generation and we've benefited from them at the University of Alabama. This book will help you understand their worldview and how they live, think, and learn. If you are a teacher, parent, coach, youth worker or employer, this is a must-read for you. Tim's honest approach will help identify alarming concerns with practical solutions."

KEVIN ALMOND · *Associate Athletics Director – Support Services*
University of Alabama

"Dr. Elmore has committed a lifetime to the development of young leaders. He models passion, intelligence, creativity, discipline, and a relentless dedication for this cause. His recent work, Generation iY, *is both profound and thought-provoking. Tim challenges all of us to be more engaged with the youth of our world to produce a fulfilling future not only for their generation but for generations to come."*

DR. JOHN GREEN · *Area Superintendent, Gwinnett County Public Schools*

"Dr. Tim Elmore's insight into this generation is mind-boggling. The statistics are clear and sobering. This is a must-read for any adult with influence in the lives of today's youth. Every parent, teacher, youth leader, coach and influencer should take a hard look at this study of the next generation. The game plan outlined in Generation iY *will leave you motivated and encouraged to impact this unique group."*

CRAIG GROESCHEL · *Senior Pastor, LifeChurch.tv and Author,* The Christian Atheist

"This book is a clarion call to adult leaders to think critically about the environment in which a new generation is developing, to create teachable moments for engaging these students, and to courageously call them to leadership—living beyond themselves and for the common good. For more than a decade, Tim Elmore's relevant, well-researched concepts on leadership, and his practical and sustainable solutions for influencing the next generation, were a tremendous resource for me as a student affairs leader working to develop students."

WAYNE BARNARD, PhD · *Director of Student Ministries, International Justice Mission*

"Our children are our future leaders. My wish is that all children would be provided a strong foundation so they could grow up to be responsible adults who love who they are, care for and respect others and enjoy what they do. This journey starts with helping children develop good character. I see so many parents starting well with their children, but as they grow, some begin to play defense, rather than offense. Tim Elmore helps us understand what young people need today—from parents, teachers, coaches and employers. This book will reveal what we must avoid and what we must embrace to enable our children to become little leaders that mature into adult leaders."

JO KIRCHNER · *President and CEO, Primrose School Franchising Company*

"Tim Elmore understands Gen Y. He also understands what our role is in leading and shaping this next generation of leaders. A cultural shift is taking place, and we must be educated, aware and prepared for our role. Generation iY provides the insight we all need."

BRAD LOMENICK · *Executive Director, Catalyst*

"Tim's mission has always been to grow leaders—when I was on a campus, I often called on him to facilitate leadership development training for my staff, so that they could provide the appropriate balance of challenge and support for university students. In my role with the CCCU, I'm on campuses throughout the nation, meeting leaders who are tasked with developing and educating the iY Generation—this book is a terrific resource for those interested in equipping this generation of students to their fullest potential."

DR. MIMI BARNARD · *Vice President for Professional Development and Research Council for Christian Colleges & Universities*

Generation iY

Generation iY
Our Last Chance to Save Their Future

Tim Elmore

Poet Gardener
PUBLISHING

Published in Atlanta, Georgia, by Poet Gardener Publishing in association with Growing Leaders, Inc.
www.GrowingLeaders.com

ISBN: 978-0-578-06355-3
Printed in the United States of America

Library of Congress Cataloguing-in-Publication Data

To the parents,
      teachers,
      coaches,
      employers,
      youth workers,
      retailers,
      pastors, and
      nonprofit executives
      who will make the changes necessary to lead this generation well.

"If you want happiness for a lifetime, help the next generation."

—CHINESE PROVERB

Contents

Foreword—Dan Cathy, President of Chick-fil-A   9

1. **A Peek into the Future**
    A Letter from a Father to His Son in the Year 2030   11

2. **Adjusting the Sails**
    A Closer Look at Generation iY   17

3. **Aftershock**
    Responding to the Cultural Shift   29

4. **Tollbooth or Roadblock?**
    Why iY Kids Are Getting Stuck in Adolescence   53

5. **Lost in Neverland**
    The Special Challenges of iY Boys   73

6. **Volcanoes and Karaoke**
    The Struggle of a New Generation of Parents   93

7. **Elephant Lessons**
    Amending the Lies We Have Told Generation iY   109

8. **My Crystal Ball**
    Predictions for Generation iY in the Workplace   125

9. **The Hinge of History**
    What We Can Expect from Generation iY Worldwide   141

10.   **A Compass, Not a Map**
      Helping Generation iY Find Their Future   155

11.   **The Care and Feeding of a New Generation**
      EPIC Ideas for Educating iY Kids   171

12.   **Saving The Future**
      Unleashing Their Leadership Potential   189

Acknowledgments

Notes

A Word about Growing Leaders

About the Author

Foreword

THE BOOK YOU HOLD IN YOUR HANDS IS A WAKE-UP CALL. It is a much needed dose of reality about the serious challenges facing what author Dr. Tim Elmore describes as "Generation iY."

This emerging generation literally is the future of America. Yet they are uneasy about the future. They are juggling way too many balls and are being ambushed by adulthood. The pressure is intense, and the stakes are high.

In many ways, I believe they are under attack -- culturally, morally, technologically, spiritually and in other areas. Tim's book explores all of these issues and how the Boomers and Gen Xers in America can better engage with the iYs. We all have an influential role to play in nurturing this next generation. We must act with a real sense of urgency and a genuine sense of purpose.

Influence is a word we frequently talk about at Chick-fil-A. There are many definitions of influence. I believe influence is simply making a difference in another person's life. This person, in turn, freely models your actions and influences others. Influence builds over time. It is boundless and fearless. It is unmistakable and undeniable. Tim Elmore's widespread work, motivated by sincere care and concern for all generations, is all about influence.

I believe Tim has been called to use his influence to pour into our children and grandchildren with the global character-building work he does. We need more Tim Elmores in the world today. I am grateful to have him as a friend and to have him in partnership with Chick-fil-A and our many endeavors to grow leaders.

Our company knows the iY generation up close. We have the best of the best working for us -- about 50,000 iY strong. We develop them, encourage them, believe in them, and empower them, resulting in CFA having the highest rated customer service reputation in the world. It is a privilege and also an awesome responsibility that we take to heart with the scholarships, camps and other initiatives we fund.

My hope is that the parents, teachers, pastors, coaches and employers reading *Generation iY: Our Last Chance to Save Their Future* will take what Tim has to say seriously and thoughtfully. Reading it is only the first step, however. The second step is essential. Apply it. Take what you learn from Tim and put it into motion. Read and apply.

I have been blessed to have a father, Truett Cathy, Founder of CFA, who is not only my role model, but who is the role model for so many others in his approach to raising families and building a business. Dad is so wise and exudes common sense and integrity.

He joins me in thanking Tim for writing a book full of insight and wisdom. He joins me in suggesting that you spread the word about *Generation iY: Our Last Chance to Save Their Future* and its relevant findings and profound truths.

May God bless the iY Generation. The future will be resting on their shoulders. Let's all do what we can to help them be the positive influential generation they can be for their children and grandchildren. The clock is ticking. We can do it...together!

Strength for the journey.

DAN T. CATHY
President and COO
Chick-fil-A, Inc.

1 A Peek into the Future
A Letter from a Father to His Son in the Year 2030

June 21, 2030

Dear Son,

Congratulations on your baby-to-be! I remember the feeling your mom and I had when we discovered you would be born, way back in 1992. I know, I know—it was another century. But I remember the anticipation and the angst we felt knowing we were about to introduce another child into this world.

I've intended to say something to you for a long time but never found the words. I guess it's easier for me to write them than to say them to your face. I know it sounds cliché, but you'll be raising your child in such a different world than the one you grew up in. Everything's changed. In your early years, life seemed so easy; you were on top of the world. We hovered over you, intending to pave the way for your college and your career. We wanted you to know we believed in you; that you were special and could do anything you set your mind to. We wanted your self-esteem and self-confidence to be rock solid.

Looking back, I realize that in our efforts to help you, we actually hurt you. Please know, we meant well. As I ponder your situation now, with your marriage contract ending this month, I can see you're in a difficult spot. What's more, because we let you move back home with us after college, you weren't prepared for the world that awaited you. We just didn't know what to do. You depended on the meds to get you through each week, you lacked a realistic plan (what with the economy in 2014), and you were as addicted to video games then as you are today. We couldn't seem to find a way to prepare you for the future you now face. Now it's too late to change things.

Son, I feel I have failed you. With all the help your mother and I tried to give you, we ended up doing just the opposite. We hindered you from becoming the best version of you possible.

All of this hit me like a ton of bricks last night. I watched a documentary on culture change, and I was shocked to see the impact my generation (parents, teachers, coaches, youth workers, retailers, and employers) has had on yours. The program painted an all-too-familiar picture of you and so many of your friends:

- *Adults living in isolation because they can't stick with their marriage contracts—even those short-term contracts that have become so popular.*
- *Social media junkies with little to no emotional intelligence or people skills.*
- *Obese adults who are stressed and don't have the discipline to eat right and exercise.*
- *Nearly an entire generation addicted to "happy pills" because of chronic anxiety and depression.*
- *A generation of adults we allowed to pass through school without really learning.*
- *People confused about their gender and identity because of the BPA you all consumed.*
- *Midlife adults who are in a "love you hate you" relationship with their parents. (I keep wondering if that's true of us.)*

All this saddens me because it's so unnecessary. With the baby coming, now it's your turn to lead, and I fear you aren't ready. We let you down.

What scares me most is the violence today. In 2010, we all began to read about the youth bulge. Your generation worldwide is huge. Remember what I told you then? When a nation's population of young people is over 30%, violence almost always follows. I'm afraid the terrorism you've seen in the last twenty years will only get worse due to the sheer size of your generation.

Son, I hope you can forgive me—forgive us—for not leading you better. But more important, I hope you can somehow make up for our mistakes. You're about to become a dad and make me a granddad. Please lead this little one well. Do better than we did in raising the next generation. It may be our only chance to save our future.

I love you,
Dad

Is the letter you've just read fiction?

Maybe.

It's a product of my imagination—but it's an informed imagination. The ideas aren't far-fetched. They represent a future that could well be a reality if adults today don't do something different to engage the generation of kids now coming down the pike.

A few years ago, I had a hunch. I met with adults and young people to talk about the year 2030. I talked to parents, educators, youth workers and employers as well as futurists who have been studying the next generation. I also met students in focus groups and wrote to thousands via Facebook, blogs, and e-mail. I especially wanted to hear what young people foresee as they peer into the next twenty years. From all those interactions, I have gotten a glimpse into the possible future of the kids who are approaching adulthood right now.

To be honest, I'm worried about what I've seen.

I have worked with young people for more than thirty years now—as an educator, a parent, a mentor, and an employer. Until fairly recently, I have remained quite optimistic about their future. But these days I'm feeling something different. I am frightened about what the world may look like in years to come and angry at how we have failed the generation who will be running that world.

They are your kids. They are your neighbor's kids. They are your students. They are your athletes. They are your young employees. They are your future. Our future.

They are Generation iY.

And I believe they're in trouble.

Introducing Generation iY

The people I'm talking about are the latest wave of what is commonly called Generation Y, or the Millennials, generally defined as those born between 1984 and 2002. The younger Millennials, born after 1990, resemble their earlier Gen Y counterparts in many ways, but in volumes of other ways they stand in stark contrast to them. (I'll discuss this later in more detail.) More than any previous group, this younger population has been defined by technology—which is why I believe it's accurate to call them Generation iY.

Why this title? It's because of the tangible impact of the "i" world (the Internet) on their lives. This population, born in the 1990s and afterward, has literally grown up online. Theirs is the world of the iPod, iBook, iPhone, iChat, iMovie, iPad, and iTunes. And for many of them, life is pretty much about "I."

The Future in a Word

What will Generation iY's future be like? After talking with thousands of students about what they think, I've come up with twenty-six phrases we could hear from adults in the year 2030. Some are tongue-in-cheek, some more likely than others, but together they paint a sobering picture of what life will be like for Generation iY unless something changes.

1. "I'm really tired."
2. "I'm distracted."
3. "I'm obese."
4. "I'm on my fifth career and ninth job in a decade."
5. "I'm overwhelmed, but I'm dealing with it."
6. "I'm impatient. I make short-term commitments."
7. "I'm finishing a marriage contract of three years."
8. "I'm reinventing myself constantly."
9. "I have no innocence."
10. "I'm seeing a therapist."
11. "I love and hate my parents."
12. "I'm bored."
13. "I'm spending money out of control— a quarter of a million each month."
14. "I'm depressed."
15. "I'm self-absorbed."
16. "I spend much of my home time online."
17. "I'm living in a greener world."
18. "I'm passionately following the reunion tour of Beyoncé and Lady GaGa."
19. "I'm stressed. I have little time to rescue my soul."
20. "I pursue instant pleasure and entertainment and will spend to get it."
21. "I'm medicated."
22. "I'm living in a virtual world. (I plan to try a virtual marriage.)"
23. "I've learned to do things faster. My pace of life is accelerated."
24. "I experiment with preferences in gender and religion."
25. "I still want to change my world, but I'm cynical about the possibilities."
26. "I'm a leader in society now, but I'm ill-prepared."

On Earth Day in 2009, you may remember a new automobile was introduced to America, the Peapod. It was, in essence, an iCar. You start the car by plugging in your iPod or your iPhone and begin interacting. It's a new world—an iWorld—and it belongs to young people who have grown up in the last decade of the twentieth century and the first decade of the twenty-first. They are connected not only by age, but by shared music, shared tragedies and crises, shared Web sites and TV programs, shared heroes, shared technology, shared wars, and shared media icons.

Ready or not, they are now entering the adult world. And unless we wake up and make some adjustments in the way we interact with them, I predict rough waters ahead. We can already see several of the unintended consequences of this new world we've created for them— a world that allows for high speed, constant connection, sedentary lifestyles, pitiful relational skills, and a large dose of narcissism.

I can't say for certain that my fictional letter will come true. If current trends continue, however, the picture I've painted might just become a reality.

But it's not too late. The future of Generation iY has the potential to change for the better if we act now.

That's why I've written this book. It's for parents, teachers, coaches, youth workers, retailers, pastors, employers—anyone in the position to lead Generation iY. Although it contains some bad news—some honest indictments about the way this generation of kids is being raised—it's primarily a book of hope. It's full of practical ideas for understanding iYers, engaging them effectively, and leading them wisely.

We've got to do it.

Their future—our future—depends on it.

> ➤ **LINKING UP** ◄
>
> For a mini-novel that tells the story of a high-school reunion in the year 2030 and vividly portrays the potential lifestyles of Generation iY, see **www.SaveTheirFutureNow.com/2030**.

2 Adjusting the Sails
A Closer Look at Generation iY

I SAW A MASTER SAILOR AT WORK IN JANUARY OF 2010, when I was part of a team that trained youth workers in Egypt. During our stay in Cairo, we got in a sailboat for a tour on the Nile River. It was interesting to watch our guide navigate his way down the river. He struggled at first, attempting to figure out which way the winds were blowing at the time. Once he did, some turns were fast, and others—not so much. It was work. Twice he stopped to rest, and we almost drifted into the banks of the river. Needless to say, he stayed quite busy—but he did get us there.

In one sense, this new generation of young people is like the wind. They are gusting in all directions, causing quite a stir in the workplace, their schools, and at home. Sometimes their overconfidence or impatience can burst out of them with hurricane force. Yep, the generational winds are blowing hard.

Now, let me ask you a question. Wouldn't it be strange for an experienced sailor to sense the wind blowing in the wrong direction and begin to yell at it? Please indulge me for a moment and imagine this scenario. Picture a sailor who gets so upset at the changing winds that he stands up in his boat and begins to shake his fist and scream in anger, lecturing the wind about proper direction and how it ought to help sailors while they are out at sea? Or wouldn't it be pitiful for the sailor to simply throw up his hands and sit down, surrendering to the wind? Or worse, what if he told his crew that since the wind wasn't cooperating, they were helpless; they couldn't do a thing but let the wind take the boat wherever it wanted?

As ridiculous as this sounds, this is what many adults have done with young people today. They have shaken their fist at the wind, or they've given up trying to do anything with it.

I have spoken to employers who told me they will never hire another recent graduate. I have heard teachers say they can hardly wait for retirement since they can't do a thing about kids today. I've had parents confide in me that they don't know what to do with their kids except scream at them.

Because I am a parent, a teacher, and an employer, I can identify with each of these reactions. But I've come to understand that the youth population is a bit like the wind on the sea—and good sailors know what to do with that wind. In fact, they actually use it to propel the boat where they want it to go.

They don't change their goal, in other words. They just adjust the sails.

And that's my whole point in writing this book—not to vent anger at kids today, but to illustrate how the winds have changed for young people and how we, as adults, must adjust our sails if we have any hope of taking our society where it needs to go. I believe there is a potential for crisis if we don't make some adjustments. But there is also incredible opportunity, and there's plenty that we adults can do—that we *must* do—to make it happen.

Let me get personal with you. I am deeply concerned, as a dad and as a leadership trainer who is in front of fifty thousand students every year, about the iY generation that's just beginning to enter the adult world. I believe in these young people, but I meet far too many adults who have given up on leading them well, and this scares me. These students have far too much confidence and far too little experience to be left to their own devices.

Generation iY has so much to offer, but they need direction—mentors who engage them in a relevant way, channel their energy, and provide them with the challenges they need.

Who Is Generation Y (and iY)?

They're the children of the late Baby Boomers and the early Gen-Xers—born between 1984 and 2002. And while experts differ on what to call them, all agree they're bound to change the way we approach life. Here are some common names for this powerful generation.

- The Digital Generation
- The Internet Generation
- Nexters
- Screenagers
- Echo Boomers
- Mosaics
- Sunshine Generation
- Bridgers
- Millennials

Portrait of a Generation

I don't know why you picked up this book, but I do know one thing: the subject of this book will affect you and everyone you know in the next fifteen to twenty years. The year 2030 is not that far away. Even if you have no interest at all, or no connection at all with this next generation of kids—you will be affected by how these kids turn out.

✱ Generation iY will be the largest in earth's history, and iY kids are the largest portion of that generation. Already, nearly half the world's population is under twenty-five years old. That represents about three billion people. In America, their numbers already rival that of the Baby Boomers, and with immigration—which is a wildcard—their population may grow as large as a hundred million, nearly a third of our total population.

Generation iY is also the most eclectic and diverse in our nation's history, as well as the most protected and observed. They are also the first generation that doesn't need leaders to get information; they have electronic access to every piece of data you can imagine.

All this will either turn out to be good news or bad news as they migrate into adulthood. In fact, let me tip my hand right now at the beginning of this journey. My research reveals there are four words that describe the reality of Generation iY. They are:

An Overwhelmed Generation

In 2007, the American College Health Association surveyed the largest randomized sample of college students since its inception. Their study revealed that:

- *94 percent of students reported feeling overwhelmed by their lifestyles.*
- *44 percent said they felt so depressed it was almost difficult to function.*
- *Almost 10 percent had considered suicide in the past year.*[1]

The stress comes from both internal and external sources. Many of these kids grew up with parents who put the pressure on them to perform. After all, the child is a reflection on their parents. Parents want a trophy to show off as their offspring enters adulthood.

On the other hand, stress can also stem from a lack of healthy pressure growing up. Children who lived with undue comfort through high school may face a shock when they enter college and face demands that are a little closer to adult life. The transition from the life of ease to a more demanding adult world can lead to stress.

Another source of stress, however, can be self-imposed. Children over the last twenty-five years have internalized a fierce competitive sense. They want to be the best. And from the time they're small, they've been told that they *are* the best—they are special, they have unlimited potential. Trying to live up to those expectations is inherently stressful.

I met Nate at the hospital last year. He was being released with instructions to stay on his medication. Nate had admitted himself when he had a panic attack and began to entertain thoughts of suicide. He was only nineteen years old.

When we conversed over a latté that day, Nate told me why he'd decided to check in to the hospital. He felt pressured and overwhelmed. He had no job and really needed one. His dad had been out of work for four months due to the failing economy. Nate's GPA had dropped, and so had his chances at getting into Georgia Tech—something both he and his mom wanted desperately. In fact, his mom was counting on it, and Nate couldn't imagine disappointing her. But whenever he tried to focus on his studies, he got grief from his girlfriend and friends on Facebook because he rarely had time to hang out like he used to.

Nate had finally buckled under all that pressure. He is among a large population of teens who feel this way.

According to researchers Howe and Strauss, 70 percent of teenagers "worry a lot" about finding a good job when they get out of school, whereas only 37 percent of adults think that teens worry about that. Four times as many high school students worry about getting good grades as worry about pressures to have sex or take drugs, and six times as many complain they don't get enough sleep.[2]

Perhaps sixteen-year-old ice skater Sarah Hughes said it best. After winning her gold medal at the 2002 Olympic Games, she reflected, "Sometimes I feel more pressure than maybe I should, because I know there are so many people who want me to do well."[3]

What if this generation grows up and never finds a healthy way to handle all this pressure? What if, as adults, they continue to seek and find artificial ways to cope? Will America have a large percentage of adults with chronic depression? Will the majority of adults in twenty years be addicted to prescription drugs as a means to handle feeling overwhelmed? What if they perpetually yearn to return to their adolescent years—to escape marriages, job commitments, and legal obligations? What if adult life just doesn't suit them well because we didn't prepare them to be adults?

I wonder if we'll see normal responsibilities today reduced to bite-sized chunks in the future: McJobs. McMarriages. McCommitments. Marriage licenses may have three- and five-year contract options. Perhaps their children will have six fathers, because each successive "dad" was only able to commit for three years. Jobs may be reduced to serial contractual projects—partly because of changes in the job market, but also as a manageable response to feeling overwhelmed.

An *Overconnected* Generation

Young people tend to respond in one of two ways to being overwhelmed.

One, they push back and get lost in a virtual world of online fantasy video games or a social world of texting, Facebook, and Twitter. It's a coping mechanism. They survive by escaping reality and becoming someone else.

Or, option two, they respond by trying to measure up. They push themselves to be a "superkid." They go online to perform. They strive for perfection.

With either response, we may have a train wreck ahead of us.

Some call this generation the "connecteds." Instead of using their youthful years to discover who they are and develop a lasting set of values to live by, they may become adults who can't make it unless they are constantly on Twitter with their friends. Noise. Busyness. Connection. Talk. Volume. Speed. When will they ever unplug and discover their own identity? Will they ever experience the solitude that enables them to think or reflect on their lives? Will they become a generation so connected that they just parrot what peers are saying in their social network? Or will they be individuals who can think and act on their own without consensus from others?

The train wreck may also take the form of miserable relationship skills and low emotional intelligence. Because so much of their life is connected by technology, young people can fail to develop face-to-face people skills. Texting, for instance, just doesn't prepare them to interact in real relationship dilemmas. Durable and lasting relationships cannot be reduced to a few words on a screen. And trying to resolve a conflict or "breaking up" on a screen is a lazy person's solution. In my opinion, screens are for information—not emotion.

✳ Our focus groups have shown that young people are short on patience, listening skills, and conflict resolution. Call me the Master of the Obvious, but it appears their generation is better at interacting via technology than face to face. We've let them become socially isolated and lethargic. Peter Eio of Lego Systems reminds us: "This is the first time in the history of the human race that a generation of kids has overtaken their parents in the use of new technology."

Rachel is a sophomore in college. She is adorable, but she's also a product of the age in which she grew up. She recently told me about a crisis she faced on the week she had a big paper due for a class. Her cell phone and PC crashed—and she crashed too. With both of her prized sources of technology down, she plunged into despair. More than that, she became paralyzed. It didn't dawn on her to borrow a friend's phone to call for help or walk over to her professor's office to negotiate a new deadline for the paper. She felt she had no options. So she took an incomplete in the course.

With each passing year, Generation iY continues to flock to new technologies, quickly becoming masters at interfacing with them 24/7. Cell phones have become pocket TVs and pocket PCs. Twitter took off in 2009. That year fourteen million folks began tweeting, many of them posting hourly updates on their life.

A common theme in all these technology advances, according to author Neil Howe, is to invite Generation iY to do something faster while also inviting them to spend more time at it. It's an interesting paradox. Most new technology claims it will save the user time. Usually, however, it beckons them to actually spend more time using it. In this sense, many of the devices that Generation iY depends on are addictive—psychologically if not physically. The very process of using them promotes dependence.

If the trend of overconnectedness continues, Generation iY risks trading the traditional value of quality relationships (face-to-face encounters that require time and energy to unpack our feelings and thoughts) for virtual relationships defined by speed and quantity. Technology without maturity can be hazardous.

An Overprotected Generation

We have given Generation iY safety seats, safety belts, and safety policies on everything. They can't ride a bike without a helmet, they've been discouraged from going places on their own, they've been shielded from financial realities, and they've spent much of their childhood inside, in front of a screen. (Some even call them "screenagers.")

Safety is certainly important. But for Generation iY, safety has often been allowed to trump growth. As parents, we don't want them out of our sight. As educators, we're concerned about liability and feel we need to avoid risk. We believe we are protecting our future by protecting them. In reality, we may be harming the future. Because of our overprotective parenting and education methods:

- *A large percentage struggle with obesity.*
- *A large percentage experience nearsightedness.*
- *A large percentage find it difficult to fulfill commitments.*

- *A large percentage wrestle with depression after eighteen years old.*
- *A large percentage discover life is hard to cope with after leaving home.*

This generation has been so sheltered by their parents, teachers, counselors, and an overregulated government that many have trouble developing strong, independent coping skills. Authors Neil Howe and William Strauss write, "Overly involved parents have become a real hassle for many educators."[4]

So what does this look like in a real-life kid? I've known Kelli since she was in middle school. She recently graduated from college. Her entire story is a picture of overprotection. While none of the turns in her life were inherently bad, together they produced a young adult who is unready for life in the real world.

When Kelli was in elementary school, her mother pulled her from public school and chose to homeschool her. I certainly understand that. My wife and I chose to homeschool our teenaged son so he'd have a more flexible schedule as he prepared for his career. For Kelli's mom, however, homeschooling was more about protecting Kelli from school pressures and controlling what she was exposed to than about preparing her for life.

And then, as Kelli grew, her mom also tightened the reins. At middle-school age, Kelli was not permitted to go on a trip to Florida (just one state over) with friends because of too many variables her mother couldn't control. In high school, Kelli wanted to go on a one-week mission trip overseas with her church youth group. She was not allowed to go because her mother worried about the safety of being in a developing nation. When Kelli started looking at colleges, the only options her mother would consider were universities two hours or less away from home.

Now that Kelli is a graduate, her mother has seen the value of cutting the apron strings, but the damage is already done. Kelli took a job four states away from home and was unable to perform. She called her mom several times a day, crying, because she was homesick. Not surprisingly, this didn't sit well with her supervisor. Later, when Kelli broke up with her boyfriend, she was devastated. Her employer insisted she make sales calls instead of texting her boyfriend through the day. Eventually the situation became more than she could handle. Kelli quit her job at age twenty-two and moved home.

Let's face it. This happens millions of times over each year. America has become obsessed with protecting children at all costs, and this generation has suffered from that obsession. We will not let our precious children do anything without a helmet, cell phone, warranty, insurance policy, knee pads, or a guarantee. And we do it out of love (as well as media-generated fear). But what kind of adults will our preoccupation with safety produce?

America was built on risk. Opportunity. Free enterprise. Failure and determination. Will these ideas be found only in our history books?

More to the point, will our overemphasis on safety and security produce a generation of kids who simply don't know how to find their way in the world?

Five Generations

Ready or not, Generation Y is entering adulthood. A new breed has entered our campuses and workplaces, and they are already influencing their worlds. Although they have evolved from previous generations, Generations Y and iY have their own distinct identity.

	Seniors "Greatest Generation"	Builders "Silent Generation"	Boomers "Pig in the Python"	Busters "Generation X"	Generations Y & iY "Millennials"
Birth years	1900–1928	1929–1945	1946–1964	1965–1983	1984–2002
Life paradigm	Manifest destiny	"Be grateful you have a job"	"You owe me"	"Relate to me"	"Life is a cafeteria"
Attitude to authority	Respect them	Endure them	Replace them	Ignore them	Choose them
Role of relationships	Long term	Significant	Limited, useful	Central, caring	Global, 24/7
Value system	Traditional	Conservative	Self-based	Media	Shop around
Role of career	Loyalty	Means for living	Central focus	Irritant	Place to serve
Schedules	Responsible	Mellow	Frantic	Aimless	Volatile
Technology	What's that?	Hope to outlive it	Master it	Enjoy it	Employ it
Market	Commodities	Goods	Services	Experiences	Transformations
View of future	Uncertain	Seek to stabilize	Create it!	Hopeless	Optimistic

An *Overserved* Generation

We live in the age of the "wanted child." That's not a bad thing in itself. The problem comes when we give our young people an overinflated idea of their own importance.

Sixty years ago, Dr. Benjamin Spock told parents to allow kids to express themselves and build a strong self-esteem. Today, we have taken this approach to an extreme—and it has worked. These kids most assuredly have developed a strong self-esteem. According to a nationwide high school survey, more than eight out of ten believe they are very important people.[5] They feel entitled to special treatment as they enter the adult world. They know that they are in the spotlight and all eyes are on them.

As this generation absorbs the parental message that they dominate America's agenda, they have come to believe that their problems are the nation's problems. They feel very special and are sure that the "key" to the future is in their hands. When asked which demographic group will most likely be the one to help America toward a "better future," teens rank "young people" second only to "scientists."

Where would they get this idea?

- *From Mom and Dad, who dote on them. Parents of the iY generation often need special orientation sessions to help them "let go" when they drop their kids off at college.*
- *From TV networks who've created entire channels just for kids—like Disney, Disney XD, Nickelodeon, Boomerang, Discovery Kids, and The N.*
- *From retailers and marketing campaigns that create products like Kids' Aquafresh, Pert Plus for Kids, Dial for Kids, and Ozark (bottled) Water for Kids.*
- *From nationwide programs, sponsored by state and federal governments, like No Child Left Behind.*

Adults have chosen to focus on and serve this generation of young people more than any in recent history. And what has being overserved done to them? Let me get practical. I just turned off the radio in my car, after listening to a pop radio station. Three of the song titles I heard were:

- *"Because I'm Awesome!"*
- *"The World Should Revolve Around Me"*
- *"Don'tcha Wish Your Girlfriend Was Hot Like Me?"*

Those three songs are just the tip of the iceberg. They help us see the side effects of being overserved. In general, Generation iY is a narcissistic or me-centered generation. (Another reason the name fits—because it's all about "I.")

A longitudinal study by Dr. Jean Twenge of San Diego State University between 1975 and 2006 showed a measurable climb in narcissistic tendencies among American students (two of six scored very high in this category) and a growing number who actually have Narcissistic Personality Disorder.[6] The majority of them believe the world would be a better place if they were in charge. The slogan back then was "I'm okay. You're okay." Today it's: "You're okay. I'm Perfect."

Dr. Twenge writes in *Generation Me*:

> In the years after 1980, there was a pervasive, society-wide effort to increase children's self-esteem. The Boomers who now filled the ranks of parents apparently decided that children should always feel good about themselves. Research on programs to boost self-esteem first blossomed in the 1980s and the number of psychology and education journal articles devoted to self-esteem doubled between the 1970s and the 1980s. Journal articles on self-esteem increased another 52% during the 1990s, and the number of books on self-esteem doubled over the same time.[7]

Accordingly, as social scientists Howe and Strauss state, the kids of this generation tend to be truly "self-conscious"— intensely aware of themselves. More than 90 percent feel "very good" about themselves.[8] But even those who don't like themselves are still hyperaware of (and often consumed with) their social standing—what their friends think of them, how they look in their Facebook photos, and so on.

One could argue, of course, that teens have always been self-absorbed. Perhaps this is true for the last three generations, but it is not true historically. We will discuss later how adults have permitted adolescents to be narcissistic far longer than they did one hundred years ago. But just one simple piece of information— one I alluded to earlier—will show the increase in generational self-consciousness.

"In the early 1950s," Dr. Twenge writes, "only 12 percent of teens aged fourteen to sixteen agreed with the statement 'I am an important person.' By the late 1980s, an incredible 80 percent—almost seven times as many—claimed they were important."[9] Such numbers have led Dr. Twenge and her researchers to conclude that the Millennial generation (including Generation iY) is the most narcissistic generation in history.[10]

How did they get this way? We just wanted our kids to feel good about themselves. Well, they do. Kids can now go to www.Celeb4aday.com to hire a fake paparazzi to follow them around and take photos of them. Hmm. Is all of this helping or hurting?

Seventeen-year-old Seth just quit his job. This is hardly unusual. Folks across the country quit their jobs every day. What makes Seth's situation unique is that this is the fourth job Seth has quit *this month*.

Seth attends a private, well-endowed prep school. He buys his clothes from Lucky Brand Jeans and Abercrombie and Fitch. He owns an iMac, an iPhone, and an iPad. He's your typical smart, good-looking, connected iYer.

I know his parents. They are good people, but they are baffled at why their son just can't hold down a job. I think I know why, though. Life has just been too easy for Seth; for most of his life he has been served instead of taught and challenged. When he needed his clothes washed, Mom did it. When he needed his bed made, Mom was happy to step in. When he needed money, Dad had it for him. When he needed a car, Dad bought it.

All of Seth's needs were met by loving parents. But did they really demonstrate love for him? It depends on your definition of love. Seth's parents have not prepared him for life because they have served him so well.

Now Seth is entering a world that doesn't share his parents' desire to meet his every need. He's expected to work for what he gets; it's not just handed to him. And Seth has no idea how to deal with those expectations. No wonder he wants to quit.

What kind of adults will lead our world if they have been raised in this manner? No one can tell for sure, but I have watched this scenario for years now. As they move from teenagers to twenty-somethings, they're often impatient, demanding, self-centered and short-tempered, with a poor work ethic and minimal sense of long-term commitment.

And here's something that really saddens me: These kids really do desire to change the world; they just don't have what it takes to accomplish their lofty dreams. When the work becomes difficult, they change their minds and move on to something else. The new term for them is "slactivists"—they are both slackers and activists. Consequently, for most of them, their involvement in causes is limited to buying a "Live Strong" wristband or signing a petition on a Web site.

Avoiding a Rude Awakening

There is still debate on what conclusions we should draw on this emerging generation of young people. I have simply furnished a portrait of them based on my experience, research, and gathering of data. The portrait is not a flattering one. As a group, Generation iY is overwhelmed, overconnected, overprotected, and overserved.

That's not the whole picture of course. Generation iY can also be energetic, confident, and capable. They dream big, they care about their friends, they thrive on activity. I can honestly say that some of my most meaningful relationships are with iYers!

But I also believe it's time for a wake-up call when it comes to Generation iY. It's time that those of us who care about these kids—parents, teachers, coaches, youth workers, employers—pay attention to the way we're shaping them.

While on the road recently, sleeping in a hotel, I had an experience I don't care to repeat. The alarm clock in my room went off early in the morning, rousing me from much-needed sleep. I turned it off, but just as I was drifting off again, a wake-up call came from the front desk.

The trouble is, I had never set the alarm and never asked for the wake-up call. In fact, it was one of those rare mornings when I could sleep in a bit before I caught my flight home.

Evidently one of my friends (and I use that term loosely here) believed it would be funny to pull a little prank. But there was nothing funny about it for me. I would much rather set my own wake-up times—and know when they are coming.

I believe we're due for a wake-up call when it comes to Generation iY. It will either be a rude awakening that comes at a time we don't expect and shocks us all, or it will be one that we set ourselves—today.

It's our choice.

And it's time to act.

➤ LINKING UP ◄

If we're to make a positive impact on Generation iY, we must approach these young people with the right attitude. Our Web site contains a brief quiz for you to check your attitude before you engage an iYer in conversation again. Go to **www.SaveTheirFutureNow.com/AttitudeCheck**.

3

Aftershock
Responding to the Cultural Shift

TERRY WALLIS WAS NINETEEN YEARS OLD, with his whole life ahead of him, when a tragic 1984 car accident put him in a coma. His family was devastated. But Terry's mother was not about to give up on her son. She opted to keep him alive through hospital technology and wait it out, hoping that one day he would regain consciousness.

The good news is, he did. The stunning news is, he woke up on June 11, 2003—after being in a coma for almost two decades. The part of Terry's story that intrigues me most was that his mom remained at his side for several days afterward, just filling him in on the major news that had happened between 1984 and 2003.

Can you imagine what that was like? The United States, not to mention the world, had experienced incredible change during that time: four presidents (two of whom served two terms); space shuttle tragedies; the fall of communism in the Soviet Union and Europe, the introduction of cell phones, DVDs, and iPods; presidential scandal; four wars; a crisis at Columbine High School; and three major terrorist attacks.

Like Rip Van Winkle, Terry Wallis had slept through a revolution. When he woke, he didn't even recognize his own mother.

I must admit that sometimes I feel like Terry, even though I've been mostly conscious for the past few decades and have actually kept up with the news. Change happens so fast these days that I often feel like someone has pushed the "fast forward" button on our culture and left me in the dust. Sometimes I feel like I'm still in the Gutenberg era while the rest of society is in the Google era.

Do you ever feel this way? Forget nineteen years—what about nineteen months? Consider just the shifts in students' preferences that took place in less than two years time:

- *Music delivery went from CDs to iTunes and MP3s.*
- *Primary communication went from phone calls to text messaging.*
- *Social networking went from e-mail to Club Penguin, MySpace, and Facebook.*
- *Entertainment preferences went from watching TV to streaming videos on You-Tube, Hulu, and a host of other sites.*
- *Personal updates went from blogs to twitter.*

In 2004, I lectured to faculty on a university campus. At a break, I found myself explaining some of the more recent social transformations to a sixty-seven-year-old professor. He just didn't recognize how different our world had become and how those differences might affect his teaching methods. As I summarized the changes for him, I'll admit the world that had emerged in the first five years of the twenty-first century surprised even me. We were two immigrants in a foreign land.

It's an Aftershock

I believe that what's happening in our world can best be explained with the term *aftershock*. I first heard this word as a kid living in San Diego, California. During my fourteen years there, I experienced five earthquakes. (I don't miss them now that I live in Atlanta.) I learned rapidly how to take cover during the rumbling of a quake. I also learned that the initial quake is only part of the story. Almost every earthquake is followed by one or more aftershocks, smaller shifts that occur just hours or days afterward. The aftershocks can be unsettling and do as much damage as the original quake.

You probably remember the horrible earthquake that hit Haiti in January 2010. It claimed the lives of more than two hundred thousand people and displaced one and a half million others. What you may not remember is that the aftershock (6.1 on the Richter scale) was almost as terrifying as the initial quake.

Allow me to let you in on a little secret. Today we're experiencing a cultural shift, and social metamorphoses are occurring at a faster rate than ever before. The world that adults created in the 1980s has come to impact us and even haunt us. That decade represents the initial "quake." The first decade of the twenty-first century represents the aftershock. It has sparked changes even within a generation of people. In other words, the students born at the beginning of Generation Y are different than the younger ones within the same generation. Let me explain.

Between 1998 and 2003, social scientists were elated with their findings on the new generation of kids they called Generation Y, or the Millennial generation (born in the 1980s). The early stats on these kids were very positive:

- *Teen pregnancy was down.*
- *Drug abuse was lower than their parents.*
- *Violent crime was at its lowest in twenty years.*
- *Education and civic involvement was at a record high.*
- *The students were optimistic about their prospects of changing the world.*[1]

Now, however, we've seen a new side to this generation. After the first thirty-five million Generation Y kids approached adulthood and their younger brothers and sisters were born, the shift began. The younger members of Generation Y (born in 1990 and beyond) look different from the older ones. Earlier, the kids were submissive, but today's kids are more likely to be mavericks. They tend to be lethargic rather than active, self-absorbed rather than engaged. Check out some of these changes within just one decade's time.

1999	2009
Teens believed the U.S. was broken, but they planned to fix it.	60 percent of them return home to Mom after college with no plan.
90 percent of teens planned to go to college.	30 percent of teens didn't even graduate from high school.
Many had dreams of transforming the world.	Many face a "quarterlife crisis" at age twenty-five.

The culture has clearly shifted—and we're living with the aftershock. Why the shift? I'll examine the reasons in greater depth throughout this book, but here are a few ideas to whet your appetite:

1. **Years of affluence and social liberation in America during the 1990s.** Though the economy has soured over the last few years, more than 60 percent of college graduates still return home with the luxury of searching their souls, savoring the pleasures of childhood, and living rent-free while they experiment with jobs and relationships. Especially with today's tough job market, many are waiting for an ideal career and mate.

2. **Damaging parenting styles that prevent kids from preparing for the real world.** It's all done in the name of love and support. The unfortunate result is that kids get ambushed by adulthood, and they retreat.

3. **Media and technology that furnish an unrealistic picture of adult responsibility.** YouTube videos are brief, TV dilemmas are solved in thirty minutes, the Internet can be manipulated, and students can log off Facebook or block a "friend" they don't like. If they're bored with it, they turn it off. This is nothing even remotely close to the world they'll soon enter.

4. **Formal education that prepares students for more school, not for the marketplace.** Most colleges are out of step with the world their graduates will enter. (In response, vocational schools such as Devry and Strayer Universities have experienced a boom in enrollment, growing 48 percent from 1996 to 2000.)[2] There are more students than ever, but fewer are ready to enter the workaday world. The jump between backpack and briefcase is huge.

5. **Postmodern thought that fosters cynicism as students grow older.** We live in a day of relativism, pluralism, and cynicism. As Generation Y graduates, they slowly get beat up by a world jaded by a postmodern worldview. Many drop their family values or walk away from their faith. As clarity wanes, so does their urgency to act.

6. **A culture that values convenience more highly than commitment.** Just observe our Western culture for a day. You'll find tangible examples of how we value speed and convenience at the expense of long-term commitment. It's hard for youth who have grown up this way to stay steady when the novelty has worn off.

A New World

I have two kids. My daughter was born in the 1980s. My son was born in the 1990s. They are noticeably different, and it's not simply a personality or gender issue. My son is an absolute product of Generation iY, more so than my daughter is. And I see a pattern. Change happens even faster for him.

Generation iY, remember, has been shaped by the pervasive impact of the "i" world—first the Internet, then the iMac, iBook, iPod, iPhone, iChat, iMovie, iPhoto, iTunes, and iPad. I'd like to suggest we've reached the point of the "iBrain," because there is mounting evidence that technology is actually changing the way our kids' brains function.

Doctors are now saying, for instance, that the pixels on the screens they stare at for hours on end have changed the way they perceive information. The "i" world also tends to foster different thought patterns. Instead of proceeding in a linear fashion (with thoughts moving from *A* to *B* to *C*), "iBrains" work more like computer screens with a choice of icons. Random, even contradictory, sequences are marks of their world. What's more, the almost-instant "i" world makes waiting very hard for Generation iY. For them, it's all about speed.

These developments have both good and not-so-good implications. Each brings unintended consequences. Shift happens—and we must respond to it. This emerging generation will not merely be more of the same. While their earlier counterparts were crying out for authentic community, organic change, and selfless service, Generation iY is okay with artificial community, high velocity, and free spending. Their battle cry is "What's in it for me?"

Case in point. College students today show less empathy toward others compared with college students in decades before, according to a study from the University of Michigan.

The university's Institute for Social for Social Research looked at 72 studies that gauged empathy among 14,000 students over 30 years. Empathy has been in a steep decline, especially since 2000. The research finds that students today display 40% less empathy than students in the 1980s and 1990s. Spokesperson Sara Konrath said one reason students are less empathetic may be that people are having fewer face-to-face interactions, communicating instead through social media such as Facebook and Twitter. Hmmm. Sound familiar?[3]

Avatars, blogs, wikis, Google—if all of this sounds like a foreign language, chances are you were born before 1980. Certainly before 1990. And even if you are a computer-literate Boomer, you do not have the same organic familiarity with the online world that Generation iY has. These kids have been online since preschool and can't imagine life any other way. The Kaiser Family Foundation reported in February 2010 that kids between eight and eighteen are spending seven-and-a-half hours each day in front of a screen. This is stunning to me. They've grown up this way—as unabashed "mediavores."

Consider how we find information for a moment. When my generation needed to locate a person or an organization, we looked it up in the Yellow Pages. Later, we called 411. The following generation began to Google...then along came Wikipedia. Today, students in Generation iY are using Cha Cha (242-242). It's a number you can text...and ask anything you want. You'll get an answer in less than two minutes. And Generation iY does.

Sexuality and pornography has been taken to a new level today. In the past, pornography was considered a dark, very shady industry. At one time it consisted of magazines and seedy theaters. Then, along came videos and DVDs. Five years ago, DVDs made up 80 percent of porn's revenue. Now the percentage is 40 and shrinking[4] because of free porn on the Internet.

Unfortunately, that's only the beginning. The thirteen-billion-dollar porn industry now has a new promoter: cell phones. Sexting, not texting, became the rage in 2008. Sexting means sending nude or sexual photos of oneself from one cell phone or laptop to another. I wish I could tell you its popularity was marginal. Sadly, according to expert Parry Afteb, 44 percent of high school boys have seen a pornographic photo of a classmate on their cell phones.[5]

Now consider how Generation iY communicates. At one time, Generation Y made cell phone calls. Today, kids still use cell phones, but mostly they text—a lot. According to the Nielsen Company, between spring 2006 and spring 2008, text messages rose 450 percent. In fact, 2007 was the first year that text messages surpassed cell phone calls in terms of frequency. The typical U.S. teen mobile subscriber sends or receives an average of 1,742 texts per month.[6]

Generation iY truly are "screenagers." Their world is fundamentally new.

Pros and Cons

As with all generations, there are pros and cons to this iY world I have just described. An 2008 article in *The Economist* succinctly sums up the cons:

> Worries about the damage the Internet may be doing to young people has produced a mountain of books....Robert Bly claims that, thanks to the Internet, the neo-cortex is finally eating itself. Today's youth may be web-savvy, but they also stand accused of being unread, bad at communicating, socially inept, shameless, dishonest, work-shy, narcissistic, and indifferent to the needs of others.[7]

Interestingly, Don Tapscott begs to differ. Tapscott is the man who coined the term, "Net Generation" in the 1990s. His book, *Grown Up Digital*, which emerged from a massive study of almost eight thousand young people in twelve countries, describes Generation iY as "smarter, quicker and more tolerant of diversity than their predecessors."[8]

While acknowledging that iY can have a "dark side,"[9] Tapscott also paints a positive picture of a generation that loves freedom, appreciates individuality and choice, and values integrity and openness. These are kids who generally work and play well together, and they bring a playful spirit with them to work. And though they spend a lot of time staring at screens, they are far less likely to be passive "couch potatoes" than previous generations because they are accustomed to interacting with a screen. Finally, the young people Tapscott describes are adept multitaskers who adapt quickly to constant innovation.[10]

A Jekyll-and-Hyde Generation?

To help you better understand this paradoxical generation, I've created a list of pros and corresponding cons to summarize them. What we must do, as mentors, is to help the kids of Generation iY capitalize on their pros and diminish the consequences of the cons.

Pros	Cons
They feel special and needed.	They can act spoiled and conceited.
They own the world of technology.	They expect easy and instant results.
They love community.	They often won't act outside their clique.
They are the focus of their parents.	They may be unable to cope with reality.
They are high on tolerance.	They often lack absolute values.
They've had relatively easy lives.	They may lack stamina to finish a task—even to finish high school.
They catch on to new ideas quickly.	They struggle with long commitments.
They're adept at multitasking.	They have difficulty focusing.
They have a bias for action and interaction.	They're too impatient to sit and listen long.
They want to be the best.	They can get depressed if they're not.
They plan to live a life of strategic purpose.	They often avoid tasks that seem trivial.
They are confident and assertive.	They can come across as careless and rude.
They hunger to change the world.	They anticipate doing it quickly and easily.

A Generation of Paradox

You may have noticed that these descriptions of Generation iY seem contradictory. There really is a bright side and a dark side to Generation iY; they're both magnetic and worrisome. As I interact with them, at times I find myself thinking they're like a Dr. Jekyll and Mr. Hyde population—a generation of paradox.

A paradox can be defined as two or more realities that seem contradictory. Our world is full of paradoxes, and I believe we will see more of them as Generation iY comes of age. They experience inward realities and outward realities that their parents and teachers don't understand. In fact, I've observed that many iYers have a highly developed capacity to accept paradox and are comfortable with conflicting realities. The following are just a few of the paradoxes I have observed in them:

Paradox #1: They Are Sheltered...Yet Pressured.

Millions of these students have been sheltered from harsh realities by their parents, yet they live with more pressure on their lives than the previous two generations. The pressure often comes from the parents as well, or it may come from sources outside the home—school, peers, and cultural expectations. Young people feel pushed to make the grade, make the team, and make the money by the dominant culture. They're under the gun to study hard, avoid personal risks, and capitalize on opportunities their family has afforded them.

Due to the pressure they feel, many of these students have made an art of cheating in school, and plagiarism has taken on a whole new meaning. Thousands visit Web sites like Best Essays or Essay Writers, where they pay by the page for a paper to be written for them. (It's all done via the Web).

Kids feel they must excel, yet researchers feel they've been coddled by their parents. How can both be true? One possibility is that parents feel they've "invested" in their kids by providing for them, but want to see a return on that investment. Another factor is that schedules are incredibly tight. I saw a cartoon recently that showed two schoolgirls leaving the soccer field after practice. One of them said to the other, "Wow! You have fifteen minutes between soccer practice and violin lessons? What are you gonna do with all that free time?"

Still another pressure on Generation iY—looming far more now than in the 1990s—is financial pressure. Jobs have been hard to come by in recent years, and both teens and young adults worry about the frightening financial picture they hear about on the news. Those who do have jobs may be underemployed or lack benefits—a sobering change for young people who have been raised to think they can do anything and have everything.

Wherever the pressure comes from, the outcome may be ill-adjusted adults. A few pages back I mentioned a book entitled *Quarterlife Crisis*,[11] which describes a situation analogous to the oft-cited midlife crisis, but among much younger people. Its authors are concerned about the alarming number of twenty-five-year olds who are clinically depressed and seeing a therapist because they didn't make their first million or reach their dream as quickly as they hoped.

The problem in my view is we've raised Generation iY on mixed messages. On one hand, they are pushed to grow up quickly, understand data and perform. On the other, they are coddled and given the message that adults will cover for them, no matter how they perform. Their lifestyle is dualistic: they are both growing up faster (in some senses), and growing up slower in others. I wonder if the comfortable, high tech world that's sped up their life exposure may actually slow down their maturation.

Paradox #2: They Are Self-Absorbed...Yet Generous.

As I stated in chapter 2, Generation iY young people tend to be self-absorbed and even narcissistic. They spend more time getting ready in the morning than Generation X and the Baby Boomers, and they spend more money on themselves as well, even when you factor in inflation. They feel they're worth it, that they are special kids. And why not? Movies, government, TV, and parents have all made this generation believe they are vital to our future. No wonder the vast majority of teens say "I feel good about myself."

The day after Mother's Day 2006, *USA Today* carried an article on what young people had given their moms for this special day. Thousands had decided to give *themselves* gifts in honor of their mothers! The gifts ranged from getting a haircut to putting money in their own bank account to cleaning up their apartment. And the mothers were pleased with those gifts! The children played such a central role in their own happiness that mothers felt good about the vicarious gift. Typically, iYers have been raised to be consumers, and many have not matured to become contributors. By overemphasizing self-esteem and underemphasizing qualities like unselfishness and responsibility, adults made it easy for these kids to be consumed with self.

At the same time, these students are happy to give their time and money away. A nationwide poll found that 50 percent of high schoolers are involved in community service.[12] They give to causes from the fight against AIDS in Africa to hurricane relief here in the U.S., and most seem to have the money to give. They appreciate the feeling of serving others and the majority find money to support their causes. Granted, it's usually their parents' money, but still, they love giving and helping others—once their own needs are met.

Paradox #3: They Are Social...Yet Isolated by Technology.

In addition to the ease with which they can stay in touch, reflect on this fact. According to research done by author Josh McDowell, nearly half of this young generation tests high on the "I" profile of the DISC personality assessment test. The "I" on the profile stands for Influencer—in essence, a people person. These kids, as a group, are intensely social. In fact, they may be the most social generation in history. They are accustomed to cooperating in teams and groups. They are also in constant contact with peers and family through text messaging, cell phone calls, IMs, Facebook, MySpace, Twitter, and all sorts of other networks. In fact, the total amount of leisure time many kids spend with such media "is the equivalent of a full-time job."[13]

But the reliance on technology to maintain relationships introduces a poignant irony. This very *social* generation is in danger of becoming one of the most *isolated* generations because so much of their relational contact comes via technology. One student confessed to me, "My generation gets to know a lot of people on the Internet, but we don't have many good friends through our networks. I think we're a socially distracted generation because of this."

Text messaging is a vivid illustration of this irony. According to "Teenagers: A Generation Unplugged," a national survey conducted by CTIA, the Wireless Association, and Harris Interactive, teens list the following as the top reasons they like to send text messages: it allows them to multitask, it's fast, they don't have to talk in person, and it's private (or secret).[14] In other words, they like connecting without really having to connect. They want to be in touch with their friends without actually having to sit still and listen, to be in touch without spending too much time on interaction or following social etiquette. It's as if they are saying, "I want the connection without the commitment. I want community, but I want control as well." Doing things online instead of in-person offers them that control.

Technology professor Greg Hearn suggests that Internet-savvy kids never need to leave home. There is nothing that can't be done online. "Humans have the same needs, and they're satisfied by the same things," he says, "but the way in which needs and satisfaction are connected has completely changed."[15] Now kids can have BFFs (Best Friends Forever) with whom they may never have spoken face to face. They may have the BOBW (Best Of Both Worlds) without leaving their neighborhoods. And they could be leading the G-SAVE (Global Struggle Against

Violent Extremists) but waging the war from a computer in a darkened bedroom in suburbia. (I know that's a bit exaggerated—but not by much!) Friends, lovers, even mortal enemies are just a click away, and messages positive or negative can quickly go viral.

Students today, in fact, are inundated with messages from every angle. I believe they're most likely to text because it allows them fast, current, relevant, personal communication with friends—but at a safe distance. The same is true for Twitter and Facebook. The ability to issue daily, even constant, updates on a screen and read the updates of others provides a form of intimacy without a lot of vulnerability.

Once again, it's a paradox. Generation iY loves using technology to communicate, but they also enjoy the isolation and control that technology gives them. In fact, one reason social media are so popular is that kids love the cyberspace fame they can achieve, even in the isolation of their own bedroom. They can keep score on how many friends they have in their online "group" or how many follow their tweets. Posting videos on YouTube can make a homeschool kid a worldwide superstar overnight.

The trouble, of course, is that it's hard to develop real relationships in an unreal world—and the world iY kids inhabit online is just that. Kids live an artificial life on Facebook, MySpace, or Flickr. "Second Life" types of online applications may soon become the new general interface medium for human activity.

Are you aware of Second Life? It's a virtual world (accessed online) where an individual can adopt a personality and character (real or unreal) and interact with other virtual characters. You can be Brad Pitt or Taylor Swift and live near the ocean if you like—what you experience online becomes, indeed, your second life.

Examine the fierce popularity of the movie *Avatar* in early 2010. It grossed over a billion dollars in its first three weeks. It's the story of people living vicariously through online personas called avatars. That's more or less what happens in Second Life and similar setups. Users get the chance to live virtual lives far removed from their own real-world lives.

And that is the problem in my view. I recognize that this technology can be used for good purposes, such as virtual school field trips. It can help develop certain kinds of motor skills and help with multitasking, but it can also hinder development of emotional intelligence. You cannot build a career via an avatar, nor can you have a meaningful relationship. Call me crazy, but I believe it's hard to build healthy people skills if the majority of your day is spent in a virtual world, isolated from actual human contact.

What Do iYers Say about Themselves?

Because Generation iY has made their lives an open book, we can study them much more readily. We decided to survey some of these students, both online and via focus groups, and let them speak their minds. Below are some highlights of our interaction with them.

- **"I only take yes for an answer. I'm used to getting what I want" (Jared, age 21).** We heard this over and over in a variety of ways. These young people have found ways to get what they're after at home and school. Their primary challenge is to discover how to maneuver or manipulate others to see it their way.

- **"I am not going to settle for less in a job, like my parents did" (Trey, age 19).** This idea was almost unanimous. Young adults today often feel that previous generations made decisions for the wrong reasons: money, pleasure and benefits. It may sound contradictory, but students from this narcissistic generation want a more altruistic motive for choosing their jobs.

- **"I despise the lifestyle, the ethics, and the greed I see in our culture" (Stacy, 18).** Female students especially abhor the hypocrisy they observe in adult leaders. The ones we interviewed made scathing judgments of the executives at Enron, Tyco, Worldcom, and others they believe have failed morally; they even blasted President Clinton and Tiger Woods.

- **"Technology is an extension of my body" (Shansel, 17).** We've already discussed this one, but let me add one thought. Technology is a tool and a fuel for Generation iY; it empowers them socially. Forbidding a young salesperson to use Facebook would be like one taking a phone or a Rolodex away from a Boomer back in the seventies.

- **"Why should I pay my dues at work? I know more than my supervisor does" (Todd, 17).** This may sound arrogant—and it probably is. Many of the working students we interviewed believed they knew more about what would sell and how to sell it than their employers did. Some told us they should become CEO of their companies within five years.

- **"My mom gets involved in my decisions about school and work; but I don't mind. She's like an agent" (Ariel, 21).** Part of the reason for this generation's confidence is their parents. They know that if they somehow fail, Mom or Dad will save them. They depend on their parents to be counselors, coaches, and spokespersons for them.

- **"I am merchandise on E-Bay. If I get fired, I will sell myself to the highest bidder" (Chen, 22).** This statement sounded brash to me. These young people are so pragmatic, many see themselves as "products." If one employer fires them, they assume there will be another down the street who will bid for them as though they're a free agent.

- **"I guess I could...but I wouldn't want to live without MySpace" (J. Ward, 23).** These kids are social—very social, and their technology allows them to be social twenty-four/seven. Social scientists say that as people age, their social circles dwindle because they don't have the energy to sustain hundreds of friends. Young people have that energy.
- **"I plan to have several careers and every one of them will improve the world" (Kris, 19).** This comment was confirmed by the majority of students with whom we interacted. Futurists agree—about the first part, at least. They say today's college graduates will likely get jobs that didn't exist ten years ago and will change jobs seven to nine times during their career. As to whether or not those jobs will change the world...the verdict is still out on that.

Paradox #4: They Are Ambitious...Yet Anxious.

This one is incredible. Some have called Generation iY a bunch of "slackers," just as they did Generation X, but iYers demonstrate far more ambition than Generation X did at their age. Thousands of them have created their own companies before they graduated from college. (Mark Zuckerberg, the founder of Facebook, is a case in point.)

The Prudential Insurance Company awards loads of these youth every year for their entrepreneurial spirit. I have met some of them, and their confidence and drive amazed me. In one recent study among students sixteen to twenty-four years old, 82 percent said they believe the "next Bill Gates" is in their generation, 51 percent said they believe they know the next Bill Gates, and 24 percent said they believe they *are* the next Bill Gates!

Why the confidence? Consider again their years growing up. They've been told all their lives that they are winners. They've been challenged to "get involved," to "save the planet," to "make a difference." And they've been told over and over again: "You can do it."

But *can* they do it? Saving the world is a tall order, and it's humanly impossible to be a winner all the time. What's more, considering today's financial landscape, it seems that winning in the future might be quite challenging. It's no wonder these very confident young people also display high levels of anxiety, especially about the future. According to Howe and Strauss, nine out of ten high school students think about the future several times a week.[16] The weight of the previous generation's expectations can paralyze them, and they fear they may not measure up.

I believe they may also understand intuitively that the world they grew up in is not at all the real world they will soon enter. In their current world, young people are encouraged to be well rounded, but as adults they'll be permitted and even required to commit to specialties. Their current world is full of support and encouragement, but that might not be true for them as adults—their bosses will likely not be clapping for them every week on the job. A sizeable chunk of their current success is measured by their ability to comply, to learn what's expected and do what they're told, but as adults they'll need to chart their own road maps. And their current schooling tends to prepare them for more school rather than for their actual future.[17]

Their current world, moreover is very structured and typically planned by a teacher or parent, whereas the future is not planned at all; it is up to them to create it. Generation iY kids are seldom required to reflect on their lives, to try to make sense of and interpret what goes on around them. In fact, many of them lead lives that are so programmed that they have little say in what they do.

This is actually true of their older Generation Y siblings as well. Emory professor Mark Bauerlein relates:

> When David Brooks toured Princeton back in 2001, he heard of joyless days and nights with no room for newspapers or politics or dating, just one "skill-enhancing activity to the next." He calls them "Organization Kids" (after the old Organization Man figure of the fifties), students who "have to schedule appointment times for chatting." They've been pro-grammed for success, and a preschool-to-college gauntlet of standardized tests, mounting homework, motivational messages, and extracurricular tasks has rewarded or punished them at every stage.[18]

I've come to believe that one of the reasons kids love participating in reality TV and video games is that these activities give them a chance to participate and "weigh in" with their opinions rather than have some adult do it for them. And one reason so many loved the movie *Napoleon Dynamite* was that it was so random; all the humor and plot to the story had no purpose whatsoever. Kids found this a re-lief. It was refreshing. It was funny. Best of all, it was unprogrammed and certainly not overproduced.

Am I saying there should be no structure in kids' lives? No. The problem, I believe, is too much structure with little or no practice in independent reflection. All of this may lead Generation iY to be unable to act on their own without seeking consensus; to be unable to act without the approval of someone. They may have trouble developing strong independent coping skills. No wonder they're anxious!

Paradox #5: They Are Adventuresome...Yet Protected.

One employer said that this generation has been to the Amazon River and climbed the Rocky Mountains, but never punched a time clock on a job. Life for them has been much like a reality TV show—exciting, yet controlled. Parents have monitored almost everything. Generation iY kids may love the exhilaration of bungee jumping and the reckless thrill of whitewater rafting, but they don't know how to negotiate adversity in the real world of people and mundane jobs. Sadly, they have caught a vision from all the information they've taken in as students, but many haven't been taught how to connect that vision to a strategy that works.

All too often, in fact, these kids have been rewarded just for coming up with ideas. Execution may never have been discussed. Consider this: Generation X struggled with authority, Generation iY often struggles with reality. I love their boldness and their faith that they can change the world. Part of their boldness, however, has come in response to parents and teachers establishing an environment where they always win.

Much of their time is spent in a protected, failure-proof environment in which they're never given the chance to lose. Their entire lives have been full of safety devices, and they have been discouraged from going anywhere alone. They also receive ribbons and trophies just for participating in activities, without having to earn anything.

Once again, I am not advocating for parental neglect. I want all kids to feel affirmed. But there's a difference between common-sense measures and over-protection. Healthy risk is a part of growing up. Being perennially protected and provided for not only tends to foster a prolonged childhood; it also nurtures a sense of entitlement.

In a survey of corporate recruiters by the *Wall Street Journal* and Harrison Interactive, students were told that there was an "E-word" that described them. Then they were asked to guess what that word was. The young people guessed a lot of words—*excellent, entrepreneur, energetic, enterprising*—but none of them guessed the right one: *entitled.*[19]

Where does this sense of entitlement come from? Largely from adults who have shielded Generation iY from disappointment and neglected to tell them "no" about anything. The National Institute on Media and Family and the Minnesota PTA have even launched a statewide campaign encouraging parents and teachers to start saying no to young people more often. They are begging parents to read David Walsh's book, *No: Why Kids—of All Ages—Need to Hear It and Why Parents Can Say It.* The campaign blames DDD (Discipline Deficit Disorder) for this generation's inflated expectations and feelings of entitlement.[20]

Paradox #6: They Are Diverse...Yet Harmonious.

Obviously, diversity and unity are not oxymorons. However, I find it intriguing that the most ethnically diverse generation in modern American history might also be one of the most team-oriented and least individualistic generations in modern history as well. They are very different, yet they seem to get along and function well in communities.

These kids have grown up playing soccer on teams and performing school projects in groups. In their preschool years they watched *Barney and Friends* and *Blue's Clues*, which taught them to love each other and solve problems in teams. Many wore uniforms in school, and they've been taught tolerance for people who are different from them. As young adults, they often date in groups. They tend to be a harmonious generation of kids, much more so than their Baby Boomer and Gen-X parents.

I have a friend who teaches the third grade. She told me that her class this year is made up of students from diverse backgrounds, but she's never seen a more team-oriented group of kids. When she highlights a student's work on an assignment, they break out into applause. Without her prompting, they encourage each other and even console each other when mistakes are made. (This never happened in my third-grade class in the 1960s.) This illustrates again how they see themselves as players on a team. They are people persons who are accustomed to doing things together and prefer it that way.

Robert Putnam's 2001 bestseller, *Bowling Alone*, summarized the differences between Baby Boomers and kids today. In a phrase, it suggests that while Baby Boomers are bowling alone on Wednesday nights, the young people of Generation iY are playing soccer in teams.[21] Their people skills may be lacking, but they love to do things together—yet another paradox.

At the same time, this team-spirited Generation iY is also the most likely to divide itself comfortably into a large variety of different groups. According to Ron Alsop, this tendency is clear on college campuses, where there has been a significant jump in racial and gender diversity. The majority of college students are now female. The Hispanic population has passed up the African-Americans in many locations. In addition, there is a huge jump in the Asian college student population across the U.S.[22]

But the diversity of the iY Generation isn't limited to traditional racial or gender categories. Generation iYers also identify with a huge variety of groups or subcultures. Researcher George Barna believes there are at least twenty different teenage subcultures existing in the United States today.[23] Teens often belong to multiple subcultures, sometimes because they are transitioning from one to another, sometimes because they have multiple interests that require variety in their tribal loyalties, and sometimes because they're searching for their place in the larger culture.

Because of the Internet, they have more access than ever before to people who share a variety of interests. They're not limited to what their schools or their communities offer. Whether they love graphic novels, birding, knitting, tattoos, skydiving, computer games, whitewater rafting, or gardening, they are almost guaranteed to find kindred spirits. In other words, Generation iY is team-oriented, but they really enjoy choosing their teams and have an almost infinite variety to choose from.

Does this mean that iY kids never feel isolated or ostracized? Of course not. There will always be kids who feel rejected or ignored by peers—definitely not part of the team. This is where the problem lies. The connectedness of the iY generation has the capacity to make this worse, as illustrated by several cases of "cyberbullying" that have resulted in suicide. And while there have been far fewer examples of school shootings by ostracized kids in recent years, they still happen from time to time. The issue here is they become far too familiar with one demographic and fail to interact respectfully with others outside of it.

Even more troubling, the kids of Generation iY tend to be connected mostly with each other. My research tells me they typically spend over 50 percent of their day with peers and only 15 percent with adults, including parents. In fact 30 percent of their day is spent without any adult supervision. As a result, many don't learn how to interface with folks from a different generation. Life for them is like an isolated compartment containing mostly people just like them. So this connected, diverse, teamwork-oriented generation is also strangely homogeneous.

This reality is more troublesome than you might imagine. Many aspects of our society distance adolescents from adults, prompting kids to choose each other instead of grownups as role models. University of North Carolina professor Dr. Mel Levine asks, "How can you emerge as a productive adult when you've hardly ever cared to observe one very closely? How can you preview and prepare for grown-up life when you keep modeling yourself after other kids?"[24]

Interaction outside of class between a student and his college instructor is at an all-time low.[25] As Mark Bauerlein puts it, "Young people have never been so intensely mindful of and present to one another, so enabled in adolescent contact. [This contact wraps] them up in a generational cocoon reaching all the way into their bedrooms. The autonomy has a cost. The more they attend to themselves, the less they remember the past and envision a future."[26]

In essence, students used to seek out adults and read the classics in order to learn. Now they're seeking more time with peers and watching video on Web sites, getting guidance from the unprepared. They are no longer interacting with Hemingway or Emerson or seeking wisdom from Socrates. Instead, they seek out each other. Sadly, their peers are seldom ready to furnish them with a healthy worldview.

Paradox #7: They Are Visionary...Yet Vacillating.

We see this all the time. The young people of Generation iY will develop a passion for an idea or a cause. They get caught up in a vision for making the world a better place, yet the vision may well be fleeting. This generation is exposed to so many possibilities, they often have trouble settling on one for very long. Many are not so much passionate as "fashionate." They get a passion for a cause for a week or a month, when it's fashionable to do so. They tend to hop from vision to vision and may never stay long enough to make a lasting difference. Instead, they remain tentative and undecided about the future, and they have difficulty focusing long enough on any one pursuit to develop a deeper knowledge or more thorough skills.

The average time it takes for today's college students to graduate is six years. Is it because they are stupid? No, it's often because they change their major multiple times or simply choose to double and triple major because they can't make up their minds.

All too often, as a result, before they can implement one good vision, they will be distracted by another. A significant percentage of recent college graduates aren't able to follow through with the planning and focus necessary to perform and execute a long-term vision. Kids today have access to a lot of information, and they can get it at the touch of a finger. However, they are rarely encouraged—and often lack the interest—to delve deeply into a subject or go below the surface. They're often fuzzy, not focused. To borrow one of the Habitudes® concepts our organization teaches to students,[27] this generation often resembles a flood, not a river, seeping out in every direction but not going far in any one direction. They are flooding, not flowing, broad but shallow, just skimming the surface.

Their reading skills are low; only half of the high-school graduates meet the benchmark for reading. In general, their study time is low as well. According to a U.S. Department of Education study, when asked how many hours they had spent on homework the day before, about 40 percent of students said they had no homework or they didn't do the homework that had been assigned.[28]

According to *World Watch* magazine, the working vocabulary of the average fourteen-year-old has dropped measurably since 1950. The average middle-school student then possessed a vocabulary of twenty-five thousand words. In 1999, the average was ten thousand words.[29]

I once heard someone say that today's students are made of Teflon—nothing seems to stick. One of our focus groups unveiled that their attention spans are about the same as their age—sixteen years old, sixteen minutes. And when they're bored, they quit. Nationwide, about 30 percent don't even finish high school.

One college dean told me he had a student ask if he could "try out" being a resident advisor in the dormitory. When the dean responded that the commitment was for one year, the student asked if he could try it for two weeks. This is the question that prompts adults to wonder if these kids are going to change the world or just keep changing their minds.

Paradox #8: They Are High Achievement...Yet High Maintenance.

As I have shown, this is a confident, optimistic generation of kids. As a whole, they are achievement-oriented. They believe they can and will improve the world...by noon on Friday. This perspective isn't new—kids are usually naïve. But this generation's expectations tend to be especially high, and they expect a lot of feedback. All too often, when they don't receive the extra attention, or things don't come easily, they give up.

Researchers report, for instance, that teen employment is down.[30] It has been for years. Kids either feel they don't need a job, or they can't find an employer who has the tolerance for them. And those who do find jobs often get canned by employers who find them too draining. We've all seen it. A high-achieving kid may also be very needy and backward.

This, perhaps, illustrates the biggest paradox of all. The iY world they live in has both accelerated and delayed their maturity. Their exposure to large amounts of data, through technology, has sped up their cognitive growth. They know a lot very early. They seem so advanced. However, this world has postponed their readiness for the real world of people, responsibility, conflict resolution, listening, and waiting. A thirteen-year-old kid may be able to program your DVR and download the latest software for you but then, at sixteen, not be able to carry on a conversation with an adult. It's easy to mistake one-dimensional maturity for fully developed maturity. In many areas, iYers may be less mature at graduation than any previous generation.

Living in the iY World

Generation iY live in a world all their own—shaped by their own choices but also by the environment adults have created for them. Some aspects of that world make it harder for iYers to transition into adult reality. For instance, their world is:

- **Artificial.** They spend much of their time in an online world, living an unreal life on Second Life, Facebook, MySpace, or Flickr. While such virtual living enhances some skills (such as multitasking), it can also hinder development of people skills, self-awareness, and ability to resolve conflict.

- **Homogeneous.** My research tells me iYers spend most of their days with other iYers—over 50 percent of their day with peers and only 15 percent with adults. Instead of learning from other generations, they get much of their guidance from the unprepared.

- **Guaranteed.** Much of their time is spent in a failure-proof, risk-free environment. Being constantly protected and provided for tends to hinder maturity and nurture a sense of entitlement. Always winning, they may never have failed at anything. They believe they deserve it.

- **Superficial.** For the most part, this generation is a flood, not a river—seeping out in every direction but not going far in any one direction. They're flooding not flowing, skimming the surface.

- **Programmed.** They've grown up in an world so structured and planned out by adults that some call them "Organization Kids." They're rarely required to interpret life on their own and may be unable to act without consensus or approval.

- **Narcissistic.** The society-wide effort to increase their self-esteem has backfired, creating a generation consumed with self. They've been allowed to be consumers, not contributors, and to be egocentric without consequence.

Getting Through to the iY Generation

What do we do with this paradoxical generation? Generation iY has the potential to reframe our realities in positive ways if we can help them resolve their paradoxes and respond well to the needs of the world around them. But in order to do that, we need to actually connect with them—and that can be tricky. How do we compete with VH1 and MTV—or, for that matter, YouTube or FaceBook, or whatever new platform has been invented while I am writing this book? Kids today are inundated with a myriad of voices vying for their minds and hearts. Because many of those voices come from well-funded marketing campaigns, we who want to capture their attention often face a daunting task.

The iY generation has so much "flash" and glitz and glamour available to them that they have developed a much more superficial set of life goals than earlier Millennials. According to Jean Twenge, a 2006 survey of eighteen- to twenty-five-year-olds found that their number-one goal is to get rich (81 percent) and their number-two goal is to get famous (51 percent).[31]

This means that those of us who believe we have something to say to this generation are in a tough dilemma. We need to remember that every time we stand in front of our own kids or a group of students, they are silently asking: *Why should I listen to you? What do you have to offer me that's different than the other options in my life?*

In short, Generation Y has become Generation Why?

I will spend the rest of this book exploring in some detail how adults can most effectively connect with the young people of Generation iY. For now, I want to start by suggesting some basic observations on how to get through to this contradictory but culturally potent group.

Observation #1: They Want to Belong Before They Believe.

Today's students don't necessarily make decisions based upon logic or statistics. They would rather join and belong to a small affinity group *before* they embrace the beliefs of that group. Their basis for making decisions is more relational than logical. If you hope to get them to embrace an idea—embrace them first.

Observation #2: They Want an Experience Before an Explanation.

Futurist Leonard Sweet describes today's culture and its young people as EPIC: Experiential, Participatory, Image-rich and Connected.[32] Teachers must remember that a lecture isn't enough anymore—or at least we cannot *begin* with a lecture. If we want to be heard, we must engage iYers' interest with an experience that captures their imagination. They want to do or see something. They want action and interaction. So instead of asking, "What do I want to say?" we should ask ourselves, "How can I say it creatively and experientially?"

Observation #3: They Want a Cause Before They Want a Course.

If you want to seize the attention of students today, plan to give them a reason for why they need to listen to your words. For instance, if I want to spark a passion for world history or international justice, I must first expose students to a cause that interacts with that issue.

Actress Angelina Jolie has confessed she grew up as a spoiled, rich girl living in Hollywood and spent much of her early life pursuing success as an actress and a model. Then she read a script for a movie called *Beyond Borders*. It was about a self-indulged woman who lived a life of privilege until she discovered the plight of refugees and orphans in developing nations. The script was a catalyst for Angelina. She took the next year and traveled to refugee camps all over Africa and Asia. She became an international spokesperson for the UN's Refugee Agency and has given a third of her income to such causes.

Observation #4: They Want a Guide on the Side Before They Want a Sage on the Stage.

Finally, keep in mind that young people today aren't necessarily looking for experts, especially if they are plastic or untouchable. They would rather have someone authentic to come beside them. When students were recently asked about their heroes, for the first time in over twenty years they did not list an athlete at the top of the list. Their number-one response was "Mom and Dad." They hunger more for relationship than for information—even relevant information. They are accustomed to learning on a need-to-know basis—but their need to know will increase if a person they trust and know well is the one sharing the information. They're looking for mentors—authentic mentors.

Observation #5: They Want to Play Before They Pay.

I find many characteristics of Generation iY healthy and fascinating. However, this one may cause trouble for them later in life. For students today, almost everything comes instantly. They don't like waiting for anything. Shows like *American Idol* are appealing to this generation because one of their peers gets to become famous overnight—and they get to determine the winner in a short amount of time. Usually, they love events but don't enjoy the process of growth. The "pay now, play later" mentality tends to be foreign to them.

For iY kids, in other words, results have to come quickly, or they may lose interest. For those who seek to influence them, this means we must connect quickly. As communicators, we have to grab their attention up front, demonstrating swiftly that our content is relevant.

Observation #6: They Want to Use but Not Be Used by Others.

Millennials love to use any means possible to get what they want—the Internet, cell phones, instant messaging, or purchasing music for their iPods. At the same time, they tend to be very wary of anyone they suspect of trying to use them. They don't want to be a project or the target of some marketing campaign. They want to take the initiative and remain in the driver's seat. They prefer it to be "their idea" and to take steps on their prerogative. Like their parents, they like being in control. And since their world has been so programmed, they feel strongly about being able to weigh in, to have a voice. For us, this means creating environments where they can come up with their own ideas and implement them—all the while moving toward a common goal for the group.

Observation #7: They Want a Transformation, Not Merely a Touch.

The expectations of students get higher and higher with each decade. Today there is a higher demand for "edutainment" than even four years ago.

Think about it. As I write, freshmen are now taking iPhones with them to college. Freshmen didn't have iPhones four years ago. And I can safely predict that in another four years students will have something new that hasn't been thought of now. All this means that adults—especially those of us who work as campus workers and teachers—cannot communicate (teach) the same way we did in the 1980s or even the 1990s and expect to be heard.

It used to be that communicators just needed to have interesting information. Next, it was good stories. Then, it was audiovisuals. Later it was to share experiences. Now I believe students want experiences that literally transform them in the process. No doubt, it's a tall order, but the bar is constantly rising.

The Future Is Waiting

To connect with and influence Generation iY, we'll likely have to adjust to them… over and over again. We'll have to rethink not only *what* we are saying, but *how* we are saying it. It may not be easy, but it's worth the effort.

One thing is sure. These Generation iY kids are products of our own invention. We created them and the world they live in. Dr. Jean Twenge reminds us: "These kids didn't raise themselves. They're doing what they're taught to do—from parents, teachers, and a lot from the media."[33]

The future is waiting. The question is, will these imaginative kids be ready to follow through on their dreams and execute them?

The answer lies in how well we lead them.

→ **LINKING UP** ←

In this emerging world, are you an immigrant or a native? Check to see if you are adapting well to the changes in the iY world: **www.SaveTheirFuture Now.com/ImmigrantorNative**.

4 Tollbooth or Roadblock?
Why iY Kids Are Getting Stuck in Adolescence

I TRAVEL ALL THE TIME, ALL OVER THE WORLD—which means I often find myself navigating a variety of road systems. Just last year, for instance, I was in California on my way to speak at an event. Without warning (at least I didn't see any signs), I came upon a tollbooth. Ugh. I was in a hurry, and now I was in a line of cars, waiting to pay some fee to drive on that road. What's worse, I didn't have any cash on me. You would have been entertained to see me scrounging through the car as I crept forward, digging to find any nickels, dimes or quarters that would add up to a dollar.

Alas, I couldn't do it. I couldn't find the money to pay the toll. The man at the booth was friendly, but he was not going to let me pass through without payment. It turned into quite an ordeal. I tried to negotiate a plan for paying the Department of Transportation later. I explained that I had a variety of credit-card options. Nope. He wanted cash.

I ended up begging the man behind me to let me write him a check for one dollar so I could pay my toll and move forward. It worked, but not until I had held up the line of cars for ten minutes.

Needless to say, no one was happy. I had not only delayed my own progress, but the progress of everyone else around me.

This is a picture of what is happening to Generation iY as it moves into adulthood. Adolescence is a lot like a tollbooth. There is a cost for passing through it and growing up. And everyone has to pay and pass through if they want to progress on their life journey.

Sadly, many of these young adults don't seem to have what it takes to pay the price. Like me, they negotiate and come up with alternatives to paying the toll.

Some even try to do it on "credit," hoping that teachers, coaches, and employers will trust in their future potential and let them keep progressing. More and more, I am finding that adults—especially employers—aren't willing to take the risk. They're not sure if that young person will ever have what it takes, and they find it too risky to float a loan.

When that happens, the tollbooth becomes a roadblock. Just as in my tollbooth experience, young people end up not only delaying their own progress, but hindering the movement of everyone else around them. And the sad thing is, many seem content to set up camp on this side of the tollbooth and don't even try to move forward.

A Postponed Generation

Since the birth of Generation iY kids, a new demographic group has expanded worldwide. The years between eighteen and twenty-five have become a distinct life stage—a strange, transitional "no man's land" between adolescence and adulthood in which young people stall for a few extra years, putting off adult responsibility. Most of these are not bad kids or troubled kids or even stupid kids. They just don't see the need to grow up because life is working for them just fine right now. They seem to enjoy a season of exploration without the demands of paying bills, or providing for someone else. And while this is true of both sexes, it manifests itself in different ways with young men and young women.

Sociologist Michael Kimmel describes the male phenomenon like this: "Somewhere between 16-29, they enter 'Guyland' and seem unable to commit to marriages, families or long-term jobs." Many ascribe to a Guy Code "where locker-room behaviors, sexual conquests, bullying, violence, and assuming a cocky jock pose can rule" over the sacrifices of growing up. Kimmel believes this is happening for a variety of reasons. First, people are living longer, so what's the big hurry of getting tied down? Second, parents make it easy for many young men to remain at home and not provide for themselves. Third, Generation iY women are often professional and competent—which is intimidating or confusing to males.[1] I'll talk more about these male issues in the next chapter.

This delayed-development issue is less common for females, and when girls do get stuck, their reasons are usually different. For instance, some may not want to lose touch with their friends. Their high-school world provides a comfortable haven of chatting, texting, Skyping, Facebooking and "hanging out." Adolescence is fun, and girls may stall because they don't want to leave their relationship haven. I know some college sophomores who continue to return to their high school each weekend.

Boyfriends can also be an issue. If a couple begins dating in high school, the girl may become accustomed to having a "boy on her arm." It feels good. It feels right. She may even love him. This guy, however, may be lagging behind her in his maturation. So, what's a girl to do? All too often, she'll lag too. They'd rather trade away their potential opportunities and assure that they maintain a boyfriend relationship at all costs.

The third reason is that the world is far more complex for a female than it was thirty or forty years ago, when their mothers were growing up. The array of choices can be intimidating. Competition between girls is high. Colleges are tougher to get into. And the adult world can be downright intimidating. Once again, why leave the cozy world of adolescence for a seemingly impossible world of responsibility?

For both genders, I believe prolonged adolescence can be fostered by an attitude that prevails among a large percentage of them. Young people often lag because they've bought into the idea that "no job is better than a bad job." They certainly don't want to get tied down to an unsuitable workplace (who does?), so they may go without work in hopes that something appealing will emerge later.

I spend the majority of my time doing leadership development with young adults. I was with a group recently on a state university campus. Every one of them was passionate about changing the world, but they made it clear that they were not in a hurry to settle down to adult life. For them, the ages between eighteen and twenty-six are a sort of sandbox, a chance to build castles and knock them down and experiment with different careers, knowing that none of them really counts. Not yet anyway.

Time magazine reported on this phenomenon and concluded that many young people are just overwhelmed with adulthood—the obstacles, the opposition, the opportunities, and especially the options. There are forty different kinds of coffee beans at Whole Foods market, several hundred channels on DirecTV, fifteen million ads on Match.com, and eight hundred thousand jobs posted on Monster. com.[2] Further, in 2009 the U.S. Census Bureau reported that there were nineteen million college students competing for those jobs.[3]

So what do young adults perceive to be the doorway to adulthood? It may surprise you. It isn't a driver's license or graduation from high school or even college. It's not even getting married. The top response in a nationwide survey was: having your first child. The median age for this milestone is twenty-seven. In Europe it is even higher.[4] Some demographers suggest that adolescence has extended into the thirties. In 2002, the National Academy of Science redefined adolescence as the period extending from the onset of puberty to around thirty years old. The MacArthur Foundation, has gone further still, funding a major project that argues the transition to adulthood doesn't end until thirty-four. Even twice-married Britney Spears fits the profile. For a brief summary of the predicament of so many of the iY generation, you can't do much better than her 2001 hit, "I'm Not a Girl, Not Yet a Woman."

So what is a society to do with these people? "The real heavy lifting may have to happen on the level of the culture itself," writes Lev Grossman of *Time* magazine.

> There was a time when people looked forward to taking on the mantle of adulthood. That time is past. Now our culture trains young people to fear it. "I don't ever want a lawn," says [twenty-seven-year-old Matt] Swann. "I don't ever want to drive two hours to get to work. I do not want to be a parent. I mean, hell, why would I? There's so much fun to be had while you're young."[5]

Abandonment or Abundance

I think there's a deeper reason for our predicament. During their childhood and adolescent years, kids often experience something traumatic. They encounter one extreme or the other: either abandonment or abundance. Many experience both.

Young people who experience abandonment are thrust into responsible roles too soon. Perhaps because of an alcoholic father or an absent mother or a self-absorbed caretaker, these children never fully form. They are exposed to emotionally traumatic situations and typically don't respond well. (Today, 62 percent of kids are being raised without their biological father.)

To be sure, some do fine. I know a woman who stepped up and became an "adult" at ten years old when her dad became abusive and then absent. Life has been a struggle, however, for her siblings. One brother, James, simply stopped growing emotionally at age fourteen. His maturation was stunted. Even today, in his forties, he is far from being healthy and well adjusted. It's as though when the child is abandoned, their emotions and spirit stop maturing. They shut down. James's body is in midlife, but his emotions are still an early teenager. He is a boy who can't seem to become a man.

The other extreme is *abundance*. It's a delightful word—we all love abundance. But when abundance is furnished and young people never learn to manage resources (money, possessions, relationships, or time), their growth can be stunted.

Certainly, every parent wishes to provide for their children abundantly, but a never-ending supply of anything reduces the human ability to interpret, manage, save, give, and spend wisely. Frankly, we become spoiled. Kyle is a young man in this situation. His parents are fearful of losing him. They're afraid he won't like or accept them. So Kyle is now in power. He's completely self-absorbed, and he's come to expect his parents to do everything. Kyle has feigned a suicide attempt, and he is rude to guests. His parents are ashamed.

Kyle was not abandoned. Quite the opposite. He wasn't expected to fend for himself at seventeen or eighteen, when he probably should have been. More important, there was no plan for giving him responsibility in increasing amounts as he grew up.

These two scenarios remind me of the ancient Hebrew proverb written three thousand years ago. The prayer says, "God, don't give me too little, or I might be tempted to steal. But, don't give me too much, or I might think I can get by without you. Give me just enough."

Sadly, iY as a generation suffers from both too little and too much. As a result, they're in danger of being "not enough" for the demands of their future life.

Let's Walk Down Memory Lane

To understand how we have spiraled in this direction, let's look at our dilemma from a historical standpoint. Let's compare how children mature today with how they matured, say, a hundred years ago. No doubt, technology and travel have changed our lifestyles in contrast to a century ago. But I'd like to examine what this has done to the minds and hearts of our young people and what we can do to remedy the problems that have surfaced.

My son, Jonathan, is seventeen years old. I love him. We enjoy a good relationship. Yet, while he's a very social creature, I call his bedroom the ASR—or Anti-Social Room. When our family arrives home after an outing, Jonathan's natural inclination is to retreat to that room...alone. Or is he? Of course he's not. I know he's texting, instant messaging, Skyping, Facebooking and calling his friends. His room is an electronic command center. And left to himself, his world is influenced mostly by the peers he keeps in touch with there.

May I remind you? Teens today spend one third of their waking hours without an adult. Oh, parents may be in the home, teachers may be in the classroom, but the adults aren't really influencing the teens. They're lost in their own world, interacting mostly with peers, not adults.

Compare this reality to life a century ago. Most young people were launched readily into adulthood because they grew up doing physical work—usually along with adults in the context of a stable family. School was either at home or in the one-room schoolhouse where they were surrounded by students of all ages. Many acquired life skills through apprenticeships that enabled them to connect with adults in their early to middle teens, and many more "apprenticed" by working side by side with their parents. All their lives they were connected to adults, and the jump from childhood to adulthood wasn't a challenge. Consequently, they looked forward to adulthood and married young, having the basic skills needed by their late teens. There was no such household term as "adolescent." A person moved from being a child to being a young adult. Initiative, responsibility and adult interaction were the norm.

Today, however, our culture has encouraged young people as a group to be more isolated from society than integrated into it. Economic changes have reduced the number of young people in the workforce. We have kept kids in school and given them cell phones. The result? We have created an environment where they can postpone maturation. Kids master a virtual world and believe they've mastered life in general.

We've also created a compartmentalized society with distinct youth subcultures. Schools, media, advertising, even churches segment their programs according to age groups. This makes sense in terms of efficiency—and who of us doesn't like content and products designed just for us? Unfortunately, I believe this increased specialization has helped hinder this next generation's growth. Because they lose influential time with adults, they come to define themselves by their peers. As a result, they're often ill-prepared for adult life. We don't expect them to "grow up" until well into their twenties or even early thirties. This self-confident, self-absorbed generation ends up stuck at the tollbooth of adolescence. For them, twenty-six is the new eighteen.

No doubt, you know students who do not fit this description. I do too. But statistically speaking, these kids are the exception to the rule. Dr. Mel Levine writes, "years of schooling and parenting have entirely missed the elusive target: work-life readiness. Our graduates may well lack the practical skills, the habits, the behaviors, the real-world insights, and the frames of mind pivotal for career startup. Their parents and teachers have unwittingly let them down. Adulthood has ambushed them."[6]

The Invention of Adolescence

How does all this compare to life one hundred years ago? First of all, the term *adolescence* had just been invented and published by psychologist G. Stanley Hall in 1904. It is taken from the Latin *adolescere* meaning "to grow up." Psychologist Erik Erikson characterized adolescence as a period of exploration and experimentation, a time when kids try on different roles, a period of coming to terms with one's personal identity. Obviously, there's a place for doing this—but there's a difference between doing it at sixteen and doing it at twenty-eight. And, there is a difference between experimenting and floundering.

I'm not suggesting it was wrong to develop this term. It helps us understand what young adults experience as they mature. However, it's now seen as an entire season of life rather than a doorway. As the term became popular, it has given permission to young people to stay in that season for extended periods of time.

Former House Speaker Newt Gingrich, writing in *Business Week*, actually suggests it's time to put an end to adolescence, that as a social institution, it's been a failure, and that it's time to return to an "earlier, more successful model" of children moving more directly into adult responsibility. He argues,

> Prior to the 19th century...there was virtually universal acceptance that puberty marked the transition from childhood to young adulthood. Whether with the Bar Mitzvah and Bat Mitzvah ceremony of the Jewish faith or confirmation in the Catholic Church or any hundreds of rites of passage in societies around the planet, it was understood you were either a child or a young adult.[7]

This was clearly true in the U.S. during the early days of U.S. history, Gingrich reminds us. At age thirteen, Benjamin Franklin was out of school and apprenticed to his brother as a printer and publisher. John Quincy Adams was sixteen when he served as a secretary to the U.S. delegation during negotiations to end the Revolutionary War. At fifteen, Daniel Boone had launched a year-long journey through the wilderness. (Today he'd be a freshman in high school.)

No doubt, life expectancies were shorter back then, but society proved that a young person could rise to a challenge if empowered to do so. Gingrich concludes:

> Adolescence...has degenerated into a process of enforced boredom and age segregation that has produced one of the most destructive social ar-

> rangements in human history....It's time to change this—to shift to seri-
> ous work, learning, and responsibility at age 13 instead of age 30. In other
> words, replace adolescence with young adulthood.[8]

I believe Gingrich is on to something. I don't know if I'm ready to outlaw adolescence entirely, but I do believe we must be more intentional about leading our
boys into manhood and the girls into womanhood.

The Problem with High Schools

But the creation of *adolescence* is not the only historical development in the early
part of the twentieth century that contributed to Generation iY's "tollbooth" problem. Another factor, interestingly enough, is the growing importance of high
schools. Today, almost everyone agrees that we need high schools—but there is a
trade-off. They represent both the good and not-so-good. Here's what happened,
according to Howard Chudacoff:

> By the 1920s,...the age grading and the nearly universal experience of
> schooling pressed children into peer groups, creating lifestyles and insti-
> tutions that were not only separate from but occasionally in opposition to
> adult power. Compulsory attendance laws, which kept children in school
> until they were fourteen or older, had a strong impact in the United States,
> where by 1930 nearly half of all youths aged fourteen to twenty were high-
> school students. Enrollment of rural youths and African Americans re-
> mained relatively low (only one-sixth of American blacks attended high
> school in the 1920s). But large proportions of immigrants and native-born
> whites of foreign parents attended high school. Educational reformers de-
> veloped curricula to prepare young people for adult life, and an expanding
> set of extracurricular...activities, such as clubs, dances, and sports, height-
> ened the socialization of teens in peer groups.[9]

Consequently, secondary school and adolescence became synonymous. With
the advent of high schools, students stayed at home with their parents longer,
yet they spent less time with their parents and more time with their peers. In
other words, one of the unintended outcomes of the high school experience
was that adolescents delayed moving out into adulthood, and peer influence was
prolonged. Teens lost close relational ties to other adults and began defining
themselves by other students, not adult role models. The quest for identity, pur-

pose, and maturity was developed within their ranks, not by the primary adults in their lives—or by their faith, as it once had been. For many, the social element replaced the spiritual.

As time marched on into the middle twentieth century, media and retailers picked up on the idea of niche marketing—and directly targeted Baby Boomers, creating movies, books, magazines, music, and radio and television shows just for them. They communicated in a way that young people would understand— and that allowed them to remain in an adolescent world. Marketing gurus drew on expert theories about adolescent insecurity and conformity to "sell goods that catered to teenagers' desires to dress, buy, and act like their peers."[10]

In the years since, marketers have gotten better and better at selling this idea. Today, our world has been increasingly sliced up into demographic sectors. Each "slice" is a market that sellers want to control...and the most-desired slice by far is the young. "They are the optimum market to be going after for consumer electronics, Game Boys, flat screen TVs, iPods, couture fashion, exotic vacations and so forth," says David Morrison, president of TwentySomething, Inc., a marketing consultancy based in Philadelphia. "Most of their needs are taken care of by moms and dads, so their income is largely discretionary."[11]

Corporations, in other words, have a real stake in keeping young people in a tractable, exploitable, preadult state—living at home, spending their money on toys. This economic reality is yet another reason why, like it or not, adolescence is now a prolonged season of life—and the tollbooth has become a roadblock. Retailers not only don't expect iYers to grow up; they don't want them to.

How Does a Kid Grow Up?

I had just landed in Dallas. My flight was delayed again, and it was late at night. As I drove my car along a service road, I noticed the headlights of a large pickup truck in my rearview mirror. He was coming up fast behind me.

I put on my turn signal and started to turn into my hotel parking lot when it happened. He swerved to miss me and screeched his tires, but he couldn't do it fast enough. Slam! He hit the back of my car. I was okay, but I could tell my vehicle was damaged. I started to get out of my car, when I realized it wasn't over. The other driver suddenly turned his engine back on and raced away.

The easiest thing to do would be to pull into the hotel, get a good night's sleep, and pay for the damage myself. But I decided I wasn't going to do the easy thing. Even though I was tired, I pulled out to follow him. All of a sudden, my night turned into a TV show. When he realized I was following him, he sped up, running a red light and turning at every corner he could. He was determined to lose me, but I was determined to catch him.

I remember feeling very calm. I wasn't angry. I wasn't looking for revenge or to punish him. I simply wanted him to be responsible for what he had done. I wanted to make the point that life is not about running away from your mistakes.

Well, the chase went on for fifteen minutes. As I drove, I scribbled down his license plate number, then called 911 and gave it to them. But I didn't stop then. I stayed with that pickup truck through parking lots, behind buildings, and through alleys. It was a little exhilarating. I wanted to help the police navigate to where he was.

Finally, my hit-and-run driver pulled into an apartment complex. As he pulled around a bend, a police squad car pulled up in front of him while I, in my damaged car, parked right behind him.

He was trapped. He gave up, and the case was solved.

Let me share with you the insights I garnered from this little episode. This driver was young (Generation iY). The police discovered he was quite intelligent. He was also drunk, and he was running from responsibility. He desperately hoped that his mistake would not cost him anything and that he would not get caught. To make matters worse, he was driving without insurance. (Guess who got called to pay for the damages to my rental car? You're reading his book right now.)

This little adventure illustrates an important point about Generation iY. This was a smart young man who did a monumentally dumb thing. How could this happen? I think I know part of the answer. It has to do with how children mature in general...and how Generation iY postpones the process. As children grow, they typically mature in four areas:

1. **Biological:** They experience puberty; their bodies change and develop physically. If they are male, their voices change. Male or female, they grow hair in new places and morph into an adult body type.
2. **Cognitive:** They mature intellectually; their intelligence moves from concrete thinking to abstract thinking. Their ability to comprehend things conceptually increases.
3. **Social:** They begin viewing relationships differently and value them for new reasons. They process interactions with others in reality instead of fantasy or possibility.
4. **Emotional:** Their view of "self" changes as well as their capacity to function independently. They become stable and their self-awareness increases.

My research on these four areas of maturity reveals some very clear conclusions when it comes to Generation iY.

First, most young people today are advanced biologically. They are growing up physically faster than ever. Puberty hits both boys and girls one to two years earlier than it hit teens thirty years ago.

In addition, young people are advanced cognitively. By this I simply mean they've consumed more data than ever. They go to school early and are exposed to huge amounts of information at relatively young ages. Most can handle multiple messages rapidly and assimilate visual information more quickly than adults.

Third, they are advanced socially. Many have dozens of friends they connect with in person at school, then hundreds of friends they connect with via the Internet. As I stated earlier, when it comes to social interaction—they multitask.

When it comes to emotional maturity, however, this generation is not nearly so advanced. In fact, our studies show they are behind previous generations in this area. A significant percentage is what I would call emotionally backward.

This is part of the reason social scientists are baffled with the iYs' Jekyll and Hyde tendencies. They're ahead of schedule in so many categories, yet behind in others. As sociology professor Anthony Campolo once told me: "I don't believe we live in a generation of bad kids. I believe we live in a generation of kids who know too much too soon."

This is yet another paradox of Generation iY. *USA Today* reports that nearly six in ten moms say children are "growing up too fast" because parents:

- *Allow Internet use without supervision (75 percent).*
- *Dress kids in age-inappropriate clothing (74 percent).*
- *Overschedule kids' lives (63 percent).*
- *Give kids cell phones (59 percent).*

At the same time, while these factors may be enabling (or pushing!) kids to grow up too fast intellectually or socially, I believe they are retarding their emotional growth. Accessing technology and going to school at three or four years old may have stimulated their brains, but people are not merely walking brains. We are whole people—with emotions, spirits, and souls. It is clear to me that Generation iY is growing up lopsided—heavy on one side, light on the other, advanced in some areas (intellect), pitifully behind in others (emotional maturity). Sometimes a student is highly gifted in an area and we mistake that for maturity. Let me say the obvious. There is no correlation between giftedness and maturity.

Atrophied Muscles in Generation iY

We all know someone who broke an arm or leg and had it in a cast for four to six weeks. When the cast is removed—the muscles underneath are deformed and reduced. It's called "disuse muscular atrophy." When muscles are not used or exerted, they shrink. This phenomena has been studied widely in astronauts who experience zero-gravity conditions.

It's surprising how fast disuse atrophy might occur. Researchers have investigated what happens during limb immobilization after injury. One study found that muscle wasting was detected in as little as three days following immobilization. The degree of atrophy experienced in a muscle depends on how that muscle is used. It's a vivid illustration of the old adage: use it or lose it.

In many ways, this is a picture of students today. The iY world is convenient, instant, simple and surreal. But this world has caused certain intellectual, emotional and spiritual muscles to atrophy. I am not down on them—I'm merely concerned that we've created a world where some "muscles" they'll need for life have atrophied through disuse.

Consider for a moment the availability of credit to youth today. America is drowning in the quicksand of easy credit and the accessibility of credit cards. The problem of course is that students not only can enjoy products and services long before they can afford them—but they finish college with huge debt and no way to pay it off except to move back home—delaying their own maturation and independence. While many may argue for the importance of establishing credit in young adults, it seems they're rarely able to delay gratification to use that credit wisely. Once again, an atrophied muscle.

Many of the common virtues our culture once celebrated are no longer visible or practiced in this emerging generation. A sample of atrophied muscles are:

Atrophied Muscle	Description
1. Patience Muscle (Delayed gratification)	The ability to wait on a reward that comes slowly.
2. Connection Muscle (People skills)	The ability to develop common ground with those unlike you.
3. Responsibility Muscle (Morals and ethics)	The ability to do what is right even when acting alone.
4. Endurance Muscle (Tenacity)	The ability to stay committed and complete a task or a goal.
5. Empathy Muscle (Compassion/perspective)	The ability to see and feel what others do.

What's Your EQ?

People who work with iY young people often observe that their development is lopsided—they mature faster intellectually than they do emotionally. Daniel Goleman began writing on this subject for the corporate world more than a decade ago and popularized the term "emotional intelligence"[12]—EQ as opposed IQ. Emotional intelligence has to do with self-awareness as well as the maturity of people's interactions with others, their sense of identity, their emotional security, and their awareness of how they fit into a social setting.

In my experience, this is the area where today's adolescents seem to lag behind; their EQ is low. Accordingly, this is an appropriate focus for adults who work with young people. I'm not suggesting this simply because we adults are weary of the emotional immaturity of a generation of students. I am begging for this because we owe it to the students. In school, success is about 75 percent IQ and 25 percent EQ. In the real world following school, success is about 25 percent IQ and 75 percent EQ. If our kids are to successfully pass through the tollgate and move into adulthood, we must focus on improving their EQ.

Pruning the Brain

There is another reason—besides cultural shifts—that teens struggle with maturation. Scientists are gaining new insights into remarkable changes in teenagers' brains that may explain why the teen years are so hard on young people and their parents.

From ages eleven to fourteen, kids lose some of the connections between cells in the part of their brain that enables them to think clearly and make good decisions. "Ineffective or weak connections are pruned in much the same way a gardener would prune a tree or bush, giving the plant a desired shape,"[13] explains Alison Gopnik, Professor of Child Development at University of California at Berkeley. Their brain is changing from a child brain to an adult brain, and there's a season when the child part of the brain has been pruned but the adult portion isn't fully formed.

Regions that specialize in language, for example, grow rapidly until about age thirteen and then stop. The frontal lobes of the brain, which are responsible for high-level reasoning and decision making, aren't fully mature until the early twenties, according to Deborah Yurgelun-Todd, a neuroscientist at Harvard's Brain Imaging Center. Adolescents who are experiencing these brain changes can react emotionally, according to Ian Campbell, a neurologist at the U.C. Davis Sleep Research

Laboratory.[14] Mood swings and uncooperative or irresponsible attitudes can all be the result of these changes occurring.

The bottom line? Students today are consuming information they aren't completely ready to handle. The adult part of their brains is still forming and isn't ready to apply all that our society throws at it. Their mind takes it in and files it, but their will and emotions are not prepared to act on it in a healthy way. They can become paralyzed by all the content they consume. They want so much to be able to experience the world they've seen on Web sites or heard on podcasts, but they don't realize they are unprepared for that experience emotionally. In terms of their brain development, they are truly in between a child and an adult. (This is the genius behind movie ratings and viewer-discretion advisories on TV.)

In chapter 3, I stated that Generation iY is a paradoxical generation, and I believe this holds for the prolonged-adolescent phenomenon as well. In some ways, young adults are hanging back from maturity when they need to be moving forward. In other ways, they are growing up too fast—bombarded with way too much information before their changing brains are equipped to handle so much. This can leave adults with a quandary of how to lead iY people in a way that helps them successfully negotiate the "tollbooth" and move forward to healthy adulthood.

A Balancing Act

So much depends on the *timing* of what young people are exposed to during this period and on the *leadership style of the adults* in their lives. What an adolescent needs is an adult (parent, teacher, coach, employer, pastor, or leader) who makes appropriate demands and sets appropriate standards for them in a responsive environment of belief and concern. In short, they need adults to display a balance of two elements—they need them to be both responsive and demanding:

1. Responsive: to display acceptance, support and patience; to be attentive to them.
2. Demanding: to establish high standards, directing them to target those standards.

Psychologist Diana Baumrind speaks of these characteristics in her groundbreaking writing and suggests that adults with too little or too much of these characteristics result in these scenarios:[15]

1. Permissive – Too much responsiveness with too little demands.
2. Authoritarian – Too many demands with too little responsiveness.
3. Disengaged – Virtually no responsiveness and no demands.
4. Authoritative – Responsiveness is matched with appropriate demands.

We've all seen it. Teens who act like immature brats because teachers or parents have failed to hold them to standards of behavior. On the other hand, we've all seen the pitiful scenario where students live in fear because adults have pressured them to perform and never communicated grace and support. They need a balance.

A Second Balancing Act

At the same time, adolescents need a balance of two ingredients that run parallel to each other. As they mature they need proportionate autonomy and responsibility:

1. Autonomy: the ability to act independently, with freedom and access to resources.
2. Responsibility: the ability to be accountable and handle tasks in a dependable way.

This requires wise leadership on the part of the parent, teacher, coach or employer. They should experience simultaneous freedom and autonomy in parallel with their ability to assume responsibility. There should be limited exposure to input they aren't yet ready to handle, but they should also be encouraged to take increasing responsibility for themselves as they grow. The young adult emerges as one who has risen to the challenges because the standard was set by a caring adult.

Like many adolescents, my son is interested in the entertainment industry. As a parent I want to stoke his passion—but help him mature at the same time. Last year, he came to me with the idea of moving out to Hollywood for a few months. We talked it over and came to a mutual conclusion about the idea. His mother would move out with him under these conditions:

- *He would assume responsibility for half of all the expenses.*
- *Any auditions that turned into income would pay back his loan.*
- *He would pay for half of the car he would need to eventually buy.*
- *He would pay for any accidents he had that didn't require insurance.*
- *He would pay for fuel he used and we would pay for insurance.*

I have a friend whose twelve-year-old son wanted an iPod. The particular one he wanted was in limited supply and he was afraid it would sell out before he had the money to buy it. My friend performed a wonderful balancing act with his son. He bought the iPod, then said to his son: "I will hold on to it, until you earn the money to purchase it from me. If I give it to you now to enjoy, you'll have no incentive to pay it off and you won't appreciate it as much as if you wait for it." Six months ago, my friend handed the iPod to his son. It was fully paid for by a grateful teenager. Every kid grows up at a little different pace. This is why adults must be responsive and demanding, and kids must assume autonomy and responsibility together. Remember, our job is to prepare the child for the path, not the path for the child.

The Marks of Maturity

Below is a list of what I consider to be the marks of maturity. It's not exhaustive, but I believe it can be helpful in focusing our efforts to help kids move past the tollbooth of adolescence toward mature adulthood.

1. **A mature person is able to keep long-term commitments.** One key signal of maturity is the ability to delay gratification. Part of this means a student is able to keep commitments even when they're no longer new, novel or they don't feel like it.

2. **A mature person is unshaken by flattery or criticism.** As people mature, sooner or later they understand that nothing is as good as it seems and nothing is as bad as it seems. Mature people can receive compliments or criticism without letting it ruin them or give them a distorted view of themselves. They are secure in their identity.

3. **A mature person possesses a spirit of humility.** Humility parallels maturity. Humility isn't thinking less of yourself, but thinking of yourself less. Mature people aren't consumed with drawing attention to themselves, and they accept the fact that they don't know everything. They see how others have contributed to their success and can even sincerely give honor to a Creator who gave them their talent and potential.

4. **A mature person's decisions are based on character, not feelings.** Mature people—youth or adults—live by values. They have principles that guide their decisions and are able to progress beyond merely reacting to life's options. They live proactively. Although they recognize their emotions as important, their character is master over their emotions.

5. **A mature person expresses gratitude consistently.** I have found that the more I mature, the more grateful I am for both big and little things in my life. Immature children presume they deserve everything good that happens to them. Mature people see the big picture and realize how good they have it, compared to most of the world's population.

6. **A mature person knows how to prioritize others before themselves.** It has been said, "A mature person is one whose agenda revolves around others,

not self." Certainly this can be taken to an extreme, but the ability to get past one's own desires and consider the needs of others is a powerful mark of maturity.

7. **A mature person seeks wisdom before acting.** Finally, mature people are teachable. They don't presume they have all the answers. The wiser they get, in fact, the more they realize they need more wisdom. They're not ashamed of seeking counsel from more experienced people, from dependable friends, or from God, in prayer. Only the wise seek wisdom.

May I Recommend?

As this book proceeds, I will offer chapters with ideas to help solve the challenges we face as we lead Generation iY. For now, however, let me recommend a few action steps that can help adolescents move smoothly past the tollbooth of adolescence and into true maturity:

1. **Lay plans to mix the generations. Intentionally set times for adolescents to spend time with adults and with younger children.** These can be social times or project times. Mingling with people of different ages and in different walks of life develops their "empathy muscles" and deepens their emotional intelligence.

2. **Teach practical life skills, such as budgeting, planning a trip, maintaining a vehicle, cooking, or preparing for a job interview.** Take the time to coach the students around you to be self-sufficient. Be patient and teach them the skills they need to do these tasks efficiently.

3. **Build in opportunities for service.** For instance, use a holiday as an excuse to visit a hospital, a nursing home, or a children's hospital with your adolescent and celebrate with patients. Take some small gifts and model how to act—listening, focusing on the people in need, and looking for ways to serve them. The combination of good modeling and practice in service will do a lot to diminish adolescent self-absorption.

4. **Give plenty of opportunity to "practice" maturity.** Create a plan for a gradual decrease in supervision and a gradual increase in responsibility and freedom throughout the adolescent years. Talk about the "marks of maturity" and have them evaluate themselves based on this list. Communicate a vision for what it means to be a mature adult.

5. **Engage kids in actively (not just virtually) helping others.** Intentionally create opportunities for them to develop the habit of helping. Mission trips,

Habitat for Humanity teams, schools, hospitals, and nursing homes all provide good opportunities to serve. Ideally, involvement should be for longer periods of time, not just short spurts.

6. **Applaud appropriately—reward real skills and actual accomplishment.** Then challenge young people to enter the next level of achievement. In areas where they have moved ahead of you (such as technology), ask them for lessons! Passing knowledge along to others is a great way for adolescents to learn and grow.

7. **Set boundaries to avoid falling into unhealthy patterns with postadolescents.** For example, limit the amount of time a college graduate can live at home without paying rent. Give them landmarks along their life journey that signal their maturity and readiness for life.

8. **Develop rituals to mark and solemnize rites of passage.** Graduations, awards ceremonies, bar mitzvahs or bat mitzvahs, "sweet sixteens," or even getting a driver's license can be celebrated as defining moments for adolescents. You can even create special events to mark milestones in a young person's development and their movement forward toward adulthood.

Bethany's Story

Let me illustrate from my own family. When my daughter, Bethany, was thirteen, my wife and I noticed it was time to be intentional about introducing other voices into her life besides our own. We wanted adult voices influencing her choices, not just peer voices. So we made what was probably the smartest parenting decision of our lives. We decided to ask six women in Bethany's life—women that she thought were cool and that her mother and I respected—to be mentors for her.

It didn't take us long to choose the mentors. Next, I called each one and asked if she would invest a day in our daughter's life. If they worked outside the home, I suggested they take Bethany to work with them. In fact, they could put her to work. All I asked was that each woman would share one "life message" with our daughter, something she wished someone had shared with her when she was thirteen.

These women were amazing. Not only did they all say yes, but they did far more than we could have asked for. Sara, an RN, took Bethany to a hospital maternity ward, where she actually helped mothers give birth. Later that afternoon, Sara took Bethany to a class for unwed mothers, many of them young teens who were far from ready for the responsibility of motherhood. Finally, at the end of the day, Sara's life message for Bethany was on sexual purity—waiting for the right man before she said yes. After the day they spent together, you can imagine how profound this message was to Bethany—much more memorable than my lecture on the subject.

Holly, another mentor, took Bethany to downtown Atlanta, where they worked in the projects all day among underprivileged families. Betsy, a flight attendant with Delta airlines, surprised Bethany by flying her up to New York City for the day. Each woman had her own special message—and her own unique environment in which to share it.

At the end of the year, we hosted a dinner and invited all the mentors to our home to say thanks. Bethany served them and ate with them. Then we migrated into the family room for a time to share about the past year. At this point, our thirteen-year-old daughter sat in the middle of the room, with her mentors all around her. To each one she read a personal thank-you card she had written, outlining the significant lesson she remembered from their time together. Needless to say, this was a deeply moving time for all of us.

When Bethany had finished reading, I opened up the Scriptures and read about how Jewish families used to give a blessing to their children centuries ago. Before I could suggest that we repeat that same act with Bethany, those women gathered around our daughter and began to speak a blessing into her life, reminding her how much they believed in her, how much they loved her, and how much potential they could see for her future. There wasn't a dry eye in the room. As the evening ended, Bethany presented each of her mentors with a gift. It was a memorable night. In fact, that year with her mentors continues to make a difference in my daughter's life.

I smiled as I tucked my son, Jonathan, into bed that night. Four years younger than Bethany, he had watched the events of the evening in wonderment. As I pulled the blanket up over him to say goodnight, he looked up at me and said, "Dad, I already picked the six guys I want to mentor me."

➤ **LINKING UP** ◄

For ideas you can use to equip adolescents and help them to mature, check out **www.SaveTheirFutureNow.com/HelpThemGrowUp**.

5

Lost in Neverland
The Special Challenges of iY Boys

I'D LIKE TO INTRODUCE YOU TO TWO TWENTY-SOMETHINGS.

The first one is Jason Russell. He grew up in an average home in California. Early on, his parents noticed he was full of promise—he was artistic, got good grades, was articulate, and loved acting in a community theatre program. Jason even directed and choreographed some stage shows as a young adult. He consistently heard from his community that he was loaded with potential.

Jason rose to everyone's expectations. Upon graduation, he elected to attend the University of Southern California and major in film production. He knew it was a highly competitive field, but he believed he could make it. He loved telling stories, he knew that was one of his strengths, and he wanted to do it through movies. During his time at USC, Jason and two other friends began hearing horrific tales about the slave trade in southern Sudan and northern Uganda. The stories gripped the heart of the three film students, who thought maybe they could do something about the problem. So off to Uganda they went, thinking they would make a film.

It was a life-changing trip for all three young men. Jason and his friends were especially touched by the realization that the primary victims in the Sudanese civil war were children. Not only had thousands of kids become refugees, but many were abducted, enslaved, and taught to kill. It was human trafficking at its worst, turning innocent children into weapons and ruining their lives in the process.

Within a year, Jason and his friends had launched a little movement called Invisible Children. Their primary method for helping the cause was to expand awareness of child refugees and child soldiers. They made movies—lots of them. They held overnight vigils in which young adults like Jason and his friends spent the night in conditions similar to the refugees they were attempting to help. In a few short years, they have mobilized tens of thousands of Americans to fight for tens of thousands of refugees and child slaves in Africa.

Invisible Children is only a snapshot of Jason's vision to improve the world. He married his childhood sweetheart, Danica, and they are both using their gifts in service to a world in need. Jason is directing, encouraging, and mobilizing others to do the same. He even wrote a movie script that got him an audience with Steven Spielberg. Not bad for a twenty-something.

What I love about Jason is this. He doesn't claim to have a corner on the market with his talent or leadership skills. He's just determined to do what he can with what he has.

Jamie is also a twenty-something. He too grew up in California in a fairly typical environment. As in Jason's case, it didn't take long for Jamie's parents and teachers to recognize that he was loaded with potential. He was the firstborn child. His IQ is over one hundred and forty. He is articulate and talented, and when he was growing up his siblings and friends consistently looked to him as an example. In fact, maybe too consistently.

When Jamie's parents divorced, he decided he was fed up with living the model life. His family and friends began hearing him say things like "I am tired of hearing about my potential all the time" and "I'm sick of living up to someone's idea of what I should be. Just leave me alone."

Jamie's grades began to drop, even though he was capable of making straight As in his sleep, with one brain tied behind his back. He began smoking and drinking and hanging around other unambitious students. When he graduated from high school, Jamie shocked everyone by saying he didn't want to go to college; at least not right away. He grew lethargic. Not bad...just lethargic. He eventually enrolled in a community college but was bored by the classes and dropped out within a year.

Jamie had lost his way. He had no vision for his life. So, what does a guy like this do? Jamie got married, then he fathered a baby. Sadly, because all this happened so quickly, the hardships of marriage and family drove a wedge between Jamie and his wife. They got divorced, and the divorce threw Jamie into a tailspin. He lost his job. Then he got arrested for DUI—three times—and spent some time in jail. Today, with the help of some friends, he is finally getting his feet on the ground, but he is not nearly where he could be. Suffice it to say—Jamie is still loaded with unrealized potential.

The contrast between Jason's story and Jamie's story is glaring. Both were kids who grew up in California, were loved by their families, and consistently heard they were full of potential. One is realizing his potential, the other has stalled.

Which leaves us to ask, "What happened to Jamie?"

The Trouble with Boys

The tragic thing about these two stories is that for every Jason, there are a dozen Jamies. This emerging generation seems to be full of young men who are loaded with potential but seem to stall out in their twenties. Why, in our educated, sophisticated culture, does this happen?

Parenting books have never been so prevalent. Education levels have never been so high. We're not stupid. Why do we experience these extremes? And why has it really affected a generation— especially the boys—so dramatically?

Let me give you some numbers. By almost every benchmark, boys across our nation and in every demographic group are falling behind. "In elementary school, boys are two times more likely than girls to be diagnosed with learning disabilities and twice as likely to be placed in special education classes. High school boys are losing ground to girls on standardized writing tests. The number of boys who said they didn't like school rose 71 percent between 1980 and 2001, according to a University of Michigan study."[1]

And nowhere is the shift more evident than on college campuses. Forty years ago, men represented 59 percent of the undergraduate student body. Now, they are a minority at 41 percent. And the percentage is dropping. Today, roughly six of ten university students are female. Margaret Spellings, U.S. Secretary of Education, believes this widening gap "has profound implications for the economy, society, families and democracy."[2]

Check out the last sixty years of trends among male college students:

- *1949—70 percent of college students were male.*
- *1959—64 percent of college students were male.*
- *1969—59 percent of college students were male.*
- *1979—49 percent of college students were male.*
- *1989—46 percent of college students were male.*
- *1999—44 percent of college students were male.*
- *2009—41 percent of college students were male.*[3]

On private college campuses, the male population is even lower. The percentage hovers around 35 to 39 percent. In some schools, the number is 25 percent. This is only the tip of the iceberg. The U.S. Census Bureau reports that *one third* of young men aged twenty-two through thirty-four still live at home with their parents—a number that has doubled over the last twenty years. And as physician and psychologist Dr. Leonard Sax points out, "This phenomenon cuts across all demographics. You'll find it in families both rich and poor; black, white, Asian, and Hispanic; urban, suburban, and rural....No such change has occurred among women."[4]

What can we conclude from these statistics? Quite a few factors may be involved. But these numbers give a strong indication that a growing population of American males is neither educated nor motivated.

Consider the ramifications of this reality for our culture. In the future, if trends continue, it will likely be the female, not the male, who is educated and the breadwinner of the home. Males could be intimidated by this scenario, which could lead to a larger percentage of singles in our society. Women may find it more and more difficult to find a male they respect enough to marry. Males may find it difficult to find a female who is compatible. Or, if males still choose to marry, they may feel the need to display their manhood with sexual exploits or through virtual experiences like video games.

I have lost count of the number of young newlywed couples I know who married for love, then somehow things changed. It was almost as though the young husband checked the "wife" goal off his list, then returned to his natural habitat— the screen. Loads of young women have complained to me about how their husband gets home from work and chooses to "veg" in front of a video game. These women are frustrated and dissatisfied, and their husbands are going...nowhere. One young woman calls herself a "video game widow."

This could be one of several factors that leads to three- or five-year marriage contracts. The woman would get the children she wanted from the man, the man would get the sex and support he wanted, and neither would have a chance to get bored or challenged for very long. (But of course neither would enjoy the comfort or growth of long-term commitment either.)

Just do a little homework and you'll discover something a bit disconcerting. In cultures where males stop setting a healthy example, there is trouble. Crime rates rise, the percentage of teen pregnancies and unwed mothers go up, the number of gangs increase, unemployment swells, and depression and delinquency rise, according to Princeton psychologist Sara McLanahan.[5]

The country of Jamaica, for instance, has been besieged with such conditions for years. Today, Jamaica struggles with a number of miserable conditions because of the lack of healthy male leadership in the home, in the school, in the church, and in the marketplace. Maxine Henry Wilson, Minister of Education and Youth, believes this issue is a major concern, especially as it relates to the socialization of boys.[6]

The disappearing male phenomenon is a global one. Even in developing countries like China, Thailand, and Indonesia that boast of higher levels of education and family planning, male involvement in family planning is very low.[7] Nonprofit organizations have been established in other nations such as the Philippines and several countries in Africa to better equip males with leadership skills, so they don't feel intimidated by the idea of leading a family or an organization.

Conversely, a lack of male role models is a factor leading young men to postpone their maturation. For millions, as we saw in chapter 4, the years between eighteen and twenty-five have become a distinct life stage—a strange transitional "no man's land" between adolescence and adulthood in which young people, especially young men, stall for a few extra years, putting off adult responsibility.

I'm convinced the problem can't be solved overnight, but we must begin to model and teach responsibility to our boys when they're young. In the last twenty years, our educational system has become obsessed with a quantifiable and narrowly defined kind of academic success. This tunnel vision is harming boys. They are biologically and psychologically different from girls, and educators must learn how to bring out the best in both genders.

Interestingly, forty years ago, it was the girls who were lagging, not the boys. When we recognized this, Federal laws were passed in 1972 that forced schools to provide equal opportunities for females in the classroom and on the athletic field. Christina Hoff-Sommers, a fellow at the American Enterprise Institute, believes that in the 1990s some misguided feminist educators continued to portray girls as disadvantaged and lavished them with support and attention. It has helped the females immensely, but the boys have been left to languish.[8]

In other words, we took nationwide action, and it has worked for the girls. I believe it's time we take the appropriate action for males.

Life in Neverland

One of the most beloved children's stories of the last one hundred years is that of Peter Pan. J. M Barrie introduced Peter in a book called *The Little White Bird*, then made him the star of a 1904 stage play called *Peter Pan, or The Boy Who Wouldn't*

Grow Up. In 1953, Disney studios transformed it into a full-length animated motion picture, and a year later the Broadway musical version made its appearance.

The story has become known by almost every kid in America. There was something magnetic about this magical world where kids fought pirates and crocodiles and no one told them when to go to bed. If you remember, Peter Pan flew Wendy, John, and Michael from their home in the real world to a faraway place called Neverland, where they met a group of "Lost Boys" led by Peter. Rapidly, their characteristics were revealed:

- *They were mischievous. (It was a world full of irreverent antics.)*
- *They looked for a mother figure. (The boys wanted Wendy to nurture them.)*
- *They were confident and carefree. (Their ideas seemed endless.)*
- *They wanted their own way. (They were often demanding.)*
- *They refused to grow up. (Their ambition was to resist adulthood.)*

In so many ways, this new generation of young people—males in particular—displays these same characteristics. They are full of potential and energy, yet somehow seem bent on postponing their entrance into adulthood. The term "Peter Pan Syndrome" was actually coined in 1983 in a book about men "who have never grown up"[9]—but it's the perfect term to describe large numbers of iY males.

Our organization, Growing Leaders, works with more than two thousand universities, schools, and student organizations. According to our findings, many male college students demonstrate the following symptoms of living in their own Neverland:

- *They are demotivated and lack the desire to assume responsibility.*
- *They are disengaged from student activities or leadership on campus.*
- *They return home after they are finished with college.*
- *They can resort to antisocial behavior if they're deficient in social capital.*
- *They lack direction and tend to postpone plans for the future.*

What Are the Reasons for Their Demotivation?

Perhaps you saw the movie, *Failure to Launch*. It opened number one at the box office in March of 2006 and told the story of a man (played by Matthew McConaughey) who continued to live at home into his thirties. Though played as a comedy, it also painted a sad picture of so many young males today. McConaughey's character hung around a group of friends, all thirty-somethings, who also lived at home. His frustrated parents were so desperate to get him out of the house that they actually hired a woman to lure him into responsibility. The people I know who saw the film believed it was funny because they all knew someone in that situation. It's everywhere. The reasons for this syndrome vary, but let me suggest six common ones based on my research and that of Dr. Sax in his powerful book, *Boys Adrift.*[10]

Reason #1: Video Games and Other Online Activity

The average teenage boy today spends more than thirteen hours a week playing video games (the average teenage girl spends about five).[11] Study after study has shown that this is not a good thing.

Some people swear that video games actually make kids smarter. I think that depends

> ### Six Reasons iY Boys May Be in Trouble
> 1. "I'm glued to the screen."
> 2. "My teacher doesn't understand what I need."
> 3. "I'm overmedicated."
> 4. "There's something in the plastics."
> 5. "My parents have too tight a grip."
> 6. "I'm confused about what it means to be a man."

on what you mean by "smarter." There's no doubt they can have a positive effect on eye-hand coordination, enabling the user to react to stimulus faster. But across the board, studies measuring the effect of video games have shown a direct and negative relationship between video games and healthy growth and development.

For instance, one undebated finding of video-game research is that the more time a child spends playing video games, the less likely he is to do well in school. It has also been shown that spending two hours a day in front of a screen negatively affects maturation. Games have an addictive quality that tends to disengage boys from the world. There is even evidence that young people who spend too much time interacting with computers or videos rather than interacting with people and learning actual physical skills may have trouble grasping simple concepts they will need to succeed.

"There is actually some disturbing evidence," writes Dr. Sax, "that boys today, on average, are less intelligent—less able to understand and solve real-world problems—compared with boys just fifteen years ago."[12] British psychologist Michael Shayer reports that twelve-year-old boys are doing only as well on certain intelligence tests as the eight- to nine-year-olds in 1976—and he blames the results on computer games.[13]

Frank Wilson, professor of neurology at Stanford, echoes this finding. He says that parents have been deceived about the value of computer-based experiences for their kids. For instance, Dr. Wilson says that medical school faculties are having more difficulty teaching medical students how the heart works as a pump "because these students have so little real-world experience; they've never siphoned anything, never fixed a car, never worked on a fuel pump, may not even have hooked up a garden hose."[14]

If all of this isn't enough, consider two more effects of video games on a screen. Boys' reading and learning abilities are being damaged by computer games and television. Too much visual stimuli has been provided, and too much work has been done for them. I spoke to one doctor who connected rising asthma rates with video games because of the long hours spent in a sedentary position. Eye specialists warn that too much screen time can impair the development of a child's vision, leading to nearsightedness.

The problem with video games doesn't stop with the dynamics, though. The actual content of these videos can be problematical. Two of the most popular games, *Grand Theft Auto* and *Halo*, each feature violent, destructive activity—and they're not the only online activities that depend on sex and violence.

When I talk to students about them, they often say, "Oh, that doesn't affect me." No? If content presented on a screen doesn't affect us, then no retailer would advertise on TV again.

Researchers at Indiana University School of Medicine have drawn a direct correlation between violent input on a screen and activation of the "thinking, learning, reason and emotional control area of the brain" in adolescents.[15] A statistical analysis of 130,000 students (elementary school through college) published in March 2010 by the Center for the Study of Violence at Iowa State University "strongly suggests" that playing violent video games increases violent and aggressive thoughts and decreases empathy.[16]

The truth is, violent images on a screen do affect us—especially boys who spend long hours glued to the screen watching them. And the same is true of sexual content, which is more readily available to young men than ever before through online sources. "Porn addiction" is now a well-documented phenomenon, and it easily applies to young males. Some young men even come to prefer online pornography to the prospect of healthy intimacy with another human being. There is no need to work at a relationship. Stimulation is easily available at the touch of a button. The temptation to remain in front a screen instead of cultivating a real relationship can be powerful.

Consider this. A male college student today has unique relationship opportunities in front of him. Unlike his father or grandfather, he's likely attending a school where women outnumber men. Even guys who are not especially good looking or socially adept have an excellent chance of finding a young woman to date. Unfortunately, as the *New York Times* recently reported in a front-page story, college administrators note that more and more young men show no interest in meeting young women. They don't want to meet anyone. The just want to "stay in their rooms, talk to no one, and play video games into the wee hours....[They] miss classes until they withdraw or flunk out."[17]

Reason #2: Inappropriate Teaching Methods

Widely publicized research reported in 2007 at the National Institute of Mental Health revealed new findings on the human brain. The researchers discovered that the various regions of the brain develop in a different sequence in girls as compared with boys and that girls develop intellectually up to two years ahead of boys. For example, trying to teach five-year old boys to read and write may be just as inappropriate as it would be to try to teach three-year-old girls to read and write. It may be just too early.

As a result, many elementary-age boys get frustrated. From the early age of six to seven years old, they learn to hate school. And as they continue in school systems that just don't teach in ways that fit their natural inclinations, the boys may continue to fall behind.

It's not enough to fill our schools with good teachers; we must teach students when they are ready to learn...using methods that fit the *ways* they learn. Most boys are naturally energetic. They need ways to expend their native energy. In their elementary years, especially, most boys are visual and many are kinesthetic learners. They want to see something, not just hear something, and they learn best through an experience, not an explanation.

As I suggested, boys just learn differently than girls do—and it's usually not the lecture, drill, test method. Most are not passive...at least at first. Boys often want to compete, to experience, to observe, to upload, and to conquer. Understandably, their mostly female teachers prefer compliant, dutiful girls--and their overpopulated, underfunded schools just want kids who will sit still and not cause trouble. It's no wonder the males eventually lose interest and take refuge in video games—where they can do what their native energy dictates in virtual reality.

Reason #3: Prescription Drugs

This is not a newsflash. Hyperactive, frustrated boys who act out in school are increasingly being medicated. If they were around today, Charlie Brown would be on Prozac and Dennis the Menace would be on Ritalin. I have no idea what Tom Sawyer would be taking for his condition!

The U.S. makes up about 5 percent of the world's population, but it consumes 90 percent of the total production of ADHD medications. And the jury is still out about the long-term effects of these medications, although disturbing evidence has begun to accumulate. Even relatively short-term use of these drugs, for just a year or perhaps less, can lead to changes in personality. Young men who used to be congenial, outgoing, and adventurous become lazy and irritable. These drugs also tend to shrink the motivational centers of the brain, and the effect of this lasts years, well after these kids stop taking their meds. [18]

The fact is, the syndrome we now call ADHD has been around for centuries. Despite claims to the contrary, it wasn't invented thirty years ago by drug companies hungry to sell more medications. You can read accounts of boys written a hundred years ago who would meet all the modern criteria for ADHD.

So why are we medicating males more frequently today? I believe there are a number of reasons.

First, as indicated below, there is a possibility that environmental factors are actually causing a higher incidence of ADHD. In many cases, if very carefully monitored, the medication may be a useful tool to help kids concentrate. But I believe this is only part of the story. I've come to believe that in many scenarios, the problem lies not in the kids, but in adults.

There has been a societal shift away from personal responsibility to outside responsibility. We prefer to blame someone or something else for our child's lack of focus or for our inability to lead our children. In many cases, I believe we just get lazy as parents and teachers. Or maybe we just get busy and overwhelmed. At any rate, we would rather pass them off to a professional psychiatrist or doctor than try to train them through good leadership.

Yet another factor is the acceleration of elementary school curriculum. School hours have been increased over the last thirty years. We expect much more from kids in school, requiring them to sit still longer and listen.

Finally, medication is more readily available today, and it's marketed by drug companies with a vested interest in selling it. One psychologist told me recently that, in his experience, only one in seven boys actually needed the meds.

Now, I'm not saying that medication is never an appropriate solution. Some boys (and girls) truly benefit from drugs that help them focus and give them a much-needed experience of success in school and relationships. I have dear friends who struggle with ADHD, and I am glad they are handling their condition wisely with the right combination of diet, exercise, and medication.

The problems arise when we inappropriately depend on drugs to do what we often should be doing through healthy leadership in the home, at school, and at the workplace. Sadly, I believe that many parents and teachers rely on drugs because they make restless kids easier to control. Medicated kids often require less energy, effort, creativity, and even money. Sadly, they also pay a price.

My son, Jonathan, showed all the signs of ADHD in his preschool and elementary school years. My wife and I discussed whether he should be taking Ritalin, Dexedrine, Adderall or Metadate like so many of his peers. (I have since discovered that a boy was thirty times more likely to be taking these drugs in 2007 than he was in 1987.[19]) Today, I am so glad we did not choose that option. We decided, instead, to focus Jonathan's energies, to give him outlets to express himself, and to give him boundaries to help him know when it was okay to make noise and when it wasn't. He has done well without prescription drugs.

On the other hand, Michael Phelps, who has won more gold medals than any Olympian in history, was diagnosed with ADHD as an elementary-school boy. His single mom made use of medication but also led him well. She tried activity after activity to identify the best way for him to channel his energy. By age eleven, Michael had found a swimming pool—and the rest is history. He asked his mom if he could quit using the drugs. He felt he didn't need them anymore. So many other boys desperately need this to be their story.

Reason #4: Endocrine Disruptors

This factor may be the scariest of all, because it's the one we have least control over. Since 2006, scientists have been discovering that many species of wildlife, from fish to mammals, are experiencing a hormone imbalance—they are being emasculated or feminized. In some species of fish, males are actually producing eggs instead of sperm. Researchers have learned that the leading cause of these disturbances is the presence of synthetic chemicals in their environment—and they've shown that the same chemicals affect humans as well.

What are these chemicals? One popular one is bisphenol A (BPA). There is some controversy over its effect, but Canada and some European nations have banned it as harmful.[20] Some refer to it as a "gender bender." It's found in plastic bottles, baby bottles, canned food linings, and some shampoos. Under certain conditions the chemical can migrate into food and water. It's been found in the bodies of over 90 percent of Americans.[21] When ingested, it mimics natural estrogen, the female hormone, with disturbing effects on human development and behavior. As Dr. Sax reports, "Scientists have just begun to recognize the pernicious effects these chemicals have on the brain—particularly the brains of boys—in ways not previously imagined."[22]

For example, the soaring rates of ADHD among North American boys in the last twenty years may be linked to these chemicals. Nations like China and India, where bottled water is far less common, have a far lower incidence of ADHD[23] And childhood obesity, one of our country's most serious health problems, may be linked to endocrine disrupters as well. Dr Sax reports that "teenagers today [both girls and boys] are four times more likely to be obese and overweight compared to teens in the 1960s and that environmental estrogens may contribute to this reality."[24]

But the most disturbing effects of endocrine disruptors on young people have to do with sexual development—and they affect males and females differently. They are almost certainly a contributor in causing females to experience puberty earlier than they did thirty years ago. (In the 1970s, females went through puberty at thirteen or fourteen years old. Today, it's nine to eleven.) These chemicals, however, seem to have the opposite effect on males.

Studies reveal that "the overwhelming majority of modern chemicals that mimic the action of human sex hormones, curiously, mimic the action of only female hormones."[25] This means they actually *hinder* sexual development in boys. Boys' testosterone levels are half of what they were in their grandparents' day. This may explain some of the gender confusion we see today as well as the lack of motivation in young men. "In boys," Dr. Sax explains, "testosterone fuels more than just sexual interest; it fuels the drive to achieve, to be the best, to compete. Successful, high-achieving boys have higher testosterone levels than boys who are content to come in last."[26]

What is most frightening is this. Scientists have discovered that exposure to environmental estrogens early in life tends to blunt or eliminate behavioral sex differences. Females become less feminine. Males become less masculine. Sexual identity becomes fuzzy and confused—which helps explain why so many iY boys opt for an extended stay in Neverland.

Reason #5: Damaging Parenting Styles

In my experience, this has become a huge issue today. We not only have a new generation of kids, we have a new generation of parents as well—and these parents often contribute to the arrested development of their children.

Parents are demanding more rules at school, and some schools in response have actually outlawed touching, handshakes, hugging, dancing and football. (Yes, I know of a school that actually banned football because an athlete got hurt doing a touchdown dance after he scored). It's absurd to me. In addition to causing the parent great stress and sending them to a potentially early grave, "hovering" may actually backfire. I spoke to a mom this week who told me she was hovering over her seventeen-year-old daughter and had done so since she was born. Her daughter now is showing signs of rebellion and resentment. Aren't those the very qualities we are trying to help them mature from and leave behind?

As I mentioned earlier, the percentage of young men who still live at home has doubled over the last twenty years. While there may be economic reasons for this, especially in times of high unemployment, often this kind of live-at-home arrangement happens because parents simply fail to lead their offspring or help them become independent. They invite their university graduates to return home rather than help them out of the nest. I find many parents who believe their child is their ultimate legacy, but by the time that child enters middle school, those parents are in a survival mode. They are weary and out of answers and they feel guilty about this. Consequently, they don't have the backbone or the courage to release those kids from the house and force them to grow up. They both just linger together—a parent without courage and young person without a compass.

In 2009, Lenore Skenazy ignited a national firestorm and inspired a movement with her book, *Free-Range Kids*.[27] Based on her popular blog of the same name, it argues that parents have to lighten up and help their kids become more independent. She talks about modern-day parents' drive to wrap up their kids in "cotton." Her site was born after she was roundly criticized as the "worst mother in the world" for allowing her son a freedom she had as a kid: to find his own way home from school. Lenore believes kids need more freedom so they can learn to survive in the world. To prove her point, she left her nine-year-old son, Izzy, in a New York department store with twenty dollars, a map, and a subway card. He made it home just fine.

Is Leonore Skenazy a common-sense crusader or a dangerously deluded mom? Though some may disagree with her choices, I applaud her plea to parents to obsess a little less on "what could happen" to kids and focus more on helping their children learn to find their way in the world. She's not inviting parents to be negligent, but to be deliberate about leading their children toward independent maturity.

Too many parents forget that their number-one job is to prepare their children for life without them. Parenting is ultimate leadership. A parent is the ultimate mentor in the life of their child. I have spotted at least eight damaging parenting styles, ways of interacting that may stunt the growth of their kids. I'll share more on this in chapter 6.

Reason #6: Devaluation of Masculinity

Perhaps it is a reaction to the women's movement of the last forty years. Perhaps there are other important causes. But manhood just doesn't get the respect in our culture that it used to.

This devaluation of masculinity has been brewing for over twenty years. *Time* magazine carried a cover article in 1994 asking the question, "Men—Are They Really That Bad?" The article stated, "It is time to talk. We must make an examination of conscience. They are saying terrible things about us. Are they true? Masculinity is in disrepute. Men have become the Germans of gender. Are we really as awful as they say we are?"[28]

The entire article poked fun at the way men are viewed by culture, but subtly asked if it were true. Incidentally, another article dated May 5, 2005 was titled the same way. There was another on July 15, 2008 and another on March 11, 2009—all posted with the same title. The problem has not gone away.

And men, especially young men, suffer because of this cultural devaluation. Outside of seniors over seventy years old, do you know what the highest suicide rate for any age group is? It is men between the ages of sixteen and twenty-six. Why? They were rewarded as little-league players just for participating, but as men they are haunted with the fear that they may not have what it takes to win in life. This may lead to the percentage who struggle with clinical depressive disorder every year.[29] Even more fight despair, though they may cover it with sarcasm, humor, and crude language.

I think I know why. Men tend to lose motivation when we are confused or when we fear we cannot win. We want to win, not lose, at work and family and life. We come home at night and quickly turn on the TV so we can vicariously win via our favorite sports team. Or, we engage in our favorite video game so we can win at *something* during our day. When our armor gets tarnished, when we're not sure what battles to fight, or when we feel that we'll be disrespected no matter what we do—that's when we're tempted to give up.

Author Gordon Daulby suggests in his book, *Healing the Masculine Soul*, that males intrinsically want to excel at four roles:

1. **Son** ("Am I acceptable to my father?")
2. **Worker** ("Am I competent to provide?")
3. **Lover** ("Can I win the affection of a beautiful woman?")
4. **Warrior** ("Can I fight and win in a cause I believe in?")[30]

Today, it seems that the lines are blurry about what it means to fulfill these roles. Fathers are often missing. Jobs come and go. Marriages fail. And we often neglect to fight for a cause bigger than ourselves. As a result, we become passive... or perverted.

This confusion is becoming both chronic and acute for iY males. Mentors are rare. All too often, they simply don't know how to become men. They are confused about their role in the home and society. There are few rites of passage. Role models are few and far between. And all the factors mentioned above—video games, inadequate teaching, prescription meds, endocrine disruptors, and damaging parenting styles may contribute to arrested development.

Instead of a healthy pursuit of maturation in his dad's eyes, a boy may refuse to grow up; he may wear a goatee and a backward-facing baseball hat until he's forty. Instead of being a competent, healthy worker, he becomes a workaholic or chronically underemployed. Instead of winning the affection of a woman, he becomes addicted to pornography. And instead of fighting for a cause he believes in, he becomes his own cause. He assumes a macho, Rambo image and fights for himself as a renegade, hurting others in his path.

Migrating Out of Neverland

Are the boys of Generation iY destined to be slackers—lethargic and lazy? I don't believe so. But we must cultivate them. We must be intentional about helping our boys become men—and not just men, but leaders. Let me take a moment and suggest some steps you can begin with if you have young males in your life who fit some of the symptoms in this chapter.

1. **Begin early to expose them to role models.** If you're a father or a concerned male, *you* can be a role model. But even if you're a single mom or a female teacher, you can be intentional about introducing young males to men who give them a vision for a career or just for what it means to be a man. Males need a target to hit—that applies both to the men you are enlisting and the boys you seek to help. Ask neighbors, colleagues, or uncles to speak into the life of the young men you know. Enlist them as one-day mentors and see if that day might lead to more. Even boys whose fathers are involved in their

lives can benefit from exposure to other male role models.

2. **Limit and monitor screen time.** Talk over the issue of video games and computer or TV time. Evaluate together what your boys are watching and playing. If they are old enough, decide together what the boundaries will be and stick to them. I simply shared the research with my son, and he was the one who suggested: "Maybe I should not play those games so much." He owned the decision because it was his idea.

3. **Provide appropriate hands-on learning opportunities.** To insure that adolescent males don't draw the conclusion they're "bad students" because they don't respond well to school, why not furnish environments where they can get some experiential learning? This could be anywhere from an insurance office to a construction site to backstage at a theater. Help them find something they love, but something they can learn by *doing*. Let males be males and exert energy, ambition, and passion whenever appropriate.

4. **Educate yourself on the effects of prescription drugs.** Some boys need them, but many do not. Don't be lazy about this issue—do your homework. My recommendation is to use drugs sparingly and look for ways to lead boys and young men with clear direction and clear goals. Consider whether there may be a link between the plastics you use and ADHD symptoms you may be spotting in your son or student.

5. **Be careful about male bashing.** I know it can be funny, but young guys see a pattern if adults (men or women) do this regularly. During dinner conversations, while watching TV, or even after movies, take some time to talk about heroes—men who serve as great examples of leadership or statesmanship in our society. This may feel cheesy, but young men need this kind of reinforcement. Most young guys think more concretely than abstractly. They need clear examples of a target to shoot for.

Jonathan's Story

When my own son, Jonathan, turned thirteen, I wanted to provide a significant rite of passage for him, just as we did for our daughter Bethany. This time, though, I decided to make it a community experience. I met with four other dads who had sons about the same age. We knew we could provide a much more memorable experience if we worked together. So we pledged to meet together with our sons twice a month for a year, focusing on building them into "champions." (The word is an acronym, with each letter standing for a virtue we wanted to build into their lives). We tried to provide what all good training provides: explanations, examples, experiences, and evaluation.

For instance, when we talked about life planning, we took the boys to a local airport and met with Dan, a local business executive. Dan is also a pilot. He took the boys up in a jet and gave them an amazing experience in the air. Along the way, he explained how a jet operates, from takeoff to landing. Later, we met in a room at the airport and talked about how a flight plan is much like a life plan. No pilot takes off without a flight plan. No person should enter their adult years without a plan either.

All through the year, we fathers introduced our sons to great men. Between the four of us dads, we made connections that surprised even us. They met sports figures such as (then) Indianapolis Colts' coach Tony Dungy and racecar driver Kyle Petty. They met a Marine colonel. They met musicians, business owners, pastors, mountain climbers, and schoolteachers. Each exposed the boys to a new experience and an unforgettable lesson.

At the end of the year, we held two significant meetings. One was just for us dads and sons, where we presented each kid with a new name and an action figure drawn by a professional artist. Then we presented them with swords and held a knighting ceremony. You should have seen those boys with their swords!

The final meeting was for friends and family. We invited them to witness the boys' rite-of-passage ceremony. We showed a video of highlights from the year and passed along a baton, symbolic of the fact that we dads were passing the baton of manhood to them. Each dad read a personal letter to his son expressing strong belief in him and his future. We gave them each a plaque to hang on their wall, and we surprised them with a personal letter from the President of the United States that encouraged them to be leaders for America in the future.

Needless to say, my son won't soon forget that year. I won't forget it either. But that rite-of-passage process actually began *before* we ever started meeting with the other fathers and sons.

When my kids turned twelve, I let each of them choose a place they wanted to visit. Each could pick anywhere in the world and travel with me to see it. Once there, we would have fun visiting sites together, but the trip would end with some meaningful talk time.

Jonathan chose Minneapolis, Minnesota. That may seem like a strange choice out of all the cities in the world, but at the time he was into Camp Snoopy at the Mall of America, and there was a particular show playing in that city he wanted to see. So we did both of those gigs.

On the last day of our four-day trip, I told Jonathan we were going to drive to one of the lakes in the area. We weren't going to do the Mall or a show. He knew something was up and wasn't sure if he liked it. I pulled into a parking lot in our rental car and stopped next to the lake. Then I turned to my son and gave him a bit of a shock.

"Jonathan," I said, "let's trade places."

I paused, then went on. "I want you to get behind the wheel of this car and drive around the parking lot a bit."

Jonathan was stunned, especially because he is a bit of a rule keeper. "Dad— no! I am only twelve. I can't drive." I smiled and encouraged him that I would only have him drive around the parking lot for a few minutes. "Dad, I can't. I am not big enough. This isn't good. Mom will not like this, Dad. Mom will not like this!"

When I finally talked him into it, he slipped into the driver's seat with fear and trembling. He slowly backed up, trying to imitate all he had seen me do over the years. Then he began rounding the parking lot. Before long, he was having fun. He's a boy, and like most boys he found driving a car natural and enticing. He was actually quite good at it, though I did stop him after a few minutes.

It was after this experience that a meaningful conversation ensued. I said, "Jonathan, how did you feel when you first took the wheel?"

He was honest. He acknowledged that he'd felt panicked, terrified that he couldn't do it. "But you found out you could do it after all, didn't you?" I said.

When he agreed, I went on. "Jonathan, those feelings are exactly what you'll be feeling as you enter manhood. You will think you can't do it, that you don't know what you are doing, but you won't want anyone to know how you're feeling. Being a man is a lot like taking the wheel of a car. You are no longer a passenger in life. You are a driver, responsible for getting to a destination and getting your passengers safely there as well. Growing up means becoming a driver instead of a passenger."

Next, we drove over to a graveyard, where we walked among the gravestones for several minutes in silence. (Jonathan thought this was morbid at first.) Afterward, we talked about the words that were on the tombstones. Single phrases described the people buried in that graveyard—they each got just one sentence. After reflecting on them, we began to talk about the sentence we would want others to remember us by. What would our sentence be if we just got one? It was a profound conversation, even for a twelve-year-old.

I told him his doctor had predicted he would grow taller than me and weigh more than I weighed. "You will fill shoes bigger than those," I concluded. His eyes grew wide. He smiled as he thought about it. Then he spoke boldly into the air, "I'm going to be bigger than my dad!"

That's my hope, son. That's my hope.

LINKING UP

For more information about the dilemmas Generation iY boys face and how to deal with them, go to **www.SaveTheirFutureNow.com/TheTroublewithBoys**.

6 Volcanoes and Karaoke
The Struggle of a New Generation of Parents

WHEN I WAS NINE YEARS OLD, I had an experience that has enlightened me as a parent four decades later. In school, our class was studying how caterpillars are transformed into butterflies. It's a metamorphosis that has fascinated me all my life. I still don't fully comprehend how a crawling wormlike creature can spend time in a cocoon and later come out as a flying creature that looks nothing like it did before.

As fate would have it, I was playing in my backyard with my friend Jay, and we spotted one of those strange cocoons in a tree. I explained to Jay all we had learned in class—that the tiny creature inside would soon break out of his dark, secluded world and emerge as a butterfly. While we talked, I removed the cocoon and held it in my hand as if I were some sort of professor elaborating on what would happen next.

Interestingly, in that moment, the cocoon actually began to stir. Evidently, the butterfly was ready to enter the world. What an amazing event this would be for two young boys to watch!

The cocoon twitched and bulged, as that butterfly worked to fight its way out of its incarceration. Suddenly, one leg pushed out, creating a hole in the cocoon. This was nature at her best, and we were observing it all in real time.

It soon became clear to us, however, that the metamorphosis was a slow process. An hour went by with little progress. And let me remind you that sixty minutes is a long time for nine-year old boys to remain still. So I decided to step in.

I wanted to accelerate the journey for the little guy inside, and I could tell he was struggling. I reached down and gently widened the opening of the cocoon. The butterfly's leg was hanging out, and I could tell he wanted to be free. We waited for at least ten minutes more while he wrestled to expand the doorway I'd created, but it wasn't enough.

Bless his heart. He needed me. So I took my fingers and again gently helped him. A few minutes later, I helped him again. And again.

Finally, it happened. The butterfly slowly emerged from his cocoon prison. That, of course, is when my lesson was learned. It was a stunning experience, but not at all like I expected. The creature that appeared was not beautiful at all. He was dark and deformed. Instead of flying, he crawled. He attempted to spread his wings as if to fly, but it never happened. The poor butterfly never really experienced life as it was intended to be. He soon died on the grass in my backyard.

I was devastated. Had I done something wrong?

I later learned that butterflies are designed to experience the struggle of breaking out of a cocoon. It's all part of the metamorphosis. The process is supposed to be challenging—it's the only way the butterfly will be strong enough to fly with those wings.

To the casual observer, it seemed all wrong not to help him as he fought and rested and then fought again. It felt cruel to let him do it on his own. I was sure I was doing him a favor by helping. I was wrong. I disabled him. The greatest help I could be was to allow him the privilege of growing up. I intruded on that privilege. I was well-intentioned in my efforts—but I interrupted his growth. I had removed the struggle and dealt a death-blow to the butterfly.

It may be that this little experience has been repeated millions of times over the years with nine-year-olds and cocoons. But it's definitely an experience parents relive millions of times each year with their children. We mean so well. We undoubtedly want the best for our children. But how many times have we disabled them from maturing into adulthood because we did too much to help them?

A New Generation of Parents

I believe we not only have a new generation of kids on our hands today, we also have a new generation of parents. I have not seen a more engaged batch of parents since I began working with students more than thirty years ago. Most of the moms and dads I meet really want to be a good parent. In fact, some are paranoid about being a "bad dad" or a "monster mom." Some are reacting to the negative parenting style of their own parents and some simply don't want their kids hating them when they're thirty.

Whatever the reason, many of the Boomer and Gen-X parents I have met and heard about from educators have become enthralled by the art of parenting. This engagement has conditioned them to make their kids almost an obsessive focus.

These kids are their trophies. Parents will do anything for them—including protect them from consequences and run interference with anyone who challenges them. (According to a recent MetLife Poll, K–12 teachers say that "parents" have become their number one professional headache.[1])

Neil Howe and William Strauss, writing about how we arrived at this place over the last thirty years, point out, "In September 1982, the first Tylenol scare led to parental panic over trick-or-treating. Halloween suddenly found itself encased in hotlines, advisories, and statutes—a fate that would soon befall many other once-innocent child pastimes, from bicycle-riding to BB guns."[2] As Generation Y began to be born first to Boomer and then to Gen-X parents, kids became top priorities. The era of the "wanted child" had begun.

At the same time, through the 1980s, national coverage about dangers to children reached a new high—behaviors such as divorce, child abuse, abortion, violent crime, alcohol consumption, and illegal drugs as well as safety concerns about everything from venetian blinds to peanut butter. The well-being of children began to dominate the national debate. Reports began coming out in the mid-1980s that confirmed our concerns, and the era of the "protected child" dawned.

By the early 1990s, elementary school kids were in the spotlight, and in the years between 1986 and 1991, periodicals for children doubled. In the 90s the popularity of TV shows like *Sesame Street, Barney and Friends,* and *Blues Clues* all skyrocketed. During the 1996 presidential campaign, both Bob Dole and Bill Clinton referred to "soccer moms" as a major voting demographic they cared about. Kids were the all-important possession to care for. The era of the "worthy child" had begun.

By the late 1990s, the first wave of these much-wanted children passed through high school, "accompanied by enormous parental, educational and media fascination."[3] When asked about their parenting skills, parents gave themselves an *A* or a *B*—but they gave all other parents a *D* or *F*. This tells us how much effort parents felt they were giving their kids, and how often they compared their efforts to the efforts and results of other families. After the 1999 Columbine High School massacre was replayed over and over again on TV, parental obsession with their kids reached a fever pitch. Many parents pulled their kids out of public schools and put them in private school, or they home-schooled them for safety's sake. Kid safety and achievement were the focus as the era of the "perfected child" moved into full swing.[4]

Today, two of three parents define the "American Dream" as leaving their children financially better off than they were.[5] This evolution of events has produced a new generation of parents more focused on their children than anything else in their lives. At times, however, I wonder if this absorption with kids is entirely healthy.

I met with a parent recently who symbolizes what I'm talking about. She is a wonderful woman who cares deeply for her son. In fact, it's safe to say that her son is her prized possession. She will drop everything to meet his needs. She'll break her back to help him succeed and reach his goals. This mother has launched a wonderful nonprofit organization and put her son in charge of the cause. He has been able to raise thousands of dollars for his cause. He has even appeared on radio and TV to promote his cause. It is obvious he loves his cause—or maybe I should say "her cause," because I'm not sure whose dream it is. He is the spokesperson for the organization, but whenever a question comes up, he defers to his mom. She is doing all the work behind the scenes, and it just makes me wonder: Is she living out her life through him?

Damaging Parenting Styles

Does everybody involved in raising iY kids fit the above description? Of course not—though the kind of excessive involvement I've described is too common for comfort. And I am convinced that we who lead young people today must pay attention to the *way* we lead if we are to correct some of the damage that has been done to this generation.

I've been enlightened by working with thousands of parents each year in PTA meetings, parent conferences, and other events where I speak. During the last few years, I have spotted eight damaging parenting styles that iY moms and dads can fall into without even knowing it. (Some are unique to this generation; others have existed for years.) Let's explore these damaging styles and see what they are doing to our culture and to the rising generation of adults.

Helicopter Parents

These are the parents I have already described—the ones who hover over their kids, making sure they get every imaginable advantage and are protected from every imaginable danger. This kind of parent has gotten a lot of press in the past decade due to its prevalence.

These hovering "helicopters" can be controlling and obsessive in their efforts to insure that everything goes well for their children and that no negative incident affects their self-esteem or their prospects. (I just heard about one parent who called her son's college president to ask him to make sure her son wore his sweater that day!) They find it difficult to trust that their child can grow without their connections and control. So they call every day during school. Some even accompany their child to college and have a hard time leaving.

Sadly, helicopter parents can damage their kids because they don't allow them the privilege of learning to fail and persevere. Like the butterfly of my childhood, which emerged dark and deformed, the child of a helicopter parent might not develop the strength for life's hardships, ironically because of their loving parents.

I recognize there is a fine line between healthy and unhealthy leadership here. Certainly, I believe parents should be involved in their kids' lives and concerned for their welfare, but in the words of an article I once read, there's a difference between "mothering and smothering, fathering and bothering." Sometimes love and leadership require that we step back and allow children to spread their wings, to fly and even fall.

The Problem: Hovering helicopter parents don't allow their kids the privilege of learning to fail and persevere. They prefer to prepare the path for the child instead of the child for the path.

The Issue: It is very possible parents can become helicopters because they possess a controlling spirit. Adults who struggle with feeling out of control or who find it difficult to trust others tend to hover and micromanage as parents. They feel it is up to them to insure life turns out well for the kids. These adults, quite frankly, must learn that control is a myth, and the sooner they acknowledge this, the more effective they'll be as parents.

I have to face this issue from time to time myself. I must realize that one day my children will enter a world where they cannot depend on me to make everything right. They must learn to make decisions and live with the outcomes without my involvement. As Frank A. Clark aptly put it, "The most important thing that parents can teach their children is how to get along without them."[6]

Karaoke Parents

Like karaoke patrons, who grab a microphone and try to sing like Barry Manilow did in 1974, karaoke parents attempt to sound like their child, dress like their child, and talk like their child. They hunger to be a buddy to their kids and emulate this younger generation.

We live in a culture that is obsessed with staying young, looking young, and acting young—and karaoke parents fall for this obsession hook, line, and sinker. Whether it's cosmetic or attitudinal, these adults will do what they think they have to do in order to come across like they're still on the cutting edge of cool. They don't like the thought of being out of style, and they work hard to maintain an up-to-date image.

While there's nothing inherently wrong about this, I've seen it create confusion with children, who wonder, "Is that adult just my cool older buddy or my leader and example?" More seriously, karaoke parents may not offer kids the boundaries and authority they desperately need.

Last month, I read about a mother who allowed her daughter to have a house full of friends over—all minors. She allowed them to drink alcohol and even bought it for them. Several became completely inebriated and damaged the house and neighborhood. The police were called, and a mess had to be cleaned up.

Why had the mom said yes to the party? She wanted her daughter to feel like she trusted her. She wanted the daughter to like her and was willing to take big risks to accomplish that goal. In the process, she risked both her daughter's immediate and long-term well-being.

The Problem: Karaoke parents often don't provide their kids the clear parameters that build security and self-esteem. They're more concerned with being liked than with being respected.

The Issue: Parents often assume the karaoke style because of their own emotional insecurities. They may worry about aging or struggle with the need to be liked or feel uncomfortable with adult responsibilities. These adults will rationalize why they do what they do, but in the end, the only remedy is for them to embrace their own age and stage in life. They must relate to the young people in an appropriate manner and focus on the kids' needs more than their own. And the truth is, kids have plenty of peers. What they need are parents they can look up to and respect.

Dry-Cleaner Parents

We take our wrinkled or soiled clothes to the dry cleaner to have them cleaned and pressed by professionals. It's so handy to drop them off and have them handed back to us looking like new. That's essentially what dry-cleaner parents do with their children. They don't feel equipped to raise them, so they "drop them off" for experts to fix them.

Frequently, these parents will be from a double-income home where both parents are either too busy for their kids or just don't feel "gifted" to work with them. They are also accustomed to a culture that allows them to drop any possession off to a professional for cleanup, correction, or repair—their car, their clothes, their broken watch... and their children. Although the home environment may have spoiled or damaged their child's character or psyche, they hope a school, counselor, soccer team, or church youth group can fix the damage. (Plus, if something goes wrong, they have someone to blame.)

Accustomed to delegating responsibility, dry-cleaner parents assume they can delegate their most sacred trust: their kids. Sadly, they fail to see that raising kids is a learning experience for all of us, but it's a vital task that demands the investment of time, effort, and presence.

Yesterday, I met with a teacher who reported the mothers of her young students are nearly all stay-at-home moms, but they often drop their kids off for extended hours. They do it because they just aren't ready for the responsibility of caring for them or because their kids are interfering with what they want to do—shopping, tennis, golf, whatever. They may leave their kids at the school for ten hours a day—just like dry cleaning.

The Problem: Dry-cleaner parents don't furnish their kids with the mentoring and personal face-to-face time they need. They prefer to pass the buck and abdicate their parenting responsibility.

The Issue: Some of these parents delegate their responsibility because they feel that connecting with kids is just not their specialty. They may have inadequacy or identity issues or just don't feel up to the task of parenting. Others, I fear, are just self-centered and oblivious. They find it too much work actually to connect with their kids, so they hide behind an array of activities, including the jobs that enable them to pay for their child's interests.

Have You Seen These Parents?

You may know parents like these—or you may be one!

- **Helicopter Parents** hover too close.
- **Karaoke Parents** try too hard to be cool. (They're not.)
- **Dry-Cleaner Parents** drop their kids off for others to raise.
- **Volcano Parents** erupt over minor issues.
- **Dropout Parents** let their kids down.
- **Bullied Parents** can't stand up to their kids.
- **Groupie Parents** treat their children like rock stars.
- **Commando Parents** let rules trump relationship.

These parents need to run toward the very challenge in which they feel they're weak. They may also need to examine their schedules and their priorities to make room for actually relating to the children they are raising. Relationships make it all happen. Parents must build bridges of relationship that can bear the weight of truth.

Volcano Parents

I'm not really talking about parents with anger issues here—although there are certainly plenty of those and kids do pay the price for parents who are out of control. But the "volcanos" I'm talking about here represent a particular variety of an overinvolved parent who "erupts" suddenly, without warning, over relatively minor issues. Because they are so invested with their children, their frustration level seems to remain at a constant simmer.

These are the parents who will write papers or do homework for their children, then storm into the school office when the child receives a poor grade. Why are they erupting? Because the boundaries between them and their child have become fuzzy. They want so much for their child to succeed because that child is their last hope of leaving some sort of name or legacy for themselves. They have unrealized dreams or baggage they never dealt with in a healthy way. These unresolved issues have built up for years and will erupt when provoked.

Sadly, these parents provide neither the model nor the healthy environment that young people need. Not only do they prevent kids from learning to do their work; they also teach their children inappropriate ways of handling frustration. All too easily, the offspring of volcano parents develop their own volcanic tendencies.

Another unfortunate result of this style is that it can lead to a counterproductive relationship with educators. Parents and teachers become adversaries instead of allies, and the children get caught in the middle. This is the opposite of the scenario I experienced when I was growing up. When I got in trouble at school, I knew I'd be in even more trouble once my parents found out about it. My parents saw themselves as partners with the schools in teaching me responsibility, and they would back up the teacher's efforts. Today, if a kid gets in trouble and the parents find out, they often march down to the school and make trouble for the teacher. They tend to assume their child is right and want to defend him or her against other adults at the school, little league ballpark, or piano studio. Rather than working together, the parents and teachers quibble over the kid, who basks in the influence they leverage with those adults.

The Problem: These parents still have some unrealized dreams from their past—sometimes an unhealthy past—and try to fulfill them through their children. They also have issues with self-control and fuzzy boundaries between themselves and their children.

The Issue: The child represents the best way for the parent to accomplish the dream he or she gave up on years earlier, even if it is vicariously done. Their behavior is often the result of past baggage.

The best step these adults can take is self-care. They must address their own emotional health and deal with their own issues, so they don't further damage a child in their wake. Once again, kids have a better chance at growing up if their parents do so first. The best way we can help kids become healthy leaders is to model it for them.

Dropout Parents

We all know what a dropout is. It's a student who fails to finish high school or college. Dropouts decide along the way that school isn't really for them, so, they quit.

In the same way, many parents become dropouts. They may start the parenting journey excited about their new baby, but along the way they realize parenting is hard. Sometimes it feels impossible. It isn't like they'd imagined. It is hard work. So at some point they simply give up—or drop out. Whether they leave physically, emotionally, or financially, they quit on the effort to raise their kids.

Over the last twenty years, we've all heard the term deadbeat dads. Sometimes, it is the mom who flies the coop in search of a more fulfilling life. Other times, the parent will remain in the home but stop engaging the children in any meaningful way. In any case, the adult will model for their kids that they can't pay the price, so they choose not to finish what they started.

I have met these kinds of parents. When the subject comes up, they either sink into guilt and make excuses, or they quickly throw up a defense like "Oh, my kids were old enough that they didn't really need me anymore." In both cases, the remarks ring hollow. I know because I've met their kids. Those children (now old enough to figure out what happened) resent their dropout parent. Even if they still love them or pity them, they have no respect for them. In many cases, the child is more mature than the parent.

More often than not, the dropout parents stay around physically but cut out emotionally. They shift into neutral and don't try to lead anymore. They focus on other priorities. Feeling a bit like a loser when it comes to good parenting, they decide to play a game they can win.

The Problem: The parent fails to provide a healthy role model of finishing what they start, and in some cases, they fail to provide the tools their child needs.

The Issue: This one seems obvious. Except for rare exceptions, it appears to be a case of children having children—and I'm not necessarily talking about teen parents! The parent wasn't really healthy or mature enough to have children in the first place. They had no business entering into that kind of responsible role. They aren't even able to lead their own lives well, much less help a child launch into the world.

These parents must ask themselves, "Why did I want a child in the first place? Was it because of my own need for affection that I hoped the child would give me in return? Did I hope that a child would help my marriage hold together?" Parenting out of one's own need usually costs a lot—and the child is the one who pays the price.

The best course for this parent is to seek out counseling and discover what's happening inside, to find out why they are unable to lead their child in a healthy way. Then, they should reengage as a parent...beginning with an apology.

Bullied Parents

My friend Russell Atherton brought this growing population of U.S. parents to my attention. In the same way that a bully picks on weaker kids at school and requires intervention on the part of a teacher or principal, bullied parents are those who have been exhausted by their own kids. They are whipped parents.

Having been beaten and worn down, these parents have given up on discipline. In response to their own children's strong will or repeated rebellion, they have opted to surrender their role of authority and adopt a laissez-faire position. Although they are not happy in the defeat of their parenting goals, they find solace in the cessation of hostilities. Life seems better once they stop resisting. Peace comes by simply allowing their children to control situations, drive the family decisions, and basically do as they wish with virtually no consequences.

These parents are often counting the days until their children leave home. Unfortunately, the children will leave ill-equipped for the world they enter. They are used to calling the shots, they have not learned self-discipline, and their attitude toward authority may prevent them from keeping a job. Unlike home, the world won't let them have their own way, and they'll suffer for it...because Mom and Dad have failed to furnish boundaries or teach them respect for authority.

The Problem: These parents lack the courage and strength to lead their strong-willed children and prepare them for a potentially harsh adult world. The children are leaderless.

The Issue: In some ways, the issues of this parent can resemble those of the karaoke parent. They may fail to lead their children and become whipped due to their intense desire to be liked and accepted by their child. I've noticed the bullied-parent scenario is likely when the child's personality is stronger than Mom or Dad's personality. The more stubborn personality is likely to fight battles that the weaker personality will simply concede to keep the peace.

This kind of parent must find some allies, a counselor or a parent support group in order to develop some backbone. They must determine what values will govern their family and choose to fight for those values. "Choosing your battles" is a term often used to refer to times when we choose not to fight over a trivial matter, but it also means that sometimes we *do* choose to fight worthwhile battles to uphold what is important. This is a lesson that bullied parents must take to heart.

Groupie Parents

Do you remember the term *groupie*? It has usually been associated with rock stars. Groupies are the devoted fans—often women—who idolize their favorite performers. They travel in groups, following their favorite performers and doing whatever they can to be close to them, enjoying the precious moments they have with those brilliant, talented performers.

Groupie parents do the same thing with their children. They view their children as "stars" who are to be honored and served and have their every whim catered to, and they make sure they are available to applaud at any possible moment. These parents never miss a performance or fail to show up for a PTA meeting. They're great volunteers as long as their children benefit directly from the attention. (They're often the "stage moms" or the infamous "pageant parents.") What they long for most of all is to bask in the presence of their glorious offspring.

They might even spiritualize the issue by saying, "These children are precious gifts, blessings from heaven, and I am called to serve them and provide for them as they grow up under my care." Those statements are true, but groupie parents fail to see the other side of that reality—their children are entrusted to them to raise to become mature, contributing adults. We parents are stewards of our children.

We only have them for so many years (although the years seem to be increasing). Our role is to equip them to give back to society; to improve the world for having been in it.

Because the child of a groupie parent in essence becomes an idol, the groupie parent's approach is almost that of worship. What the child wants, the child gets. More than merely being spoiled, the child is venerated as the center around which the family revolves.

I recently spoke at a college commencement ceremony and heard about some groupie parents in the audience. These parents had kids who didn't graduate magna cum laude or even cum laude (with honors). Consequently, their graduation robe didn't include the "honors" cords and tassels. Since these parents felt their children deserved those honors, they created their own set of cords for the kids to wear. I would assume this was embarrassing for the graduates, but who knows? If you're accustomed to being idolized and catered to, you might not even understand when such behavior is out of line.

The Problem: These parents fail to recognize that kids need leaders, not servants. They enjoy their precious moments with their children, but they fail to equip them for the future.

The Issue: I have observed that this type of parenting style is often a reaction to a past experience. Due to the absence or neglect of their own parents, they may swing the pendulum to the other extreme, determining to never miss any milestone their child experiences. This motivation in itself is noble. The problem lies in their failure to see the big picture. By lavishing too much time and attention on a child and never denying the child anything, groupie parents can increase that child's self-image to an unhealthy level. How can anyone surrounded by groupies avoid becoming bloated with self-importance?

Sadly, these kids, who are used to being the center of attention, may never learn to function when the spotlight goes off. They may also become relationship-disabled, unable to manage the give-and-take for a healthy relationship.

These parents must work to grasp the reality that loving their children means treating them as people, not idols. It means learning to say no when appropriate and requiring them to serve others...as well as learning to work well even when the focus is not on them. And perhaps the best gift any married parents can give their kids is to keep that marriage healthy. The kids will be happiest when they know they're a welcome addition to a family, not the center of family life.

Commando Parents

These parents have been around for centuries. They have frequently been called "military parents" because of their authoritative style. This parenting style is almost always well-intentioned but can cause damage when it offers more rules than relationship. In this style, one or more parent adopts the role of a drill sergeant who expects perfection from both parent and child. Allen Vehey, professor at Hope College in Holland, Michigan, worries that society is beginning to see "the duties of parenting as making perfect children rather than in terms of uncalculating nurturance."[7] Instead of flexing with the messes that come with raising kids, these parents demand perfectly clean rooms, perfectly diligent study habits, perfect performances at sports and academics, even perfect behavior at playtime.

The discipline imposed by commando parents is not bad in itself. In fact, it can be a breath of fresh air in light of the many other damaging parent styles, and it can be very helpful in preparing children for the practical demands of the world. What's wrong is that it typically offers law without grace. It's about rules and routines and can produce a child who's afraid of anything short of straight As on a report card.

A friend told me about how his dad used to play ball with him in his backyard. The man would challenge his son to catch every pitch perfectly—fifty times in a row. Then the dad would purposely throw the last pitch in the dirt, preventing the boy from meeting the challenge. His dad's logic? He didn't want his son to ever stop shooting for perfection. Good goal—horrible method. This man now struggles with a poor sense of identity and a feeling that no matter how hard he tries, he will never measure up—an all-too-common fallout of commando parenting.

The Problem: These parents are focused on attaining compliance and perfection instead of growth and improvement. Their children may live in anxiety, frustration, or exhaustion just trying to meet expectations.

The Issue: Commando parents have their own issues. Perhaps they never felt love or approval while growing up. Maybe the only model for parenting they know is a drill sergeant who pushes and pushes the child to perform. The commando parents I know also feel their own reputations depend on their children's performance. They cannot stand a poor showing on the Little League field or in the classroom because they feel it makes them look bad. I suggest they watch other families, consider other models, look for opportunities to practice being less rigid, and take baby steps toward flexibility. They need to see that life is about love and empowerment, not command and control. High standards are good as long as they fit the young person and are balanced with equal levels of responsiveness to what the young person needs.

Let's Keep the Drama on the Stage

My son loves participating in a community-theater program here in Atlanta. He is a true thespian. He loves the drama of a Broadway show. He loves the drama of television or movies. He loves the drama of a powerful play. Unfortunately, he's seen a little too much drama from the adults involved in the program. If parents in this community-theater program feel their child wasn't cast appropriately, if someone doesn't affirm their child's talent when her self-esteem is low, or if the theater doesn't spotlight the son's abilities when the talent scouts are present, these parents can turn into guerillas.

There's nothing more intimidating than a mom or dad who is determined to fight for their kid's rights. I cannot tell you how many times the parents in this community theater program have embarrassed me by their immature behavior. They fail to lead themselves well, much less their kids. I find myself thinking, *Please...let's keep the drama on the stage.*

There have actually been times when I've felt the kids are more mature than the adults who are trying to lead them. I see parents who consistently behave like spoiled children, yet when they're confronted for their behavior they cry foul or act hurt, playing the victim. It's a sad commentary on the most educated generation of adults in U.S. history.

But the real issue, of course, is not education. These parents generally have sound minds. Our problems are issues of the heart—emotional issues that prevent us from leading well at home or in the classroom.

And what is the result? Kids can grow so accustomed to adult interventions that they miss out on lessons in self-reliance. They may never successfully emerge from the "cocoon" and fly.

Mara Sapon-Shevin, an education professor at Syracuse University has had students tell her they were late for class because their mothers didn't call to wake them up that morning. She has also had students call their parents from the classroom on a cell phone to complain about a low test grade, then pass the phone over to her in the middle of class because the parent wanted to intervene. She often hears parents play the money card. They point out that they are paying a lot of money for their child's education and imply that anything short of an *A* is an unacceptable return on their investment.[8]

It seems to me we've experienced a pendulum swing over the last sixty years. During the 1940s, Dr. Benjamin Spock reacted to the damage done by rigid parents. They were distant, structured, and legalistic, and they were producing children who were anxious, neurotic, and repressed. Dr. Spock wrote to correct this. He urged parents to let children be "little people" and express themselves. They needed to feel love as well as discipline, and they needed a boost in self-esteem. Of course, other child psychologists have built on Spock's theories over the decades. The pendulum has swung back and forth.

Today, we may need another pendulum swing. The damage we often do is intervening too much; we are into "hyper-help" mode and need to allow our kids to grow up and make it on their own.

Adults Can Grow Too

I should be clear on the fact that I believe there are millions of healthy parents around the U.S. and across the globe. I applaud their efforts and their example. Yet, even healthy parents can lean toward one of these styles and benefit from some self-correction. I believe this is also true of teachers and other adults who interact with young people. I want to encourage my fellow parents and educators to address the issues that might be holding us back from authentic leadership in the lives of our children and to grow toward a healthier, more mature style of leading young people.

Over the years, I have observed my own parenting style, a style I naturally assumed as my kids grew through various stages of childhood. Now, as I write this book, my daughter is in her twenties and my son is in his teens. While my values haven't changed over this period, my parenting style certainly has. I've had to adjust my approach to reflect my children's needs and yes, to correct some past mistakes.

Interestingly enough, I've also had to adjust my style when it comes to being an educator and mentor. When I began to teach students in 1979, I tended to relate to the kids as an older brother—with maybe a hint of a karaoke style. Within a few years, I realized I needed to change the way I was relating to them if I was to be effective, so I moved into more of an uncle's role. Some years later, I remember consciously choosing to relate as a father figure. I'm certainly old enough to be a dad to the students I teach today. I must embrace this and give them what they need, not necessarily what feeds my own ego or need to be cool.

In the same way a corporate executive might manage one team member differently than another, parents and other adults who work with kids need to pay attention to both individual temperaments and life stages and lead accordingly. A teenager or young adult doesn't need to be parented the same way a toddler does. One child in a family might require a different approach than another. As the kids grow, the approach might need adjustment. Mine certainly has. Both of my children are good kids, and I, like many other parents, hope I haven't done too much damage as my wife and I attempted to raise them.

The truth is, no parent, teacher, or adult involved with young people will get it all right all the time. I believe, however, that healthy leadership from healthy parents and teachers produces healthy students who become healthy leaders themselves. I am haunted by the truth that James Baldwin once penned: "Children have never been very good at listening to their elders, but they have never failed to imitate them."[9]

Wouldn't it be wonderful if what our children learn to imitate is to fly strong and free—like a healthy butterfly.

➤ LINKING UP ◄

For a quiz on what kind of parent you tend to be, see **www.SaveTheir FutureNow.com/ParentQuiz**.

7 Elephant Lessons
Amending the Lies We Have Told Generation iY

WE CAN LEARN SOME VERY INTERESTING LIFE PRINCIPLES FROM ELEPHANTS.

That may sound strange, but let me explain.

A few years ago, in the African bush, it was discovered that some young elephants had strayed from their herd. They were lost for quite some time. A search was launched to find them and restore them to their families. It took time, but when they were found, researchers gleaned some new insights into their species. These young pachyderms were no longer babies. They had grown a bit and were now bullying other animals they came in contact with. In fact, they were even killing other animals, seemingly for fun.

This was strange—very unlike the normal behavior for elephants. Typically, elephants only kill to protect their herd or perhaps to guard their territory. It's as though these young elephants had become rebels.

The lesson was quite simple. Once these young elephants were removed from their older counterparts, they had no models to follow. They had no one to guide them, or to show them how to act. They were renegades. They were making up their own reality and because of their size, they got away with it for a season.

But that's not the end of the story. Another observation about these elephants was even more enlightening to me. When they came upon a pond of water to drink, they would reach down and stir the water with their trunks, making huge ripples and even waves. Only then would they lean over and drink the water.

Researchers became curious as to why they performed this little ritual before drinking. After months of observation, they figured it out. When those elephants looked down into the water, they were distracted by their reflection. They didn't like what they saw. Sometimes they appeared repulsed by seeing themselves, so they stirred the water to remove any likeness of themselves. Distortion is what they were after, and making those waves seemed to help. The bigger the ripple, the less they had to face what they really looked like.

In many ways, these accounts of "lost" African elephants inform us about ourselves. I believe we have a generation of young people on our hands—Generation iY—who desperately needs mentors. Like the young elephants, young people who spend most of their time with peers may drift into a lifestyle that won't work in the real world. Many are truly lost and need to find their way back to a path that leads to maturity.

Even when these young people do find themselves on the right path, they often run into another problem because, all their lives, they've been taught to "stir the water." They've even had the water stirred for them! (This little analogy gives new meaning to "making waves.")

What do I mean? Simply that so many Gen-iY kids have grown up without ever seeing a clear picture of themselves. Adults have muddied the waters for them and given them a distorted view of reality.

Let's face it, this "muddying the waters" is just another name for lying to kids—and we've done it for years. Some have done it to sell goods or to promote ideas. Some have done it to get elected. Parents and educators have done it in the name of healthy self-esteem or happiness. (I admit I've done that too.) We have lied to manipulate, and often we have lied out of love. We've even taught young people to lie to themselves—to muddy the waters in ways that will eventually sabotage them as a young adult.

I've come to believe something about human nature. There is nothing easier than to believe a lie about ourselves or our situation. There is often nothing tougher than to face the truth.

Liar, Liar, Pants on Fire

I recognize what you might be thinking. *Lies? Me? I would never lie to my children or my students or my young employees. I am an honest person.*

You think so?

Lying to our kids is rampant in our nation. It happens for a variety of reasons:

- *Because we're insecure. Telling the truth, even gently, requires a deep level of emotional security. The person we tell the truth to may reject us or may not like us enough to confide in us. Our need to be liked cannot be allowed to eclipse our pursuit of their best interests.*

- *Because speaking the truth takes time and work.* There may be only one truth, but many possible ways to "spin" an issue. Sometimes we lie because it gets us out of a jam. Sometimes the lie just seems to make things easier.
- *Because the truth can be painful.* The truth can hurt and be much more painful than a charming lie, at least in the short run. To most of us, pain feels like an enemy.
- *Because facing the truth makes us responsible.* Lies sometimes let us off the hook. They allow us to pass the blame to someone else, or avoid facing something we'd rather not acknowledge. Often we'd rather trade in long-term consequences for short-term benefits.
- *Because we've lost sight of the truth ourselves.* As we'll see later in the chapter, the Baby Boomers and Gen-Xers who are raising the next generation have their own set of misconceptions that can affect our ability to be truthful. Sometimes we tell lies because we believe them too.
- *Because we genuinely want these young people to be happy.* Most of us want our kids happy all the time, so we'll sacrifice the truth a bit in order to medicate the moment.

My daughter, Bethany, is a well-adjusted twenty-one year old. She's a psychology major and serves as a leader on her university campus. But three years ago, Bethany went through a bout with depression. Almost overnight, she became a different person.

Needless to say, we were worried. We tried everything from family talks, to counseling, to prayer, to activities—you name it—to help pull Bethany out of her low state. And I can't tell you how tempting it was on certain days to take shortcuts, to try to stimulate her out of the depression and just make her feel better that day, even if it meant telling her lies.

Eventually, we realized the problem was a chemical imbalance that required a small dose of medication. This, coupled with truth telling within our family, proved to be crucial. To our relief, we finally saw results. The key, however, was not to patch things up, but to make things right. It was truth our daughter needed, not well-meaning lies.

When I say we have "lied" to this young Generation iY, I don't mean we have done so on purpose. The last thing we would want to do is harm our kids. All too often, however, we have fed them "lines" to help them feel good about themselves or to bolster their confidence or to get them to try a new sport or ballet or piano. At the time, it seemed like a noble thing to do—or at least a harmless and useful falsehood. But in the long run, lies are far from harmless. Lying to young people, in fact, can harm them deeply.

I recently had the privilege of interviewing author Laura Fraser. A warm, authentic writer in her mid-forties, she has personal knowledge of the damage that well-meaning lies can do in a person's life. In an article for *More* magazine, she relates much the same story that she told me:

> By the time I was five or six, I had heard it often—I was always young-er than everyone around me and ahead of my peers....I thrived on being called "smart" and "cute." A psychologist said I had an IQ of 165....I whizzed through school, skipping grades, racking up awards and hon-ors....All the way back in third grade, my teacher told me I would become a great writer—at an early age, of course—and that's just what I figured would happen.[1]

But it didn't happen—not the way Laura expected. She's done well profession-ally, yet the dazzling career predicted for her has not quite materialized. At midlife she has watched others pass her by, and she has often struggled with "a nagging sense of failure."[2] Laura told me that despite her accomplishments, she some-times feels like she hasn't really lived up to her potential. She tends to dismiss her achievements as not good enough because they pale against her supposedly spectacular promise.

As I spoke to Laura, I felt someone was finally talking honestly with me about the kind of childhood dilemmas we tend to sweep under the rug. When she arrived at college, for instance, she was shocked to find there were hordes of "smarty pants" just like her. It's likely they too had heard from parents and teachers that they were on their way to the top of the heap. Like Laura, they were probably shocked to find themselves square "in the middle of that heap."[3]

"Early aptitude doesn't necessarily predict adult accomplishment," Laura writes. "In fact, the opposite may be truer." She quotes author Malcolm Gladwell as saying that few childhood prodigies ever become successful, and she adds, "That's because there's a huge difference between talent and the application of talent....If everyone tells you when you're 10 that you'll become a great novelist, you just sit back and dream about your book jackets. Not only don't precocious kids think they have to work hard, but deep down, they believe true effort entails too much risk."[4]

Seven Lies That Can Disable a Generation

Laura, of course, is a Baby Boomer, not a member of the iY generation. But I believe what she experienced as a result of well-meaning adult lies may increasingly be the future of the iY generation. That's because what she experienced as a "precocious" and obviously gifted child—a constant stream of accolades, compliments, and predictions of greatness—is par for the course for many iYers. In fact, I believe we are in danger of disabling a generation because we keep muddying the waters.

Because of our lies, too many are reaching adulthood emotionally unstable and socially naïve. Shame on us, not them. It's now time for action—a new kind of action, one that's not merely about inflating the self-esteem of iY kids, but equipping them to face an uncertain world. It's about bolstering their confidence, but in a way that is based on reality. It's time we stopped lying to these young people with our thoughtless words and led them in a thoughtful manner.

Here are some of the most harmful lies we've told to Generation iY:

Lie #1: "You Can Be Anything You Want to Be."

This is one of the most popular lies today. Parents and teachers say it to children daily. It's considered part of the American dream, and I certainly used to believe it. Now I consider that lie a particularly dangerous one.

We see signs of it on reality shows like *American Idol* when well-intentioned kids by the hundreds of thousands show up to audition before the judges for a spot on the show. Most of them have no business being there...and end up making fools of themselves on national TV. Why do they try out? All too often, it's because some friend or some adult has lied to them. Someone has said, "You have a great voice. You can be anything you want to be!" And they really, really want to be the next *American Idol*.

The trouble is, wanting something is not the same as being able to achieve it. Desire is not the same as talent, and talent is not the same as accomplishment. The truth is, I will never be an opera singer no matter how badly I want to be. My gifts simply don't match that desire. Unless I can match my dreams with my actual strengths, I will be doomed to failure.

The reason that adults, especially parents, tell kids the lie of "you can do anything you want to" is that they want their kids to think big. They don't want them to be ruled by fear. But telling them they can do anything is simply setting them up for later discouragement—because the truth is, they *can't* do anything they want. None of us can. We all have strengths and weaknesses, true potential and true limitations.

Consider the young person who really believes she can do anything she sets her mind to. If she begins working in an area outside of her strengths, she'll likely be de-energized by the experience. (People are usually energized by playing to their strengths.) Not only will she need to invest extra time and intense focus to achieve what she's working for, but the pleasure of accomplishing it will pale in comparison to the pleasure she could find by working within the scope of her natural strengths.

Our greatest chance for fulfillment, for personal growth, for results and for impact on others will always come from working in a strength area. Working in a weak area will only foster the feeling of exhaustion and failure.

Megan is good example. She'd been told she "could do anything" she wanted, so she assumed that was true of her desire to go to college. The trouble is, she wasn't very academically oriented; her strengths lay more with the mechanical and the hands-on. The gap between Megan's expectations and her gifts set her up for failure. She flunked a number of courses and changed her major six times until she finally landed on one with courses she could pass. She did manage to graduate—after eight years! But by the time she hit on a career path that suited her strengths, she felt she was ten years behind. She ended up taking a job she could have gotten without college. While I am proud of Megan for her tenacity, I can't help regretting the time she wasted. She needed a target that fit her strengths, not her imagination.

Lie #2: "It's Your Choice."

We live in a culture full of options. Generation iY has grown up constantly choosing between breakfast cereals, TV shows, Facebook photos, fast-food combos, and YouTube downloads. All they have to do is point, click, pluck it off the shelf.

I believe this vast array of choices—and the assumption that all are equally available—can be harmful. It can create a self-centered paradigm, a lie that I get to suit myself all the time, that it's about me. A young person who grows up believing this is in for a rude awakening when he hits the real world and discovers it *doesn't* revolve around him or offer him infinite choices.

Alex hit a wall emotionally because of this lie. Once he graduated, he took a job close to the university he attended. He was on top of the world when he started but soon learned the team he worked with had some rules. Some things were done a certain way, and there wasn't much room to improvise or adapt. Alex chafed at these restrictions. Although his work fit his gifts well, he quit after five months, telling his boss he needed more freedom and options. I think that not having alternatives to choose from made him feel claustrophobic. He was conditioned to having things his way; he had been led astray by the lie that he had a choice in everything.

The truth is, not everything is an option in the real world. Sometimes, there really is one right answer, only one good choice. Sometimes—quite often, in fact—someone else may decide what we will do, and we must go along with that decision. That is simply reality. It's not necessarily a bad thing, because having too many choices can be unhealthy and overwhelming. I know of parents and teachers who offer a wide range of choices to children far too young to handle them. The adults were well-intentioned but not wise. In my opinion, young people need the number of choices they're offered to increase slowly in proportion to responsibilities and maturity.

Too many choices too soon in a child's life can be just too much. Have you ever seen a kid crying at Disneyland? Seems like an oxymoron, but I've seen it many times, and I think I know why it happens. There are so many options, so many things to do, and the little ones quickly become overwhelmed. They are not emotionally prepared to make all the choices. Then, when they make a decision that doesn't work out, they aren't prepared for the disappointment. Hence the tears.

No doubt, learning to choose wisely is part of growing up, and it's part of our job as adults to give young people practice in making good choices. But we must also help them learn the truth that not everything is open to decision or debate. Sometimes there really is no choice, and kids will be better prepared for adult life if they understand this.

Lie #3: "You Are Special."

This is a message that most members of Generation iY have heard since they were very small. Parents and others say it because they want the kids to know they are loved and cherished and unique. And it's true that each human being is a one-of-a-kind blend of talents and abilities. But it's easy for kids who are bombarded from birth with "You're special" to get the message that they are truly outstanding and extraordinary—more talented and accomplished than their peers. That simply cannot be true of everyone—and kids will eventually figure this out. Like Laura Fraser, they may eventually go to college and be shocked to discover that thousands of students are more talented than they are. Some may realize it even sooner.

What happens then? Certain temperaments can spiral down into depression when they realize they're not really that special. Overachievers and perfectionists may buckle under the pressure the word *special* implies. And some will simply begin to question the judgment of adults who insist on calling them special. One student told me, "My mom is like the Easter Bunny or Santa Claus. She always does nice things for me, but I don't take her seriously."

David is seeing a counselor at age twenty-seven. He told me why. He has this love-hate relationship with his parents. He's grateful they cared enough to try to encourage him, but he also resents them for painting him a picture of life that just isn't real. David struggles with feeling paralyzed, unable to try much of anything for fear of revealing that he really isn't special after all. Mom and Dad meant well, but they borrowed their parenting style from Barney the Dinosaur. David would have been better served by parents who pointed out his strengths and affirmed them but also prepared him for a real world where not everyone will think he's special.

Lie #4: "Every Kid Ought to Go to College."

I used to say this to the teens I worked with each week, and I still hear adults say this to kids all the time. They don't want students to set their sights too low. They want them to believe they can do what, perhaps, their parents were unable to do— to get a degree and really become somebody. They want these kids to believe in themselves and value their own abilities.

The intent is good. But I have come to believe that the actual statement is a lie.

Like you, I want the best for this generation of students, but I have come to believe that a four-year college degree isn't for everyone. In fact, I have seen some young people spiral downward when they realize that a liberal-arts education does not fit their gifts, interests, or aspirations. It isn't that they are stupid or unable to successfully navigate a career, but rather that the career choice which suits them best calls for a different kind of preparation.

But won't a college degree be required to get a decent job in the future? Not according to Edward E. Gordon, an internationally recognized expert on education reform and the future of the labor market. He writes, "Many economists believe that 70% of the good jobs in the current and future American economy will not require a four-year college degree; rather, they will require some form of additional training and education, such as an associate degree or technical training certificate."[5]

In other words, the widespread assumption that a four-year degree will guarantee a place in the marketplace or the lack of such a degree will automatically hinder a young person is simply not true. As W. J. Reeves writes in *USA Today*,

> Moms and dads, who foot the bill, delude themselves that going to any four-year college will make their sons and daughters literate, analytical, culturally aware, technologically advanced, and therefore employable. In America today, there exists a goal that the majority of the nation's youth should go to college and that access should be the byword for higher education. On the surface, this sounds like a great idea; in reality, it is not.[6]

Carey would agree. His parents pushed him to go to college all through his high-school years, and he assumed they knew what they were talking about. After a miserable freshman year, however, he was afraid to tell his mom and dad he hated school. Further, he felt like a failure. He doubted his intelligence and his ambition. It was only after he had wasted two years of tuition payments that he mustered the courage to talk to his parents and go a different route.

The lie that everyone needs to go to college has unhappy repercussions not only for the students who would do better elsewhere, but for the colleges themselves. According to author and professor Thomas C. Reeves,

> The impact on college and university campuses of legions of unprepared freshmen is never positive. Millions of dollars must be spent annually in remedial education. And the rate of failure is still extraordinarily high. The ACT estimates that one in four fail or drop out after one year. A third of the freshmen at the relatively select University of Wisconsin-Madison do not return for a second year. I toiled for decades on a Wisconsin campus on which a mere 18 percent of the entering freshmen ever graduate. The financial costs, let alone the emotional toll on the young people involved, is scandalous.[7]

The truth about advanced education for the iY generation is that there is more than one path to a successful future. Four-year college (and graduate schools) may certainly be a fruitful option for some, but community colleges, tech schools, and vocational institutes may be more appropriate for many. We must guide Generation iY into the appropriate path for their aptitude and gifts, not for the satisfaction of our egos.

Lie #5: "You Can Have It Now."

This is a phrase we all love to hear. Generation iY has heard it all their lives. They get their music—now. They get their text messages—now. They get their money—

now. They get their fast food—now. They use Google and Bing and ChaCha and get their information—now. They update their Facebook page—now. They use Netflix streaming to get their entertainment—now. They post their YouTube video—now. They send out tweets to all their followers—now. They're accustomed to living this way, and they have a low tolerance for waiting.

And the truth is, adults in our culture are not much more patient than the kids. *Wait* is a four-letter word for adults too. We pace in front of the microwave oven and shake our fists at stoplights. But if we cannot teach Generation iY how to pay now and play later, we're in for trouble when they lead the world in twenty-five or thirty years.

Corey has a bad temper, and it surfaces every time he doesn't get his way. That's fairly typical for a child—but Corey is no longer a child. He's in his twenties. His anger flares when he has to wait on anything—from traffic signals to waiters, from slow cars on the road to slow printers in the office. As a boy he was fed the lie that he could have what he wanted immediately, and his growing-up years confirmed that this was true.

Corey's problem, of course—and the problem of many in his generation—is that he has never learned how to wait. He expects instant gratification, he is quick to give up when answers are slow in coming, and his lack of self-discipline is already causing him problems in his personal relationships and his job. The truth is, the cult of instant gratification is costly to young people because it fails to teach them qualities such as persistence and self-discipline, which may well be more important to their success than intelligence or talent.

Nobel laureate economist James Heckman writes,

> Numerous instances can be cited of people with high IQs who fail to achieve success in life because they lacked self-discipline and of people with low IQs who succeeded by virtue of persistence, reliability and self-discipline. Our analysis challenges the conventional point of view that equates skill with intelligence, and draws on a body of research that demonstrates the importance of both cognitive and non-cognitive skills in determining socioeconomic success.[8]

How can the "noncognitive skills" of persistence, reliability, and self-discipline be developed? Heckman and his colleagues suggest two critical factors—early intervention through active child development programs and development of adequate role models. In other words, we who are raising the next generation must be intentional about teaching young people how to cope with non-instant results and how to persist when answers are slow in coming. We must value their ultimate welfare more than their immediate gratification—or ours.

Lie #6: "You're a Winner Just Because You Participated."

A change swept across the nation between 1990 and 2000 in Little League baseball, kids' soccer leagues, Pop Warner football, even pet shows and science fairs. Parents began insisting that there should be no losers. Everyone who participated in a sport or competition would be declared a winner. I am certain that at first this was a refreshing perspective for the kids, a reminder that winning isn't everything. Over time, however, the insistence that "everyone is a winner" has diluted the value of achievement.

I'm pretty sure I used the "everyone is a winner" line on my son when he was six years old, standing in the outfield at a baseball game and staring at his glove. I didn't want his self-esteem to be dashed because he was not as good as the pitcher on his team. I suppose this "everyone is winner" phrase is okay to use when they are young. But by late elementary school and middle school, those kids are well aware that is a lie.

Kids are not stupid. They can see that some of the players on a team or participants in a competition are far more capable than others. Ignoring this reality simply robs kids of motivation. The less accomplished kids have little reason to strive to be better, and the more talented kids can have little motivation to improve.

Last year, I visited a friend whose son, Scott, had just finished another soccer season. I asked him, "How'd you do?" Scott looked down at the ground and muttered, "Great." I could tell he wasn't convinced of his own remark. So I suggested we go up to his room so I could see the trophy he just got. I walked into a bedroom full of ribbons, trophies, plaques, and team photos. It was like the Hall of Fame... only bigger!

Well, I'm kidding about that. But this young kid had gotten an award of some sort for every team he'd ever played on and every season—whether the team had won or lost. And I could see that these awards were almost meaningless to him. There were eighth- and ninth-place ribbons on the wall. There were trophies that didn't say anything on them. Generic...just like the way it made him feel. When I asked about the newest trophy on his shelf, Scott just pointed at it silently. Instead of a feeling of pride, he had a room full of meaningless, trite expressions.

And that's the problem with the "everybody wins" lie. What it means, in reality, is that nobody wins. Kids have nothing to strive for, nothing to feel genuinely proud of. And when they launch into the real world, where there really are winners and losers, kids raised on "everybody wins" may be in for a rude awakening. What will they think when their boss doesn't reward them just for participating?

"Everyone wins" is obviously a lie—but there is a counter-lie that can be just as damaging. It's the one that says, "If you can't win, you might as well not play." I hear this all the time from parents. It's the "gotta be a winner" syndrome that tempts some kids to give up before they even participate. Playing in a band or orchestra or playing on a team and not being the best player can and should be very rewarding, even if you're not the best. In this case participation is, indeed, winning. You don't have to be a star to benefit from being part of a group effort.

Lie #7: "You Can Get Whatever You Want."

This lie may sometimes come from family members when kids are growing up, but it's also fed to them relentlessly by the media. It falls into that category of something that's been said so many times we perceive it as true, even if it isn't. Of course, for many iY young people, it's also been confirmed by their experience. Growing up, many of them really have gotten just about everything they wanted.

There was a time when one's childhood was localized to a neighborhood, a school, or a small town. Not today. Generation iY will shop, research, phone, text-message, and write to each other at any time, any place, to find what they want—and they expect to get it. Students in a focus group we sponsored at Growing Leaders confirmed: "We rarely take no for an answer. And what's cool, we rarely have to."

From the time they were babies, the kids in this generation have received attention, toys, technology, money and options. Over and over again. Sadly, they've been set up to expect the same in their futures. This means they've been set up for disappointment because none of us get everything we want! Like other lies, this one nurtures unhealthy

Lies and More Lies

This chapter lists the most pervasive lies we've told Generation iY—the ones I encounter most in my work with kids. Here are some others that are almost as common—and can be equally as destructive:

- "You shouldn't worry about what anyone else thinks."
- "Everyone is equal—we're all the same."
- "You can change your life in a few easy steps."

Intrigued? To read about these and other lies we've told Generation iY, go to www.SaveTheirFutureNow.com/Lies.

adults who cannot delay gratification, who feel entitled to the best all the time, and who quit when something doesn't turn out the way they would like it.

Lying to Ourselves

The lies we tell the younger generation can cost them, no matter how well-meaning adults are at the time. Author Lynn Austin learned this one day when she took her little boy to visit the planetarium.

> My five year old son had been looking forward to visiting the planetarium while on vacation, but when we arrived, we learned that children under age 6 were not admitted.
>
> "Let's pretend you had a birthday," I told him. "If the ticket man asks you how old you are, I want you to say, 'I'm six.'"
>
> I made him practice it until he sounded convincing, then I bought the tickets without any problems. When the show ended, we moved on to the museum. There, a large sign read, "Children 5 and Under Admitted Free." To avoid the $5 admission fee, I had to convince my son to forget his pretend birthday.
>
> The consequences of my lie became apparent as we walked up the steps to our last destination, the aquarium. "Wait a minute, mom!" my son said with a worried look. "How old am I now?"[9]

As sweet and innocent as this story is, Lynn puts her finger on something important for every adult. Eventually our lies, which were intended to help our children, actually begin to confuse them. This is true with each of the lies I included in this chapter. Lies and false beliefs are not a healthy way to produce a generation of upstanding adults.

So why do we lie in the first place? How did we get into this mess?

At the beginning of this chapter, I outlined a few reasons why the current generation of parents, teachers, coaches, and mentors have fallen in the trap of lying to kids. We lie to kids because we're insecure, because lies are easier, because we want to avoid pain and responsibility, and because we want the kids to be happy. But I think perhaps the main reason we lie to our kids is that we have our own set of generational baggage that muddies the water for all of us.

Let's face it. Parents typically begin having kids and educators begin their careers before we have mastered our own lives. Both Baby Boomers and Gen-Xers have had to process through their own baggage as adults. We have our own issues and we're influenced by our dominant culture just as our children are. The kids of Generation iY are not the only ones who hunger for instant gratification or assume the world should adapt itself to them. Our example has not always been stellar for our children.

In essence, we lie to our kids because we too are blinded by a set of lies. I recently spoke with a father who confessed to me he was terrified of being a "bad dad." Such paranoia can lead us to do things that defy common sense and logic. We don't want to fail, so we parent "defensively" rather than leading our kids well. A lie has blinded us—the lie that parents must be perfect in order to raise kids successfully.

Our preoccupation with safety, which I've mentioned before, is another obsession that has guilted many of us into poor training habits. We fear our kids will be harmed if they're allowed to do anything risky or potentially harmful. And many other lies can be chalked up to our own failures or unfulfilled dreams. We tell ourselves we have young people's best interests at heart when we are really trying to live through them. Another lie.

So how can we reach past our own brokenness and give Generation iY kids the tools they need to be happy, productive, real-life citizens of the future? I have an idea.

What if we tried telling them—and ourselves—the truth!

Moving toward Truth

Dr. Chris Thurman has said, "The number one cause of our unhappiness are the lies we believe in life."[10] I think he's on to something. Growing up requires facing the truth and embracing reality, and this is an important challenge for Generation iY kids and the adults who are leading them. But the good news is that living in the truth makes us happier, healthier, and more productive human beings. Truthful relationships are more stable. A truthful approach to problem solving gets to the root of the problem more effectively. A commitment to truth makes all of life simpler and more fulfilling.

So how do we get there?

Thurman later imagines the response of the American public if the following ad were placed in a hometown newspaper:

The Truth about the Truth

The truth—what a concept! It's a requirement for emotional health, the only sure foundation for building a life, the only pathway to lasting relationships and satisfying careers. I'm convinced it's the dependable solution to so many looming iY issues. We who are leading the iY generation toward the future must make a radical commitment to telling them the truth—but we would do well to keep the following realities in mind as we strive to become truthful guides for Generation iY:

1. **The truth can hurt.** The truth helps us, but at first it may feel painful—like a successful surgery. To me, this means the commitment to tell the truth must be accompanied by a commitment to be as gentle as possible and to work through the discomfort with the person who is receiving the truth.

2. **The truth can be eclipsed by a thrilling lie.** Even when some young people know the truth about life, they still may choose to believe a lie. Why? Because lies can be far more enticing than truth. Altered reality may be more fun, more exciting, or simply easier to handle, at least in the short run. This is something to keep in mind when an iY kid seems to resist the truth you're trying to tell. Truth telling may require persistence.

3. **The truth can be difficult to identify**—especially for a generation that's been raised on fantasy films, computer-generated effects, virtual-reality games, "reality" TV, and all kinds of social communities where they learn to project a doctored version of themselves. Media and corporations often deliberately blur the truth in order to sell something. A commitment to truth, therefore, might include exposing some of the "altered" realities, which can be just another kind of lie.

4. **The truth can allow healthy doubt.** Doubt doesn't have to be the enemy of the truth! In fact, telling kids the truth may make it possible for them to intelligently and honestly assess their talent, competence, or status in a given area. It could motivate them to invest their energies in pursuits that best match their interests and abilities. Committing to truth telling might include reassuring someone that such doubt can actually be healthy.

5. **The truth will stand forever.** Note that here I am differentiating between facts and truth. Facts change; they are relative. The truth is timeless. And while facts are important, truth is very important. In order for iY kids to fulfill their future and have their most positive impact on the future—and for us to help them—we must all must learn the truth about ourselves. This may take courage, but it's definitely worth it!

6. **The truth will eventually set us free.** This age-old statement is valid even today. Lies forge emotional chains, but truth breaks those chains, releasing us from bitterness, resentment, or unmet expectations. Even when the truth hurts, embracing it leads to a better life.

New Psychosurgery Technique Developed: Personal Maturity Now Possible Without Any Effort. Unbelievable Press International (UPI)—Doctors at Happy Days Hospital in Nirvana, New York, have developed a new method of surgery that can create mental health and maturity in people in a matter of hours. The technique involves going into the patient's brain with a laser scalpel and removing all of the patient's faulty beliefs, expectations, and attitudes. The patients who have had the procedure have reported a total absence of depression, worry, anger and guilt after waking from the surgery. They have also reported feeling a strong sense of acceptance of themselves and others for the first time in their lives. Dr. I. M. Deluded is the surgeon who developed the technique. He hails the discovery as, "What everyone has been looking for all along—all the benefits of mental health without any hard work!"[11]

Sounds pretty appealing doesn't it? Who wouldn't want to undergo such an operation or, better yet, escort certain young people we know into the operating room? If only there were a technique that could get these results.

The bad news, of course, is that there isn't. And I'm sure you've guessed that there is no Dr. I. M. Deluded and that no such magical psychosurgery exists.

The good news? There is indeed a process for challenging Generation iY kids to embrace truth and live more hours in reality than in virtual reality. But I won't lie to you. It requires good, old-fashioned hard work and a commitment to some honest-to-goodness truth telling.

Like the young elephants in the beginning of this chapter, our young people must return to the pack to learn some timeless values and relationship skills. There's no room for renegades. There's no splashing the water to hide who we really are. And there's no need for virtual reality. Generation iY needs a healthy dose of *actual* reality.

If we truly love them, we'll make sure they hear the truth.

➤ LINKING UP ◀

For suggestions on the truths we must communicate to this younger generation, check out: **www.SaveTheirFutureNow.com/TelltheTruth**.

8

My Crystal Ball
Predictions for Generation iY in the Workplace

I'VE ALWAYS LOVED WATCHING THE CLASSIC 1939 MOVIE, *The Wizard of Oz*. And there's an inconspicuous scene in it that's become one of my favorites.

Early in the story, Dorothy decides to run away from home. En route, she meets a traveling fortune teller named Professor Marvel. He is a kind person but also a bit of a con man—his predictions of the future are based more on intelligent guesses than any psychic ability. But he can tell that Dorothy is troubled, and out of the goodness of his heart, he decides to help her get back home. Asking her to close her eyes, he rummages through her belongings, trying to find a clue to her life so he can say something relevant to her circumstances. He finds a picture of Auntie Em and soon knows exactly what to say to Dorothy.

It's a winsome scene in the story that also prepares us for this chapter—because I'd like to do a little fortune telling here. So many employers I've spoken with seem baffled and frustrated by workers from this generation. They just don't seem to understand how these kids think and what motivates them. So this chapter is especially for the current and future employers of Generation iY.

I will be the first to admit that I'm a little like Professor Marvel. He didn't have any real psychic abilities that allowed him to see the future. What he did was look at the evidence (the photo in Dorothy's basket) and put some clues together as to what was going on.

In the same way, I have been a student of this culture and this generation for quite some time. Our organization, Growing Leaders, works with fifty thousand students and staff each year on campuses across the nation and worldwide. Based on what I've found, I have some predictions regarding iYers in the workplace. They're not written on tablets of stone, and they don't come with some guarantee.

However, I can say with some sense of certainty that unless some changes are made, the realities I outline in this chapter are what we will see over the next five to ten years, as Generation iY takes its place in the American work force.

Eight Predictions

Stop and think about it. This generation will be entering the doors of our corporations, nonprofits, and other workplaces for the next eighteen years. It may be too early to tell exactly how they'll mix with the previous two generations who manage the office, but based on the first wave of graduates, this is my educated guess—along with some practical ways employers can best respond to these trends. (Space does not allow me to list all of my predictions here. For more thoughts on how Generation iY will fare in the marketplace, go to www.SaveTheirFuture.com/Predictions.

Prediction #1: Job-hopping in Search of the Perfect Career

Sean Aiken is a twenty-something who graduated from college in 2007. At dinner one night he told his dad he was seeking a job he could be passionate about. His dad told him that at age sixty, he'd never had a job he felt that way about—which started Sean on an interesting quest. Sean determined he would try a different job every week for a year to find one he loved.

To document his efforts, Sean began a Web site and blog page called One Week Job (www.oneweekjob.com). When he began to get offers, he started traveling all over North America, working for one week at a time to check out a variety of jobs. He decided to work for free, recruiting sponsors to cover his costs and sleeping on the couches of fellow bloggers to save money.

Sean finally finished his yearlong job experiment in the spring of 2008. His weekly jobs included stints at UPS, Starbucks, GAP, Enterprise, and Apple. He worked for a dairy farm and a Manhattan filmmaker and served as a yoga instructor. In the process, he reports, he has learned much about himself.

In a sense, Sean Aiken illustrates what employers are about to see coming down the pike. Not that they're likely to do exactly as he did. But he has lived out what so many students in Generation iY long for—a passionate search for the perfect career.

This is a generation that believes their parents "settled for less" in terms of work, and they are determined not to settle. They want a job that fits their passions and strengths, something they can throw their heart into. What makes this noble pursuit a bit complex is that, by and large, this generation doesn't want to "pay their dues" by starting at the bottom of the ladder. They want to launch into their dream job right off the bat.

This explains in part why so many graduates move home after college. They want to use their twenties to explore, not settle down. (Remember, for Generation iY, adulthood begins at twenty-six, not eighteen.) And they resist the idea of working just to make money; they are waiting for the "right" job. This may be the reason that, in a random sampling nationwide, 30 percent of working young adults said they were presently looking for a new job.[1]

The good news is, college-entry scores are up as students master core curricula. Teachers, tutors, and guidance counselors have found ways to zero in on the bottom line and push those test scores up, helping students get into college. The trouble is, according to the testing firm ACT, too many of those students will spend their time mastering the wrong skills. The data shows there is a serious disconnect between students' top career choices and the occupations that will need workers when they graduate. For instance, college majors that lead to careers in entertainment are increasingly popular, while according to ACT, the greatest needs are for computer scientists, engineers, and systems analysts.[2] There is a disconnect, in other words, between a Generation iYer's desire and our nation's need.

How can employers best respond to iYers' job-hopping tendencies? Here are a few suggestions:

- *Build an authentic relationship and earn your right to give them counsel. Then help them simplify their lives and goals.*
- *Do what you can to help them keep their expectations realistic. (Remember, while Generation X typically struggled with authority, Generation Y struggles with reality.)*
- *Help them to focus and discover what their true passions are.*

Prediction #2: Innovations in Use of Technology

Generation iY doesn't seem to be limited to present rules for how things get done. They are constantly looking for new ways to do things and in the process are challenging past practices of the older generation. In the future, I believe these kids will redefine how technology is used for both communication and work. Their scope of usage will be larger than our current one, and they will feel free to suggest out-of-the-box ideas to a team that might be stuck on one methodology.

This new generation is bold and feels more comfortable with new technology than either of the previous two generations. (That's no surprise, since they've been "wired"—or "wireless"— almost since they were born.) Like Facebook founder Mark Zuckerberg, some will invent new ways of applying technology while they are still in college.

Communication via technology is a vivid example. Most iYers today would define "e-mail" as a way to communicate with older people. Among themselves, they're more likely to text, IM, tweet, or use Facebook and MySpace.

Employers should look for this generation to be bold about technology and innovative in using it. They will likely surprise employers with their perspectives on the technology they have at their disposal. But they will also resist rules about how they may use technology in the workplace.

One major characteristic of young people is they tend to be "hands on"—about everything. They learn hands on. They want to explore technology in a hands-on way. They want to jump into work projects hands on, the way they do with a video game. It's all dynamic for them. And they're connected 24/7. While the Baby Boomer boss values seeing them get to work on time, clocking in and clocking out—they value task more than time. They're willing to work off and on throughout the entire twenty-four hours of the day. They sleep with their cell phones on.

How can employers make the best use of iY's technical capabilities? I suggest the following:

- *Try not to get defensive when someone from Generation iY questions your present methods or use of technology.*
- *Try reverse mentoring—be emotionally secure enough to ask for their input. It really is possible they know more than you do when it comes to technology.*
- *Create a team to do some innovative brainstorming, then invite your young members to participate on that team. According to our focus groups, they love employers who value what they say from day one.*
- *Stay open to change and be ready to embrace new ideas, especially when they come from young employees.*

Prediction #3: Waves of Depression and Disappointment in the Workplace

I am concerned that few people see this one coming, and it could be a significant occurrence for Generation iY in the workplace and for their employers.

Keep in mind that this generation is accustomed to getting their own way. They've seldom heard (or accepted) no as an answer. They have little or no experience with failure, and they have high expectations regarding the speed of their climb up the corporate ladder.

What happens to these kids when they encounter frustrations on the job? Obviously, their supervisor may not be as intent on protecting their self-esteem. Being reprimanded for inferior performance or low production may well send them into a tailspin.

In addition, kids who may have never worked or punched a time clock may find it emotionally difficult to have to do the unglamorous. They may feel stuck and frustrated because, as so many have said to me, "work is different than I expected."

According to Ginger Murphey of *Arizona Living*, a new study conducted by Dove beauty products and Columbia University has found this sense of disappointment especially true for young women. Twenty-something females "are so engrossed in having it all by the time they are 30, they are not fully enjoying what they achieve. These women are being pressured by their inner voice to keep pushing for the next goal. This non-stop pattern of negative narration [is] called inner critic syndrome."[3]

Several chapters ago, I mentioned a recent book called *Quarterlife Crisis*. Yes, you read that title correctly. It isn't "midlife crisis," but "quarterlife crisis." It describes the large percentage of twenty-five-year-old professionals who are now seeing a therapist because they haven't made their first million as fast as they expected nor found the perfect mate.[4] Some of them are devastated. And depression is a natural response to such disappointment. We already see signs of this in today's twenty-somethings. Sales of depression medication in this age group have risen acutely over the last five years.

What can employers do in light of this trend? I am not suggesting that employers adopt doting "helicopter" tactics or coddle their iY employees. Sooner or later, they must come to terms with living in the real world. However, in order to get the most out of this new generation of workers, I believe bosses should be prepared to play the role of a coach, not just a supervisor. My suggestions?

- *Treat this generation as young leaders you are mentoring. Let them know you believe in them and have their best interests in mind.*
- *Give them short-term commitments to put some wins under their belts and acclimate them to the realities of working in the real world.*
- *Take the time to affirm what they do well before launching into improvements they need to make. Celebrate with them when they do perform well. I believe this generation will respond well to "bad news" when this kind of relationship is established with them.*

- *Be alert to signs of depression or other stress-related illnesses in young employees, and steer them toward any appropriate employee-support options your company offers.*

Six Simple Suggestions for Finding and Keeping the Best iY Employees

1. **Foster friendships.** Draw on their teamwork skills and strong peer affiliations.
2. **Provide purpose.** Help them understand how their work can make a difference.
3. **Offer options.** Allow as much flexibility as possible in terms of where they work, how they work, and when they work.
4. **Value volunteerism.** Offer them opportunities to make a difference in the world while making a contribution to your company.
5. **Challenge them with change.** Make creative use of their energy and desire for new things.
6. **Make the most of their strengths.** Be intentional about using what this confident, tech-savvy generation has to offer.

Prediction #4: Parent Involvement in Their Children's Work Life

Throughout their childhood and adolescence, iY students have reported that their parents are the number-one influence in their lives. Some 90 percent of young adults surveyed say they are "very close" to their parents.[5] Forty-eight percent of eighteen- to twenty-nine-year-olds say they communicate with their parents every day.[6] This seems to continue even into the workplace. The iY generation wants to or feels they must include Mom or Dad in the important aspects of their lives—including their work life.

And parents of iY young people seem all too happy to remain in this choice spot. As we have observed, they've been overinvolved since their kids were small. Again and again, they've removed opportunities for their children to fail and learn from the failure. It's little wonder that they expect to be right there as their son or daughter interviews for their first job.

I have spoken to employers who verify this. A few are even seeing a therapist themselves because they are not sure how to handle the helicopter parents who insist on negotiating a salary for their adult child. One employer told me not only did a mom join her son in the job interview and ask questions of her own, but six months later she returned to the employer's office to ask why her son had not gotten a raise. She was, in essence, acting as an agent.

Even when a parent doesn't show up in person for the interview, they make their presence known. Many employers report that young people being interviewed ask questions that seemed random and prerehearsed; they didn't arise naturally from the flow of the conversation. I think I know where those questions came from.

Needless to say, this is another symptom of the phenomenon of prolonged adolescence we examined in chapter 4. Sometimes neither the parent nor the child sees the long-term effect this could have on the child's development. Both would rather grab all they can now, than struggle to learn during those young adults years. In other words, the parent would rather "give them a fish than to teach them to fish." It's tough to cut those apron strings.

Obviously, this trend can be frustrating for employers and supervisors, who expect to hire adults without parental "agents." Here are some ideas for handling an interview where the parent shows up (or other experiences of parental intrusion into the workplace):

- *Clearly communicate respect and admiration for the parents' desire to be involved in their young adult's life. At the same time, let them know it is not appropriate to have the parent join them in the interview.*
- *Make the interview a learning time. Share the value of standing alone and assuming responsibility—and yes, even the value of failure.*
- *Persist in communicating that you want to know the young person's opinion and preferences, not someone else's. Give him or her dignity as they interact with you as an adult.*
- *Use the interaction to learn whether the potential employee is even ready to stand alone on the job and take initiative and responsibility or whether parental involvement is likely to be permanent.*

Prediction #5: The Expectation of Change and Amusement

Young men and women of the iY generation are accustomed to being entertained at the click of a button and to click off what fails to hold their interest. This mindset is a mixed blessing.

Many employers are learning that iY workers can be energetic and highly creative. They can multitask with aplomb and handle a variety of projects on any given day. Just don't make them sit still for long!

As we've seen, iYers want and even need lots of challenges coming at them. The problem is, they might have difficulty performing when asked to perform menial tasks or stick with a project past its initial novelty.

Generation iY simply doesn't subscribe to the standard assumptions about work—that you must endure work you don't like, that you must put in your time and earn a promotion, that you have to work a set number of hours to get a job done. When it comes to work projects, I believe they will rethink the "how," not just the "what." Remember, it's task, not time, that's important to them on a job.

This generation is willing to work long hours, but they also want some leeway as to when they spend those hours. As Penelope Trunk points out, "It feels normal for Gen Y employees to check in by Blackberry all weekend as long as they have flexibility during the week. For example, Microsoft's telecommuting program, Sun, has kicked into high gear in response to Generation Y's demands. Today, more than half of Sun's employees work remotely."[7]

Flexibility is about as valuable to iY young people as money—because it gives them power over time. One young person said to me, "You can always get more money, but you can never get more time."

There may well be an unrealistic expectation on a young employee's part as to how fun or exciting their work should be. Their teachers discovered this at school, now employers will do the same. Earlier, I stated that in 2000, 90 percent of this generation planned on going to college.[8] By 2006, however, 30 percent of them didn't even finish high school. Typically, it's not because they are stupid. I believe it's mostly because they are bored.

Certainly, supervisors can simply fire young employees who don't complete projects or who shirk the inevitable menial, unglamorous tasks, or they can refuse to hire easily-bored iYers in the first place. I spoke with one manager who employs hundreds of twenty-somethings. He now refuses to hire anyone straight out of college because, according to him, they just don't get the working world. If employers do this, however, many of these young employees will simply sell themselves to the highest bidder down the street, someone who needs an energetic, multitasking worker.

What can employers and supervisors do instead? Here are some ideas:

- *Try to do more coaching than bossing. These young employees are hungry for mentors. If they find them at work, those mentors will earn their loyalty.*
- *Be patient with young staff members. One manager told me he needed to be half diplomat and half shrink in order to connect with his young team.*
- *Explain the "why" behind tasks and show how important they are to the company's overall goals.*
- *Be flexible about time issues if possible (while still expecting quality work). Options such as comp time or projects geared to deadlines instead of "office time" will appeal to iYers and may get better results.*

Prediction #6: A Search for Meaning, Not Just Money

This one is very important for employers to understand. This generation wants meaning to come with their work. Young job seekers today want to work for organizations they believe in, to be part of a company that matters. They don't just want to make widgets; they want to know how those widgets will make the world better.

I recognize this may sound cliché, but it's true. Twenty-somethings desire their work to be transformational and not merely transactional. They seek jobs they have a passion for...with companies that are about more than just generating a profit. One student said it best in a focus group I led: "I feel pretty confident I can make money. What I look for is a job that can improve our world in some way, a job that meets a need I recognize as an important one."

And yes, this is a bit of a paradox—from a paradoxical generation. They certainly can be self-absorbed and are used to getting their own way. But the media content they have absorbed since childhood has convinced them they are supposed to change the world and save the planet—and they take this responsibility seriously.

According to one survey I read, 69 percent of young people aged thirteen to twenty-five said that when they shop, they consider the company's environmental and social commitment. Further, 83 percent said they'll trust the company more if it is socially or environmentally responsible.[9] When these young people look for jobs, they carry this social awareness with them into the workplace, and 61 percent of them say they feel personally responsible for making a difference. So, they want a cause to participate in, even if that cause only requires a little bit of their time and energy. Even as young people, they are already concerned about their legacy.

One more caveat. These Generation iY kids are people who don't simply want to talk theoretically about changing the world. They want to feel they're in the middle of it. When they're old enough for a career, they will seek out companies where they can get personally involved, not just send their money. It's amazing. The same young person who loathes cleaning their own bedroom may willingly go to the inner city and work in the projects all day long—without complaining.

During high-school, about 50 percent of this generation participated in community service projects. While this is often a school requirement, iYers (yes, these same slacktivists) also appreciate opportunities to volunteer on the job once they graduate. A recent Deloitte survey found that more than half of twenty-something workers want to work at companies that provide volunteer opportunities. And software company Salesforce.com, which pays their employees to volunteer

1 percent of their work time, reports that their on-the-job volunteer program has "dramatically" improved both recruitment and retention of new employees.[10]

What's the best way employers can respond to this concern for meaning on the part of their employees?

- *Make sure young employees are aware of your company's participation in chari-table or community endeavors and offer them the opportunity to be involved.*
- *Look for new ways your company can give back to the community and include young employees in the quest. You might explore dates on your calendar when you permit and even encourage employees to participate in fund-raisers, 10K runs, even "service vacations." Another possibility is to let them choose a charity they love and match any money they give to that charity.*
- *Don't forget simple and basic strategies such as putting a container in the break room for recyclables.*

My Passion Profile

Because Generation iY hungers to identify and work in an arena they have a passion for, Growing Leaders offers an assessment tool to help clarify the depth of their passion for local and global issues. To check this instrument out, go to: www.MyPassionProfile.com.

Prediction #7: Low Tolerance for Jobs That Fail to Provide Speedy Rewards

Because kids from Generation iY have been gamers and are a part of the "instant generation," they will find it difficult to work at a job that fails to provide speedy rewards and results for their effort. Once again, consider their earlier years at home. Remember that a large percentage of these students were raised by a parent who gave them constant and instant feedback. They've rarely been criticized and have often been praised for merely coming up with an idea (forget implementing it). The video games they've played for hours on end have also provided immediate feedback on their progress. They are used to lots of adult attention and interest in them, and communication has almost always been positive.

Consequently, jobs that fail to keep them updated on how they're doing will quickly lose their luster for iYers. In fact, the jobs may go from sizzle to fizzle in a matter of a few months. When that happens, young employees will typical-ly terminate their involvement just as they would end an Xbox game or log off Facebook. If they don't like the job, or if their supervisor doesn't give them the feedback or a reward they seek, they will likely just go looking down the street for something better.

I believe this low tolerance for job frustration is part of the reason so many from Generation iY are entrepreneurs. A study on Millennials by Northwestern Mutual Life revealed that 3 percent of college graduates have bypassed "getting a job" and simply started their own businesses.[11] Our research tells us it might be closer to 5 percent. They'd rather start something of their own and make up their own rules than fit in with a system that's already irrelevant in their eyes.

Thousands of these Generation iY kids are starting new companies each week in America. It's an experiment that sounds better to them than getting "tied down" to a boss. When they do take a job under a boss, the experience can be a challenge and an adventure for both. According to a recent survey, "more than half of the Massachusetts executives queried named Millennials the toughest generation to manage. Only 17 percent said the same of Generation X."[12]

What can employers do in light of these realities?

- *Launch these young employees with as much communication and feedback as possible. Remember to communicate the positive and the negative.*
- *Where practical, give young employees a chance to give feedback as well about how the job is working out for them. In the long run, allowing them to vent may be cheaper than running another job search.*
- *Earn loyalty and the right to criticize by developing a relationship with them. You don't have to be a buddy or a guru. Just be intentional about coaching them on the issues with which you have some insight and experience. Make time for them, and they'll give time to you and the job.*
- *While it's not your job to "make work fun," consider ways to keep iYers engaged and interested in their jobs. Special short-term projects, friendly employee competitions, and opportunities to work offsite or vary workday tasks can all help keep young workers productive and present.*
- *Talk about the future with young employees. Offer a plan for growth and give them an idea what they could do if they chose to stay and play a major role on the team. Be realistic about what this will take (including time), but make it clear that they are part of a dynamic team that is going places.*

Prediction #8: The Pursuit of Both Influence and Affluence

Influence and affluence are both important to Generation iY. Yes, they may want to change their world, but they can also be self-indulged narcissists. They don't want to give up too much free time, but they want to do work that matters—that has a measurable impact on their world. They are used to getting what they want—new clothes, new technology, even right grades in school.

At the same time, iYs are intensely aware of many of the deep needs in the world because they are so media savvy—and because so much "big stuff" has happened in their lifetimes. They have grown up with the Oklahoma City bombing, the terrorist attack on September 11, 2001, the Indian Ocean tsunami of 2004, Hurricane Katrina in 2005, and the devastating earthquake in Haiti in the spring of 2010. In fact, such tragedies have come to be almost expected among the teen and twenty-something population.

Their response? They want to help. They want to solve problems and make a difference...*but* they want to do it over a weekend or, on a short-term mission trip. And they don't want to wait until tomorrow to do it. After all, they have lots of other things they want to accomplish in their lives.

The earlier kids born into the Millennial generation tend to be more self-sacrificing and a little less materialistic than their younger brothers and sisters. They want to influence their world, but affluence isn't in the center of their radar screen. But both influence and affluence are front and center in the minds of Generation iY. As I mentioned earlier, a recent survey revealed that their number-one goal was to become rich. Number two was to become famous.

In other words, Generation iY does want to make a difference to the needy world around them; they just want to do it with a six-digit salary...and they'd really like to record it on YouTube. Unless their course changes, their spending as adults will be out of control. Today, the average teen spends about a hundred dollars a week.[13]

The best word that describes this young generation is *passionate*. It's a word they use often, much more than Generation X before them. They are determined to "find their passion" and devote their life to it—or, should I say, part of their life. Reports indicate that they may develop more than one passion and experience multiple careers in their adult life. It's hard for them to narrow it down. If they possess five passions, they may pursue five careers. But, they always want to be about a "passion" in the moment they are living right now. They don't want to do anything halfway.

How can employers harness Generation iY's energy and ambition?

- *Leadership guru Max DePree writes, "The first responsibility of a leader is to define reality."[14] Help your iY workers understand that both influence and affluence require time and lots of hard, unglamorous work.*

- *Show them the big picture. Connect the tasks they are asked to do with the legacy they might already be thinking about leaving.*
- *Help them see that service to the world, not fame or wealth in the world, is ultimately the most satisfying mission in life.*

Face Off: Navigating Our Way through the Differences

I am sure you've already guessed that there might be some clashes between a company's current team and this new species of workers I call Generation iY. But while some of my predictions for iY in the workforce are negative, I actually remain quite positive about their potential. I believe there is a lot that employers (and parents and educators) can do to help young iY workers overcome their weaknesses and capitalize on their strengths.

Remember, Generation iY will lead the way into the future. No one understands how to reach them and sell to them like they do. No one is better at relevant language and no one will be better at developing products and services for their peers. I am optimistic about the future, if we can manage to work out our intergenerational differences.

Let's take another look at the generations we interact with every day. Note the variety of perspectives and the values each one brings to the table. This can be a strength, not a weakness. I believe teams need to share a vision, but a variety of perspectives and gifts can be valuable.

A quick perusal of the chart on page 138 will suggest both the changes and challenges employers may face as you lead this new generation in the workplace. It's meant to remind you of the stunning opportunities you will have as you welcome a new generation to your team. If you hope to be relevant to the world around you, you'll need to invite Generation iY to work on your mission with you. They will likely appear at your front door looking much like a "free agent."

Leading a Generation of Free Agents

Not long ago, I had an intriguing conversation with an Atlanta businessman. He told me he's at the end of his rope—about ready to see a shrink. The reason for his duress? The college graduates he recently hired. They were driving him crazy. (He was not the first one to say this to me). When I inquired about what made his new employees so challenging, he noted some of the realities we have already seen:

Generational Diversity—We Can Work Together!

	Builders	Boomers	Generation X	Generations Y & iY
View of Life	"I am grateful for it."	"I will conquer it."	"I will endure it."	"I will change the world."
Work	"I see work as a duty and privilege."	"I live to work."	"I work to live."	"I work to make a difference."
Work Style	Commitment, tenure-oriented	Seek personal fulfillment and status	Tentative, divided loyalty	Network, team-work, opportunistic
Relationships	"I'm loyal but private."	"I network to get ahead."	"Friends are my family."	"I'm connected globally."
View of Self	"I'm humble, resourceful."	"I am the center."	"I'm lonely and need community."	"I play a role on a team."
Family	Close family	Dispersed family	Latchkey kids	Looser family definitions
Marriage Patterns	Married once	Divorced, remarried	Single parent	Desire lifelong partner but cautious
Purchasing	Purchase with cash	Purchase with credit card	Struggles with purchases because of debt	Purchase online
High Tech	Slide Rule	Calculator, TV	Computers	Smart phones
Money	Save it now	Buy it now	Want it now	Get it now (online), struggles with debt
Morals	Puritan ethics	Sensual	Cautious	Tolerant, but scrupulous
Landmark Issues	radio, prohibition, stock market crash, depression, the New Deal, WWII	TV, rock ' n' roll, civil rights, Vietnam, space race, nuclear threat—indulged kids	Watergate, ERA, high-tech, MTV, AIDS, PCs, "Me generation," artificial everything	Internet, volatile economy, terrorism & 9/11, dot coms, Columbine tragedy, tolerance, Hurricane Katrina

- *They had high expectations for mentoring and relational time with him.*
- *They wanted time off to travel and participate in volunteer organizations around the world.*
- *They expected a raise within the first six months just because they showed up for work on time.*
- *Their mothers actually set an appointment to negotiate the raise for them.*

More and more, I am meeting corporate leaders who share the same basic story. This new population of Generation iY kids demand a different work environment than the previous two generations. In essence, they have a different attitude toward authority:

- *Baby Boomers were "antiestablishment"; they **questioned** authority.*
- *Baby Busters were smaller in number and tended to **ignore** authority.*
- *Generation Y (and iY) are increasingly **choosing** their authorities. (It's a buffet.) Their expectations are high, and they are in demand, with so many of the Baby Boomers retiring and leaving space atop the corporate ladder.*

Let me give you an analogy. More than thirty years ago, the game of baseball experienced an amazing transition when Curt Flood of the St. Louis Cardinals ushered in the era of free agency. He was the first player successfully to negotiate the right for input on where and how long he played with a club. Following Curt Flood's arbitration, professional players began to expect to spend some of their career as "free agents," having a choice about such things. It was a new day for major-league players.

This same phenomena has occurred among iY twenty-somethings entering the job market—they see themselves as free agents. They fully expect to dictate some of the terms of their working conditions, and they may quit if they don't get what they want. Because more than half of them have moved back with their parents after college, they have a cushion of support that gives them the freedom to choose the job they really want. And in the future, as the Baby Boomers start retiring, a shortage of labor may give them more power to demand what they want.

Beginning in 2008, however, this picture began changing just a bit, bringing both good news and bad news to both Generation iY and employers. The bad news was an economic crisis that has affected just about everybody. The good news was that the suffering economy imparted a fresh realism to the newest wave of iY graduates. Things are not quite as easy nor quick as many had presumed they would be. This is a good time to meet them in the middle between their free-agency ideals and the reality of the market.

Finding and Keeping the Best iY Talent

So how do we deal with these new workers? We can't avoid them—they will be entering the workplace for the next several years. We must stay informed as new information about iY characteristics emerges and implement the strategies that have been discussed from a variety of sources. The key to attracting the best among them and keeping them as employees is to create an environment that is familiar and intriguing.

Yes, there will be difficulties. Sometimes interviewing and supervising young iY employees may feel like a crosscultural exercise. However, I also believe this could be the most exciting era in modern history if we will choose to mentor these young leaders wisely and well. I believe this generation can be both inspired and inspiring as they mature and take their places in the workforce. This hope is stoked by stories such as one I recently heard about an iY high-school student who recently walked into a convenience store. He said his cell-phone battery had died and asked to use their telephone.

The store manager pointed to the phone, and because he'd never seen a teenager use a pay phone, he listened in on the young man's conversation. He was astounded to hear the student say, "Hello. I heard that you were looking for a clerk who's a hard worker, who takes initiative, is responsible and has a great attitude. I am interested in the position." He was silent, as the employer responded. Then he said, "Oh, I see. You already have someone who meets all the criteria? Okay, I will call back later."

At this point, the student hung up the phone. As he walked out, the manager stopped him. "Excuse me, son, but I couldn't help overhearing your conversation. If you really are a hard worker who takes initiative, is responsible, and has a great attitude, I'd like to hire you right here and now. Are you looking for a job?"

"Oh, I wasn't calling because I'm looking for a new job," the student replied. "I was just checking on the one I already have."

If I were to gaze into my crystal ball concerning that student's life, I'd predict his future is very bright.

➤ LINKING UP ◄

For more ideas on how to work with Generation iY in the workplace, check out: **www.SaveTheirFutureNow.com/Work**.

9 The Hinge of History
What We Can Expect from Generation iY Worldwide

You may remember reading about the Black Death in history class. It refers to one of the deadliest pandemics in human history, peaking in Europe between 1348 and 1350. It is widely thought to have been an outbreak of a bubonic plague that started in Central Asia and reached Europe and North Africa by the middle of the fourteenth century. Probably carried by fleas residing on the black rats that were regular passengers on merchant ships, it spread swiftly and killed mercilessly. The Black Death is estimated to have killed 30 to 60 percent of Europe's population and reduced the world's population by a hundred million in less than a hundred years.

Needless to say, the Black Death had a profound impact on the course of European history. In addition to reducing the population, it changed social mores, religious ideas, and economic life, not to mention dramatically influenced the mood of the day and people's view of the future. It took one hundred fifty years for Europe's population to recover.

The problem with the Black Plague was its highly infectious nature—the fact that it spread so fast and grew so large before anyone knew how to deal with it.

I remind you of this for one simple reason. We may have a similar situation with the problems of the iY generation.

I'm not saying these kids are a disease.

I'm just pointing out that we have a rapidly spreading worldwide phenomenon on our hands—with international ramifications that could make the Swine Flu of 2009 seem like a simple case of chicken pox.

The combination of characteristics that defines Generation iY is indeed contagious. It has spread around the world and reached epic proportions. This generation is huge, and I know of no magic elixir that will cure all its problems.

However, a sound understanding of what is happening can help us capitalize on the positive qualities of the iY generation and minimize its complications. That is what I'd like to address in this chapter—the worldwide impact of Generation iY and what we can do to help make that impact a positive one.

In This Thing Together

Much more than their predecessors in Generation X, young people from Generation iY seem to be acting as a generational group. The university students I talk to across the U.S. and around the world feel they belong to each other. Their attitudes and ideas are comparable. They face many of the same challenges. And they are truly connected, via technology, across the globe.

François de Waziéres, who recruits employees worldwide for his company, L'Oréal, agrees that these Millennial kids are surprisingly similar.

> One thing I find to be very universal is that they have international experiences, are eager to take on the world and value their relationships... whether they are from Malaysia, India, France, Argentina, or the U.S., they wear similar clothing, have the same iPods, and mix and connect easily. Two hours after meeting, they're probably best friends on Facebook.[1]

This, of course, doesn't sound bad. What's wrong with a tight-knit demographic group like this, especially one that seems friendly and energetic? The problem is that when a population is this large and homogeneous, its weaknesses tend to be magnified.

Take for example a Gen-iY characteristic we've discussed at some length: the "Twixter" tendency to delay assuming adult responsibility. American parents, educators, and employers aren't the only ones who are frustrated with this behavior. In some countries, it's even worse!

In England, for example, the Twixters are known as KIPPERS, an acronym for "Kids in Parent's Pocket Eroding Retirement Savings." In Canada, they're called Boomerang Kids, named after their tendency to fly back home after school. In Japan the term is "Freeters," a combination of *free* and *Arbeiter*,the German word for worker. It describes an unmarried young adult who job hops and lives at home. (The trend has even been debated in the Japanese parliament.)[2]

In France, the problem is dubbed "Tanguy Syndrome," after a 2001 film about a charming twenty-eight-year-old who refuses to move out of his parents' apartment. In Germany, they are called *Nesthockers*,which translates literally as "nest squatter." (One study attributes the reluctance of young Germans to go out on their own to the fact that they regard their parents as friends.) Italy, too, has their own term for Twixters: *Mammone.* It's a description of young adults who can't make themselves leave Mama's cooking behind. The number of them living at home has grown nearly 50 percent in the last decade.[3]

The Twixter phenomenon, in other words, is not limited to iY youth in America. It seems to be sweeping the world, or at least the developed world. The same is true of this generation's other iY characteristics.

What will this mean to our future? Unfortunately, with my ear to the ground, I am picking up some signals that could mean trouble if we fail to respond well. There is definitely a downside to the globalization of this new generation. Their growth, behaviors, and connection is causing concern among sociological experts—especially when their numbers grow in a geographical or social trouble spot. Let me tell this story beginning with Generation iY in America.

A Rising Generation and a Retiring Generation

It's widely known that the Baby Boomers are the largest generation in America's history to date. But Generation Y is rapidly catching up with them and with immigration will likely outnumber them. Some social scientists say their numbers could reach 100 million, almost a third of our population. In between the Boomers and the iYers is Generation X, which is measurably smaller than either of the other two generations. Here in a nutshell is the challenge we face as a result of this "generation sandwich":

- *Young people (Generation Y) will be entering the marketplace in greater numbers and more quickly than we can prepare them.*
- *Older people (the Baby Boomer generation) will be retiring in greater numbers and more quickly than we can replace them.*

This is one of the most crucial tests we'll face in our lifetime. It is a global challenge with consequences right here at home. It will have an impact on everyone, though few seem aware of the dilemma it presents for our future. Unless we raise the standard for kids today and help them to think and act like authentic leaders, they won't be ready for the responsibility thrust on them as they enter young adulthood.

Americans will feel this problem acutely in a few short years. According to the U.S. Department of Labor, by 2025, 76 million Baby Boomers will have retired, and there will be only 46 million younger workers waiting to take their place. Generation X is just not big enough to replace them. Generation iY is the fastest-growing segment of the workforce.[4] But if current trends continue, at that point iYers may not yet be prepared to fill the gap and take their place as effective leaders in the workplace or in the community.

The first wave of Baby Boomers has already begun retiring, and Boomers will continue retiring for the next eighteen years. In fact, during the next decade, about 45 percent of the workforce will vanish without replacements.

Stop and think about your own community and circumstances. Most of the established leaders you follow are likely from the Baby Boomer generation. Imagine large groups of these folks disappearing over the next several years, vacating leadership positions in hospitals, in government, in education, in the military, in churches, on mission fields, and in corporations. Now imagine those positions being filled by Twixters who are still barely getting started in terms of maturity, who still live in their parents' basements, and are still insisting that everyone cater to their needs.

Do you see my point? Whether or not our kids today will be ready to face this complex world will be up to us. Adult coaches, parents, employers, teachers, counselors, and religious leaders must take up the challenge to prepare them. We must build bridges they can cross over into adult leadership roles.

Right now, I'm afraid, we're not doing a very good job of that. So many of us are operating in survival mode, hoping to merely get through the week. We're glad that we've made it to Friday, and we're still alive! Hopefully we still have a house and a 401K. Hopefully our kids are not on drugs. Hopefully there is something in the house for dinner. Many of us are overwhelmed by economic hardship. Many struggle to stay healthy. Company executives are focused on making it through the next quarter without falling into the red. Who has time to think about preparing Generation iY for leadership? No one. Unfortunately, if we don't, who will be prepared to lead our businesses and government and families in another decade?

The Fear Factor

Our survival mode is due in large part to the uncertain season of history where we find ourselves. Is it just my imagination, or has this generation been assaulted with more than its share of tragedy?

No doubt every generation experiences memorable crises that shape them as they mature into adults. But I think it's safe to say that no cohort of American youth has ever experienced such mass catastrophes in the harsh, inescapable glare of a 24/7 media environment. As the sidebar on page 145 shows, these kids have been shaped by trauma in their formative years, and yet they have not been broken.

"The Millennial generation has every right to be the Melancholy Generation," writes Sharon Jayson and Maria Puente in *USA Today*, "and the wonder is that it's not."[6] In fact, when studies are done on the students growing up in our world today, one reality surfaces regularly: This generation of kids is resilient. They are a remarkably irrepressible, optimistic bunch, say social scientists, psychologists, and generational researchers such as Neil Howe and William Strauss.

As we reeled from the shock of the Columbine tragedy or the terror of 9-11, those of us who work with students noticed something interesting. The attacks scared American parents to death. They began pulling their kids out of public schools and protecting them from any potential danger that might arise.

The kids, on the other hand, had a different response. The attacks on the World Trade Center seemed to galvanize them, and they sought involvement. Many visited Ground Zero and wanted to dig through the rubble to restore what we'd lost.

A Snapshot of the Turbulent iY Years

- **1990–91:** Socialist governments collapse in Europe, shaking up the world economy.
- **1995:** A truck bombing at the Alfred Murrah Federal Building in Oklahoma City kills 168.
- **1996:** A terrorist bomb explodes at the summer Olympic games in Atlanta, killing two and wounding more than a hundred more.
- **1999:** Fifteen die in a shooting spree at Columbine High School in Littleton, Colorado.
- **2001:** Hijacked jets crash into New York's World Trade Center, the Pentagon in Washington, D.C., and a field in Pennsylvania. Nearly three thousand die in the largest terror attack in U.S. history.
- **2003:** The Columbia space shuttle breaks apart, killing all seven astronauts aboard.
- **2004:** A massive earthquake in the Indian Ocean triggers devastating tsunamis in east Asia, killing about 225,000 people in fourteen countries.
- **2005:** Hurricane Katrina devastates New Orleans and the Gulf Coast states.
- **2007:** Thirty-three people are gunned down on the Virginia Tech campus in Roanoke, Virginia.
- **2010:** More than two hundred thousand people are killed in an earthquake in Haiti and another 1.5 million are left homeless.[5]

Protecting Instead of Preparing

Generation iY's disposition to get involved may be a typical youthful bias, but it deserves to be supported and encouraged. Sadly, fearful parents from both Generation X and the Baby Boomer generation too often have sought to protect their kids from the hardship and messes that come with involvement.

Many Baby Boomers remember the 1960s, when chaos reigned on college campuses and in the streets of urban America. Their response today? "I don't want my kids to see that." Even though Boomers experimented with marijuana, alcohol, riots, and cigarettes, we want to prevent those poisons from ever contacting our kids. We want to protect the children from the stains and pains of life.

I understand that. I'd like my kids to never have to experience the dark side of this world. But if they never see it, how will they ever change it?[7]

Let's face it. Many adults today have unconsciously chosen one of two extremes when it comes to handling their kids:

1. **Isolation.** This is a response of fear and caution, the urge to remove the children from the evil world around them and protect them. My question: If you don't touch the world, how can you transform it?
2. **Saturation.** This is a response of surrender and exhaustion. It's the temptation to allow children simply to absorb the surrounding culture because, after all, what can you do about it? My question: If you only imitate culture, how can you transform it?

My suggestion is that while both these responses are understandable, neither of them represents what Generation iY needs from adults. I believe we must choose a third response instead:

3. **Interpretation.** This is a response of wisdom and concern that involves teaching young adults how to think critically and translate current events. They must interpret both the good and bad in a culture in order to transform it.

Our Challenge Worldwide

Preparation of Generation iY for leadership becomes even more critical in light of what is happening around the world among the younger population. The global challenge we face involves much more than a worldwide case of arrested development, a national workforce challenge, or a generation shaped by tragedy. The size and scope and the connectedness of the iY generation simply amplify a far bigger challenge. If history repeats itself with this new, mammoth, connected generation, we could see the largest expression of revolt the world has ever seen.

As we consider what to expect from Generation iY worldwide, I want us to examine two major facts:

Fact #1: Almost half the world's population today is twenty-one years old or younger.

While people are living longer, the birthrate is passing that of older generations— in some countries, at an alarming rate. The average age in China and India, the two largest nations in the world, is midtwenties. This represents more than a billion young people. Many people in African nations won't even see their thirtieth birth- day because of the AIDS pandemic. This means African young people are serving as teachers, nurses and postmasters long before they're ready because there is a shortage of healthy people who are older. Even in America, where birth control is widespread and abortion is permitted, the Millennial generation will likely become the largest in our history. The earth's population is growing younger, and these kids desperately need guidance.

According to the U.S. Census Bureau, in 2009 the population of kids world- wide from birth to college age was 2,987,230,232. That's nearly three billion peo- ple—almost half of the world's population. So while a huge generation is retiring in the U.S., a huge generation is just getting started around the rest of the world.

Fact #2: Historically speaking, where there is a bulge in the youth popula- tion, violence follows.

Gunnar Heinsohn, a social scientist at the University of Bremen (Germany) has uncovered some startling patterns. He writes that when fifteen-to-twenty-nine- year-olds make up more than 30 percent of the population, violence occurs. When large percentages of the population are younger than fifteen, violence is often imminent.

The specific causes for the violence seem to be immaterial. Whether the country is rich or poor, whether they experience good conditions or bad, violence typically follows a bulging population of young people. This explains Ireland ninety years ago. It explains Africa over the past fifty years. It explains Latin America in the 1980s and Europe in the 1500s. For that matter, it explains the violence America experienced in the 1960s. (It was primarily the young Baby Boomer population rioting on the university campuses or in the streets.)

Today, there are sixty-seven countries in the world where a "youth bulge" exists— that is, more than 30 percent are young adults or kids. Sixty of those countries are presently in civil war or are experiencing mass killings.

Heinsohn's eye-opening book, *Sons and World Power*[8] documents this history of youth and violence. According to Heinsohn, it's not a matter of whether countries are civilized or not. It is more about the next generation finding a place to express their identity and frustrations. Without healthy guidance, they'll tend to latch on to any available cause, and violence will be the predictable result.

It's Happening Now

A quick look at some of the world's hotspots would seem to support Heinsohn's thesis. In Christopher Caldwell's *Financial Times* article entitled "Youth and War, A Deadly Duo" published in January 2007, he stated that "Since 1967, the population of the West Bank and Gaza has grown from 450,000 to 3.3 million, 47% of which is under 15." He went on to report "Gangland slayings in the Palestinian territories this week have pitted the Islamist gunmen Hamas against the secular forces of Fatah. The killings defy civilized norms...and political common sense. The violence—previously justified with the cause of a Palestinian homeland—continues as if nothing had changed, merely finding its outlet in a new set of targets...The violence is, in a strange way, about itself."[8]

Iraq is another example. Like many of its neighbors, Iraq has a young population—nearly half is under eighteen. And according to *Newsweek* magazine, these kids are growing up "uneducated, unemployed, undereducated, traumatized and, among boys in particular, ripe for the vengeful appeals of militias and insurgent groups."[9] Hassan Ali, a sociologist at the Ministry of Labor and Social Affairs predicted, "These children will come to believe in the principles of force and violence. There's no question that society as a whole is going to feel the effects in the future."[10]

More recently, a normally peaceful Kenya has experienced violence. Why now? "As in so many other African countries, Kenya's exploding violence can be traced to an exploding population that goes unnoted by local and international media alike."[11]

Consider the turmoil in Yemen. Approximately 50% of its population is fifteen years old or younger. They have no unifying ideology except for their anger against the West.

From the Middle East to Europe to the Americas, violence may well beget violence around the world for years to come. French scholar Gilles Kepel, author of *Jihad: The Trail of Political Islam*, warns that many of these young people, raised on anger and fear, are potentially rebels without clear causes. "What will their jihads become?" he asks. "Are they going to grow up to kill each other, or will they turn their weapons against the West?"[12]

Growing Global Leaders

The stakes are high for Generation iY worldwide. To avert tragedy in the future, they need to develop strong, positive leadership *now*. Our organization, Growing Leaders, has chosen to respond to this crying need. Our goal is to turn ordinary students into growing leaders who will transform their world. And in addition to our work on U. S. university campuses, we have chosen to work internationally in areas where we see a youth bulge—specifically Asia, in Arab countries, and in the Persian-speaking world. We are building partnerships with like-minded organizations worldwide to train young people in leadership. To read about our strategy, go to www.SaveTheirFutureNow.com/International.

They Long to Find Expression

The danger of violence in "youth bulge" cultures is exacerbated by the fact that we've conditioned this generation to be an "upload" generation. They are accustomed to finding ways to express themselves. We have encouraged this by the technology and environments we have created for them. We have invited it. But what if their expression is not pleasant for the adults in power? Will Generation iY be too big and too loud to suppress? Will we be prepared to respond well as their leaders? The sheer size of this generation should sober us.

Very often we assume that conflict results from poor living conditions. But this is not always so. In El Salvador, for example, the explosion of political killing in the 1970s and '80s was preceded by a 27 percent rise in per capita income. In that situation, the real problem was that there were not enough positions to provide many young men with prestige and standing. They wanted to be known for something, so they acted out.[13]

When economic times are difficult, of course, societies become especially vulnerable. While it's not the chief factor, poverty does add to the tension. With a waning economy, with the job market low and opportunities for employment weak, any culture, including the United States, could be a powder keg waiting to explode.

The Perfect Storm...or the Perfect Story?

Like every generation of youth, Generation iY wants a voice. They long to make a difference. One way or another, they will find a way to speak. The question is what will they say—and how will they say it?

Will their response to coming challenges be that of positive optimism...or ultimate destructiveness and nihilism?

Somehow, I believe we must enable this generation's positive potential to counter the negative possibilities. We must equip Generation iY to find positive ways to express their energy and vision, or we could experience a social disaster. The hinge of history could swing either way in coming decades, and Generation iY will determine which direction the hinge will swing.

Students of history can readily spot this pattern. A swelling youth population leads to a shift in how culture looks and feels and ultimately the direction it takes. When there is a disproportionate population of young people, the course of society will inevitably change.

In my own research, I've concluded that this redirection is often brought about by three typical characteristics of emerging generations—characteristics that seem to apply to the iY generation as well:

1. **Arrogance.** As young people hang out and interface primarily with each other (as opposed to interacting their elders), they develop an attitude. We saw it in the Baby Boomers during the 1960s, and we're seeing it now with Millennials. Spawned by their confidence and esteem and sparked by high-tech savvy, their general demeanor conveys, "I've mastered this. I know more than my professors or my parents or my boss." As their population swells, so does their pride.

2. **Dissidence.** Pride and arrogance typically lead to dissidence in a youthful population. They begin to feel their oats and challenge the norms of society. This is not necessarily a bad thing. The clash of new ideas against old can actually invigorate a culture, and conflict handled well can lead to growth and improvement. But dissidence can be a problem when it is accompanied by anger and arrogance. This is especially likely when the dissenters don't feel heard or understood. As anger builds, the conflict between opposing views stops being constructive and may become dangerous.

3. **Violence.** Once again, violence doesn't always stem from poverty or injustice; it may simply grow out of young people's need to express themselves and their sense that there's not enough opportunity to do so. A general

frustration with life can make things worse. Jobs may be scarce. Families may be unsafe places to communicate. Friendships may only be virtual in nature. Such uncooperative circumstances coupled with arrogance and dissidence spells trouble. Youth may not have the patience to wait for the right opportunity to express themselves. Civil disobedience and simple protest may morph into violent demonstrations where emotions rule and everyone begins to look out for himself.

Is such a scenario inevitable? I hope not. In fact, I've invested my entire career building kids into life-giving leaders. And it seems to me there has never been a better time to invest in students. The time is right and the generation is ripe. Generation iY is still in the process of being formed, but the cement is quickly hardening with time. In fact, in some parts of the world, the situation is desperate.

The elements are combining to form either the perfect storm...or the perfect story of a new generation of leaders.

How we respond will make all the difference.

Size Matters: The Reason We Can't Ignore the iY Generation

I am certain you've heard some of the same stories I've heard over the last ten years. In communities around America, local hardware stores have been driven out of business by the entrance of a new Home Depot in town. Communities feel a similar impact when a Walmart sets up shop in town. Local discount stores just can't compete with the new store's low prices.

Have you ever stopped to consider what these stories have in common? One word: *size*. The reason Walmart's prices are so low is the sheer volume of products they offer. Similarly, Home Depot trumps local competitors because it has the advantage of being a large chain.

Let's face it. Size matters.

The same is true for Generation iY. Regardless of what we think about the intelligence, emotional maturity or even the leadership skills of iY young people, they will impact the world for the mere reason of their numbers.

We cannot ignore the issue. We cannot pretend they won't affect our future.

If we're serious about transforming the world, we have to be serious about investing in this next generation. What we do today as adults will no doubt determine who they will become as adults.

I believe the greatest investment I can make—as someone who cares about the future of the world—is to equip a young person to think and act like a leader.

How Will We Respond?

Here are some questions to consider as we consider the challenge of the global iY phenomenon:

- How can we meet Generation iY's need for social capital (influence)?
- How can we let them find expression, yet keep them focused on solutions?
- When are they most ready to learn and accept guidance from adults?
- How can we instill timeless values in a pluralistic world?
- What are the biggest issues to resolve worldwide as they enter adulthood?
- Where can we steer them for leadership skills and mentoring?

It is not enough that we have nice kids. We must build a generation of kids who possess vision, who plan well, who set healthy priorities, and who practice good people skills—men and women who know how to lead the way.

I also believe this is not just an economic issue or a social issue, but also a spiritual one. We need leaders who lead from their hearts, not just their heads or their wallets or their political ambition. I hunger to see leaders whose vision is for a future well beyond their lifetime. I want to see a new generation of leaders whose faith guides them and gives them courage to stand for what is right, even in the face of great risk.

In government, this means they are statesmen, not politicians.

In education, this means they are mentors, not just faculty members.

In business, this means they are philanthropists, not just capitalists.

I challenge you to join us at Growing Leaders to invest in this next generation. Become a mentor for at least one young person, if not a community of young people who desperately need someone to show them the way. I urge you to:

- *Find a time. (It won't happen if you don't plan a regular time to meet.)*
- *Find a team. (You must choose the young people with whom you wish to connect.)*
- *Find a tool. (You must decide what resources will guide you.)*

In the remainder of this book, we will discuss exactly how to do this. We will look at some workable models for engaging young people and suggest practical ways adults can be a part of a healthy solution for the next generation.

Remember, we cannot do anything about our ancestors, but we can do something about our descendants.

Let's start a new, positive, viral pandemic.

➤ **LINKING UP** ◄

For six case statements on why we must commit ourselves, as adults, to invest in this next generation, go to **www.SaveTheirFutureNow.com/Case Statements**.

10 A Compass, Not a Map
Helping Generation iY Find
Their Future

WHENEVER I HAVE TO TRAVEL TO A NEW CITY, I want to have a map or, better yet, a Global Positioning System in my car. These tools can keep me from getting lost and direct me to my destination. I can't tell you how many times I've been in a new territory and that GPS saved me.

There was a time, however, when I found myself in a place where neither a map nor GPS could help. I was in a remote part of Canada where there were no signs and not even any roads. No maps were available for this territory, and if I had had a GPS device—which I didn't—it would have had to furnish directions using landmarks like trees or hills. I was, quite literally, in deep weeds. Conventional tools couldn't help me navigate in that situation. The only tool that could've guided me was a compass.

No matter where you are, a compass can tell you where your true north is. It can direct you when all else fails. And that's what you and I need as we interact with Generation iY today, because we are now in uncharted territory. We've never faced a challenge quite like this rising generation, nor have we faced quite so many baffling questions—including the ones rolling around inside of me as I write this book:

- *Has constant exposure to technology lowered the emotional intelligence of a generation?*
- *Does our kids' premature launch into school (at ages four or five) foster a postponed launch into adulthood (at ages twenty-six or later)?*
- *Is the early affirmation that kids receive from adults causing narcissism and depression for them later on?*
- *Has the increased time playing video games lowered the grades that boys make in school?*

- *Does the heavy access to social media (Facebook, Twitter, and so on) impede the development of mature relational skills?*
- *Have antiquated teaching methods caused a disconnect between adult and student generations?*
- *Do the lies we adults (especially parents) tell our kids actually return to haunt them in the form of anger and disillusionment?*
- *Will the expanded population of Generation iY in a challenged worldwide economy spark violence and antisocial behavior?*

Then there's the $64,000 question: What do we do to steer Generation iY back on course and keep them there? How do we prevent ourselves from being overwhelmed by the problems? Where do we begin to address the issues?

Let me tell you a story that may suggest an answer to this dilemma—or at least a way to approach it.

Run to the Battle!

In 1862, a young man named Joshua Chamberlain from Bangor, Maine, signed up to fight for the Union army. He had no training as a soldier; in fact, he was a college professor by trade. But there was a civil war going on, and the Union needed him, so he enlisted and was commissioned as a lieutenant colonel.

In the summer of 1863, Chamberlain was ordered to march his troops to Gettysburg in pursuit of General Lee. By this time he was a full colonel and had seen firsthand the horrors of battle and its aftermath. He'd negotiated with disgruntled soldiers, buried the dead, tended the wounded, and prayed with the survivors. He thought he'd seen the worst of war. But more was yet to come.

The Battle of Gettysburg proved devastating for Colonel Chamberlain and his regiment. In wave after wave of confederate attacks, he lost all but eighty of his men and all his ammunition. But when several of Chamberlain's officers asked when and where they should retreat, he shook his head. *Retreat* was not in his vocabulary. He had the men sit down so he could think.

It was during these hours that the Confederates were joined by two new regiments from Alabama and Texas and decided to attack. A Union lookout boy saw them coming and signaled to Colonel Chamberlain.

It was at this point that Joshua Chamberlain commanded his men to do the illogical. You might even call it the impossible. With only eighty men and no ammunition, he sounded the cry to attack. His soldiers were stunned, but they followed his orders, jumped the wall, and ran to the battle.

To the shock of every one of his men, they won. The Confederate soldiers saw those Union soldiers running toward them at full speed, shouting at the top of their lungs, and they became paralyzed. They laid down their guns and surrendered.

Moments afterward, a young Union private was holding a hundred confederate soldiers at gunpoint. When Colonel Chamberlain walked by, the private whispered to his officer, "I don't got no ammunition!" Leaning into him, Josh Chamberlain whispered back, "I know it, but don't tell them that!"

I love that story for many reasons. First and foremost, however, is its pertinence to the challenges we face with Generation iY. We can learn some valuable lessons from Josh Chamberlain:

- *He knew that to sit still and hope for the best was sure death.*
- *He took risks and seized opportunities by choosing to take initiative.*
- *His success came because he approached life as a leader.*
- *His contribution to history was far greater than his job or profession.*

If we could talk to Joshua Chamberlain today, I suspect he'd tell us he shouldn't have been able to do what he did. The odds were stacked against him. Like us, he felt he had little to work with. He had no formal training for what he was required to do. He was outnumbered and outresourced. But somehow he knew that to run or to hide wouldn't solve the problem. He decided the best defense was a good offense, and history has confirmed his decision.

That's exactly what I believe we adults need to do as we consider the challenges of guiding the next generation. To simply sit still and hope for the best would be disastrous. To run and hide would be worse. We must play offense, not defense. We must take whatever action is necessary to secure a healthy future for our kids and for ourselves.

The Best Way to Help Them Find Their Way

My premise for the rest of this book is simple. We must prepare Generation iY for the future. The best first step is to enable them to discover their vocation— to recognize their passions and strengths and use them to engage the world around them.

Did you know the word *vocation* is taken from the same root as *vocal?* It means calling. The implication is that each of us who have a vocation possess more than a job. It's a mission. To pursue a vocation is to work in a natural "sweet spot" and master it.

When we enable Generation iY to discover their vocation, that's when they'll become people of influence, true life-giving leaders. This is the compelling message that Generation iY needs to hear. Sadly, all too often we have failed to translate this message. Our message to Generation iY has been more about safety and maintenance than about adventure and calling. We have been protecting them rather than preparing them and coddling them instead of calling them out—challenging them to seize opportunities and make a significant contribution.

We've insisted on playing defense when what we really need to do is forge ahead and equip Generation iY to be our future leaders. If we will, they'll come alive—and have incentive to become the best version of themselves.

The Wrong Kind of Message

When I began working with students in 1979, I noticed the way adults typically approached kids. It seemed like one message bellowed through schools, YMCAs, Boys and Girls Clubs, youth groups, and scouting troops: "stay off drugs and don't get pregnant."

It was a relevant message. We certainly had a drug and teen pregnancy problem in our country, and we tried to address it. Nancy Reagan's famous "Just Say No" campaign in the 1980s focused on preventing kids from doing drugs. By the 1990s, several character-building programs in our elementary and middle schools nationwide begged kids across the nation to be nice, to be respectful and courteous, and not to be bullies.

Those are all noble goals...but they don't cut it anymore. The problem is, they just don't motivate students. Kids are savvy. I have not met a single adolescent who gets motivated by the challenge to "not bully," and "just say no" sounds lame to them.

A defensive message is insufficient. While all the campaigns were well-intentioned, they focused on preventing kids from doing something wrong instead of challenging them to do something right. All we cared about was avoiding trouble. It wasn't enough then, and it certainly isn't enough today.

Consider character-building programs in schools that use a "word of the month" to help kids learn to be good citizens. Beyond elementary school, do you know one student who is engaged by this approach? And while "be nice" and "be courteous" and "be respectful" are good thoughts, will a typical middle school or high school student find them compelling? I don't think so.

If we want to successfully guide Generation iY into the future, we've got to do more than just challenge them to stop doing bad things. Playing defense just doesn't work. As author Dan Pink describes it in his provocative book, *Drive*, we must move from "Motivation 2.0" to "Motivation 3.0," which is a move from punishment and reward to purpose.[1]

Purpose—that's what we must focus on as we seek to lead Generation iY. We must ignite them with a vision for their future, based on what is inside of them.

Zach Hunter is a vivid example of what can happen when we do that. I've known Zach for four years now. He's a relatively quiet, unassuming teenager, but what's happened with his life is quite remarkable.

As a young teen, Zach became aware of the phenomenon of modern-day slavery. Every year, he learned, millions of children and adults around the world are bought and sold by traffickers who trade them like commodities. Zach was amazed to learn this happens even in the United States. Zach's parents encouraged him to do something more than just write a paper about the slave trade. So, he began to study the issue, go to Web sites, do interviews, and eventually to study the historical roots of the slave trade. He learned about William Wilberforce, an abolitionist who fought against the slave trade in England back in the late eighteenth and early nineteenth centuries. Wilberforce became a hero to Zach, a role model. In fact, if you ask Zach Hunter to introduce himself, he'll say, "My name's Zach. I am an abolitionist."

Zach launched a grassroots movement called, "Loose Change to Loosen Chains." He speaks at high schools all over the country, raising money to buy slaves and set them free. He has appeared on CNN, *Good Morning America,* and other national broadcasts, raising awareness and challenging people to step out of their own comfort zones and help. His ultimate goal is to stop slavery entirely. And the movement he started is no longer a small endeavor. Tens of thousands have jumped on board and are involved now.

When I last spoke to Zach, I observed, "You are quite a leader." He looked down and shook his head. Zach Hunter doesn't see himself as a leader, but he is one, and he's effective because he's leading the way in an arena where his passion and strengths lie.

Zach is a young man of stellar character. But he wasn't compelled to be a good boy by some word-of-the-month program. He was challenged to solve a problem, to lead the way and make a difference. And he responded. He said yes to a call... and he's changing the world.

Called, Not Driven

It's important for me to clarify what I am not saying. When I talk about challenging Generation iY to something great—to a life of contribution—I am not talking about calling them to a driven life. Kids today know better—they realize the lives of driven Baby Boomers are out of balance. A calling may look like "drive" on the outside, but it is an inward passion, not an outward compulsion. It's a burning desire to serve, not to earn; to make a difference, not just a buck.

Liz Worth's life supplies a vivid portrait of what I'm talking about. Liz grew up "instilled with the importance of career aspirations, success and overachieving." So she threw herself into journalism school and also worked nonstop to grab as much real-work experience as she could. She built her portfolio and then, a few years after graduation, found a great job in a busy PR office. She made lots of friends and found an apartment she loved. "But even though I had accomplished everything I set out to do," Liz writes, "I constantly found myself thinking: so this is it?...When everything is so contrived, you wake up one day and realize you have the job you wanted, but that job isn't everything. Not even close."[2]

I believe Liz speaks for many in Generation iY. They love to throw themselves into something—but they must believe in it. They must feel it makes a difference. For so many iYers, it's not just about mortgages. Or maintenance. Or money. It's about a mission.

A Work, Not a Job

Consider this. When you scour the pages of history and discover the people who powerfully affected their world, you find it was people who did more than fulfill a job description well. In fact, many were folks who labored for a cause completely separate from their livelihood.

They were fulfilling a calling not just drawing a paycheck. They were doing a work, not just a job.

I'm not just playing with words here. There really is a difference. A job is basically a source of income, whereas a work is a calling, a vocation. Consider some of the other distinctions between a job and a work.

- *Jobs are about what we can get. A work is about what we can give (and who we are). With a job, you basically trade your time and skills for money. Accomplishing a work is more about making a contribution to our world.*
- *Jobs come and go, but work ties a life together. Young people may have six to eight jobs before they reach midlife. Their work, however, should be the single,*

common thread that runs through each of their jobs. It is the central mission they are accomplishing with their life.

- **Jobs enable us to be consumers, but work enables us to be contributors.** *A work can be defined as the most important contribution someone will accomplish before they die. Pursuing a work ignites the passion inside of a person. It harnesses their gifts and causes them to think (and act) long after the job is over.*

- **A job is often motivated by competition; a work is usually motivated by compassion.** *This represents the primary difference between being driven and being called. One pushes, the other pulls.*

- **When people do a job, they walk the mile they are compelled to walk. When they do a work, they walk the second mile, above the call of duty.** *In other words, we do a job because we have to, but we do a work because we want to.*

- **A job is about selling a product. A work is about solving a problem.** *A work is motivated inwardly, which means that motives are purified and collaboration can be intensified. For this reason, a work tends to pull like-minded people forward together.*

- **Jobs are about making a living. Work is about leaving a legacy.** *If the only thing kids are remembered for is that they made a lot of money or had a good 401K or owned a nice home—will that really be satisfying to them? Not the young adults I know. They are already thinking about how they'll be remembered. They're pondering their legacy.*

A work is almost always bigger than a job. It is rarely reduced to a job description that someone else asks you to complete. On the other hand, a job can certainly be a place where a person discovers and pursues a work. Ideally, it should be exactly that—a venue for a vision.

It doesn't always happen that way, of course. Sometimes a person's calling or work has little to do with the job he or she is holding down at the moment. The job is just a source of much-needed income, though that income may help make the work possible. And iY young people who resist settling for "just a job" may need to face that. Grownups do what's necessary to put food on the table. In the long run, however, we must help Generation iY to find and do their calling—not just get a job.

Five Decisions to Help iYers Find Their Future

How do we do that? One of the best ways adults can help iY youth find their future is to help them think through five critical decisions. Everyone ends up making these decisions, by default or design. But if they're made on purpose—and in the right order—they can become a kind of compass to help them steer a course in life. These five decisions are great topics for discussion between students and their parents or mentors.

Decision #1: "What Are My Values?"

This decision is priority one because values keep a person on course as he or she pursues their vision. When people fail to determine their values before they pursue their vision, they may compromise the person they want to become. The end will justify the means. They might reach great goals, but at the expense of their moral integrity.

We've all seen leaders who got into trouble when their integrity didn't keep pace with the momentum created by their giftedness. Do you remember the gifted leaders at Enron or WorldCom or Tyco in the first few years of this century? Did you watch Tiger Woods fall from grace in 2010? These people didn't have a skill problem. They had an integrity problem. Either their values were out of whack, or they didn't live by them.

I firmly believe we must help young people determine their values before we can talk to them meaningfully about their future. This means asking them questions like:

- *What do you want to be remembered for?*
- *What qualities in other people do you most admire?*
- *What statement will be written about you in your obituary?*
- *What are four to six words that most describe the person you wish to be?*

Just as all of us have an IQ (our intelligence quotient) and an EQ (our emotional intelligence), we also have a certain amount of moral intelligence—a sense of right and wrong. For Generation iY this can be a problem. Most believe they are ethical people, and they want to live lives of integrity. But ethics is a mixed bag for them. There is no set of absolute morals or values they all embrace.

According to research done by Northwestern Mutual Life, most Millennials don't trust present leadership in business or government or representatives of organized religion. Generation iY tends to give these leaders a *D-* or an *F* on their moral report card.[3] What's interesting is, according to the same study, most young people believe littering is wrong, but only half of them think it's wrong to exaggerate experience on a resume or not declare income to the IRS. Perhaps they caught a vision before they've set the values.

The good news, however, is that character can be taught and learned. We all know that humans are born "lingual," meaning we have the capacity to learn and speak a language. According to social scientists, we are also born with the capacity to be moral. However, just as humans learn language only after being around people who use it, young people can develop good morals and character only if they are exposed to these things. This means we must model positive values and ethics for them as well as work with them to clarify their own values.

Decision #2: "What Vision Do I Want to Pursue?"

The second issue Generation iY must consider is that of vision—their big-picture goal or mental picture of a better tomorrow. This issue is second only to values, because a vision furnishes incentive for every other decision. Once a young person embraces a dream for their future, his or her incentive to finish college, do an internship, or learn new skills is high.

According to our research at Growing Leaders, most young adults have a dream for their lives and their careers—and they tend to dream big. There are exceptions, of course, but I meet more students today who embrace a big vision for their future than at any time since I began working with students. In fact, their most common problem is not that they don't have a vision, but that they have seventeen of them. They can become paralyzed by so many ideas.

To help them focus on a central vision (or help them catch one), try discussing questions like:

- *What do you see yourself doing in five years? How about ten years?*
- *What do you most want to accomplish in your lifetime?*
- *If you had no fear of failure, what would you attempt to do?*
- *Of all the goals you considered for yourself, which is most important?*

Young people can be crushed when adults fail to listen and affirm their vision. Far too often we will tell a five-year-old, "You can accomplish big dreams!" but then, when the same kid turns twenty-five, we'll say, "Don't get your hopes up!"

Adolf Hitler entered this world as a promising young leader on April 20, 1889. He was one of three children born to Alois Hitler and Klara Pölzl. Klara was protective and smothering, and Alois was hot-tempered and hard-headed. At age twelve, Adolf told his dad he wanted to be a priest, but Alois firmly rejected this career choice. Later, young Adolf talked about wanting to become an artist. Alois insisted Adolph could never make a living that way.

After Alois Hitler died suddenly in 1903, fifteen-year-old Adolf traveled to Vienna to pursue a career in the fine arts, but the art school rejected him for lack of creativity. He didn't want to return home, so he hung around in homeless shelters, with lots of time to read the anti-Semitic books being circulated among the poor and homeless in Vienna. Finally, after experiencing rejection after rejection in Austria, Hitler decided to return to Germany and enlist in the army. He fought in World War I, and for the first time he felt part of something great—but Germany lost the war. Feeling bitter and defeated, Hitler vowed that one day he would avenge himself and his country. The rest, as they say, is history.

I have wondered, over the years, what might have happened if anyone had taken young Adolf Hitler's dreams seriously. What if he'd had an adult to guide him and focus his magnetic personality and big dreams in healthy ways? What would the world have looked like if someone had helped him leverage his vision for a worthwhile cause?

Decision #3: "What Is My Virtue?"

We often think of *virtue* in terms of morality, but it also means strength. In ancient Greece, the word actually was translated "power." And this, too, is an important issue for Generation iY to grasp. Each of them must ask: What primary strengths do I possess, and how could I use them to improve the world?

I am convinced each of us has a set of strengths. Usually, we possess a primary strength that enables us to add value to a team or an organization as well as work toward fulfilling our personal vision. Authors Marcus Buckingham and Don Clifton identify a "strength" as a combination of talents, gifts, knowledge, and acquired skills.[4] Using our strengths on a given task leads to consistent performance. Matching our primary strength to our daily work can almost feel like magic. When we're working out of our strength, we usually love what we're doing, we're good at it, and we're able to bring value to others.

Think, for example, of Michael Jordan. He decided in high school to pursue basketball, even after he got cut from the varsity team. He intuitively knew basketball was for him. He loved playing it. Though his skills were still unpolished, he was good at it, and he could imagine that one day people would want to see him play. And he was obviously right. Folks eventually paid hundreds of dollars to watch him dunk a ball through a hoop at the United Center in Chicago. No doubt, Michael Jordan is a gifted all-around athlete. He can play a number of sports. But when he plays golf or baseball, he knows he is good, not great. Playing basketball is his primary virtue.

Finding and playing to our strengths is a key to satisfaction in so many areas of life, especially where career is involved. The problem is, most people don't stop to consider this when they're making plans.

When the Gallup organization sought to find out why so few Americans love their jobs, they stumbled onto an interesting insight. Knowing that no job is perfect, that every job has a few components that aren't energizing, they decided that an ideal job was one that allowed the worker to play to his or her strengths at least 75 percent of the time. Then they polled large numbers of American workers to find out how close their jobs came to that ideal. What they discovered was pitiful. Only 20 percent of the workers they polled said that their strengths "are in play every day" in their jobs.[5]

This helps explain why so few people truly flourish in their work. Most people are living out someone else's life—badly. They fail to thrive because they're trying to follow a pattern laid out by someone else. They never discover what they're wired to do, and they never go where they're really supposed to go...because they never stop to ask, what are my virtues, and how can I arrange my life to make the best use of them?

Interestingly enough, though iY kids tend to be very self-confident, they often need help determining their primary strength. I've found it's helpful to ask them questions like these:

- *What do I do best?*
- *What do others tell me about my strengths?*
- *What do I enjoy doing the most?*
- *What have I done in the past that really got results?*

Hopefully a young person will find some overlap in their responses to the questions above and pinpoint one significant activity or ability. This strength—not what pays most, what daddy did, what friends plan to do after college, or even what they like—should guide their choices. When young people make right decisions about their strengths based on right motives, they will thrive.

In my book, *Nurturing the Leader Within Your Child,*[6] I tell the story of a boy named Jimmy. He was a different sort of kid who grew up a bit of a misfit among the neighborhood boys. He much preferred playing in his room than playing baseball or football outside—and much of the time, he was playing with his socks. This seemed strange to his parents, but Jim was very creative using different pairs of socks and other clothing to create characters and tell stories.

Mom and Dad decided to nurture his interest. They got him more socks. Today, I am so glad they did, because Jim Henson grew up and made a living out of playing with socks. He created an entire industry with Muppets, an idea that began

Five Decisions to Help Generation iY Find Their Way

1. **Values:** These come first, because they're the moral compass.
2. **Vision:** This usually comes next because it is your blueprint for life.
3. **Virtues:** This is next, since it reveals your best tool to influence and serve.
4. **Venue:** This follows because now you're ready to find a suitable context.
5. **Vehicles:** Finally, you can choose the actions necessary to reach the goal.

in the mind of a kid and grew when he insisted on working out of his strengths.

Decision #4: "What's the Best Venue for Me?"

This question is about the location or context in which young people will use their virtues and pursue their visions. It's about *where* they will live and work. Because iY kids tend to value aesthetics and community and are very contextually aware, the *where* can make a big difference in their ability to function at their best. Venue can make or break their careers.

For instance, a student may find that teaching is her strength and may choose to use that virtue in teaching younger children, but the specific venues for this could vary. She could do this in a suburban school, in an urban neighborhood with underprivileged kids, at a Boys and Girls club, a church youth group, or a kids' camp. She may choose to do it in the town where she grew up or across the country.

According to *Time* magazine, young adults aged eighteen to twenty-nine move around a lot. Twenty-five percent of them have had three addresses in the last five years. Twenty-two percent have had four or more addresses in the last five years.[7] The environment, for some, may be as important as what the mission is of the organization. It's quite possible for a young person to be clear about her vision and her virtue and still feel out of place if the venue isn't right. Help them consider these venue questions:

- *In what context do my skills and strengths fit best?*
- *With what group of people do I feel most at home?*
- *Are there environments that allow me to be at my best?*
- *Where do my personality and my style seem to flourish?*

Julie was a college student who came to talk to me about once a month. Something wasn't right. She was confused about her "life calling." In our sessions we went back and forth talking about her passions, her gifts, and the problems she felt compelled to solve. One day, however, we began talking about her opportunities. She had always loved speaking Spanish and was studying it in college. She was using it to tutor high-school kids in an ESL program and to volunteer at a local Boys and Girls Club, but she still felt out of place. She wondered if she'd chosen the wrong major in school or just wasn't gifted enough to make a living with her degree.

Then, I asked her what other opportunities she had in front of her. She began revealing how many mission trips she made each year to Mexico, working in Tijuana, San Juan, Mexicali, Cabo San Lucas, and Mexico City. Suddenly, I said the obvious: "Julie, have you considered your best venue to use Spanish might be Mexico?"

Today, Julie is serving as a missionary in Mexico, using her Spanish every day and loving every minute of it. She's now found her vocation...and her perfect venue.

Decision #5: "What Vehicles Will I Employ to Help Me Reach My Goal?"

A vehicle is simply a means to reach a destination. Just as a car is a vehicle that carries you to a physical address, a well-chosen action (or actions) can carry a young person toward her goals in life. Vehicles, in other words, are the day-to-day choices and activities that will enable a person to fulfill his or her vision. Vehicles have everything to do with the daily grind. They are, essentially, items on a to-do list. And they can only be chosen wisely after values, vision, virtue, and venue have been decided.

The analogy to actual transportation is clear. A car is a vehicle that can transport you to a location if there are roads. Jeeps are better if there are no roads. Neither works very well if you must cross the ocean. In life, vehicles can get you to a place you want to be, but you can only select the appropriate one after you know where you want to go.

I wish you could meet my young friend Micah—a young man with a mission. He graduated from college, as so many do, with a million ideas on what he could do with his life. Like many of his fellow iYers, he moved back home to get his bearings. But what he did after that made his story quite different.

Micah's parents and his mentors advised him to look at the world around him and catch a vision for something he could do to solve a problem in the world—then set to work solving it. Micah grabbed some friends and did just that. They recognized how so many from their generation tend to get stuck in front of a screen, wishing they could make a difference but somehow unable to actually get it done in the real world. Micah and his team decided to launch a networking Web site called Roov. The entire purpose of the site is to network young adults online, in order to get them offline and actually get involved in the real world. In fact, that's sort of a slogan they use: "Get online so you can get offline and do something."

Users of Roov connect with new friends who share their passion for under-privileged kids or for the homeless or for unwed mothers or for the environment. Then the new friends arrange to meet and do something together. Roov fans are making connections not around typical social networking issues like "What's your favorite movie?" or "What did you do last weekend?" but rather, "What do you like doing or want to do that makes a difference?"

They saw results fast. For instance, a group of people who enjoy an alternative style of music found each other and actually collaborated on an album. Another group began serving underprivileged kids in a rough part of West Dallas. Each of them had felt apprehensive about working there alone, but once they found each other online, they had a team who could back each other up. The Roov idea has helped people connect and act together.

You can imagine, of course, that bringing such a mammoth vision to life was a little intimidating. Where to begin? This is where vehicles became critical for Micah and his friends. The Roov team, a group of twenty-somethings, drew up a list of what was necessary to accomplish their vision and began implementing them one by one. They gathered investors, raised money, drew up a business plan, met with key influencers, hired extra help, and chose how to advertise. And while Roov was a short-lived vision, it became a springboard for other ventures.

Here are some questions Generation iY should be asking regarding vehicles:

- *Once you know your vision, what are the wisest actions to take to fulfill it?*
- *On your "to do" list, what are the top, most productive priorities?*
- *What are possible activities that are tempting but less productive?*
- *What are the next steps you should take to move toward your goal?*

Often, the vehicles are the elements that are forgotten when executing a personal vision. For many, it is easy to come up with a lofty goal and even to find the right context for their talents. Actually reaching the goal may be another matter entirely. Vehicles insure that the lofty vision gets translated into practical action. If young people execute a good list of vehicles, chances are good they will ultimately fulfill their vision.

Doing Well and Doing Good

It is my goal to enable Generation iY to *do well*—to navigate their way into adulthood and successfully enter a career. At the same time, I also want to help them *do good*. It's about more than just making money or getting ahead to insure their own success. I believe a satisfying and successful life is one that positively influences others and improves the world in some way—to lead the way in some area and leave behind a positive legacy.

Arthur was a young twenty-something in 1752 who felt the same way. As he wandered the streets of Ireland one night, he noticed all the people who flocked to the pubs each night to get drunk. It was as though they had nothing more to live for than alcohol; their life had no direction.

Arthur began to think, what if someone could create a beer that was actually healthy to drink? What if it tasted so good that folks would love to drink it but was so rich in nutrients that they'd have trouble getting drunk on it? This seemed a worthwhile venture to young Arthur.

His godfather had left him a hundred pounds in his will, so Arthur put that money to work and, after four years, had saved enough to begin brewing his "new idea." In 1759, he acquired a nine-thousand-year lease on a four-acre brewery at St. James Gate. And it wasn't long before Arthur's new recipe made it big. It was originally full of vitamins and so healthy that doctors prescribed it to pregnant women.

A satisfying and successful life is one that positively influences others and improves the world in some way

You've probably heard of Arthur Guinness's brand of beer. Guinness is now the number-one brand of beer in Ireland and a worldwide icon as well. Yet the success of Arthur's recipe is not the best part of the story.

Sometime later, Arthur recognized there was more good to be done in Ireland. Talking to a friend one day, he inquired of him what he was spending his time on. His friend told him he'd become consumed with the latch key kids of Ireland; there were thousands of orphans without a home or living in poor conditions. This was all Arthur needed to hear. He began funding the construction of orphanages in Ireland for these children. This, of course, spread his name even further across the country, and soon he was able to "evangelize" others to join him in the cause.

Arthur Guinness is a vivid example of what real work is all about. He made sure he was doing good while he was doing well. As an entrepreneur, he established his commitment to improving the lives of people in communities where Guinness did business. The Guinness Company was one of the first businesses in Ireland to provide proper pensions and healthcare for its employees and their families. Over the years, it has donated land to create public parks and recreation areas and provided low-income housing and educational initiatives. Why? For Arthur Guinness, it was about both money and mission. He possessed both a job and a work. For him, his job and his work provided three outcomes:

- *It improved the world in some way.*
- *It generated revenue to give away.*
- *It provided a platform to empower others.*

May we enable Generation iY to do the same as they steer their way forward into the twenty-first century.

LINKING UP

To weigh in with your greatest concerns about this generation, go to **www. SaveTheirFutureNow.com/DiscussionBoard**.

11 The Care and Feeding of a New Generation

EPIC Ideas for Educating iY Students

I RECENTLY VISITED A FRIEND WHO RUNS AN ANIMAL CLINIC IN MISSISSIPPI. As she showed me the variety of pets she was caring for in her clinic, she singled out Moe. Moe was quite a character—a temperamental ferret who was recovering from some minor surgery. Generally, ferrets are furry, fast, and always on the move. Moe was, well, unusual. All the other animals loved attention, they were mostly congenial, and they had predictable feeding times and habits. Not Moe—or Moody Moe, as he was dubbed at the clinic.

Moe wouldn't eat the same food as his counterparts—or even at the same time—and what went down often came back up. He was finicky, like a cat. He was lazy, like a cow. At times he was impetuous, like a puppy. And he was always changing, like a chameleon.

Sharon, my vet friend, had quickly discovered she couldn't care for Moe the way she did the other animals. At times, I would hear her talk to him in exasperation: "Okay, Moe, you can just go without. If you won't eat this stuff, I'll it give to someone else. It's up to you."

But Sharon was determined to meet the daily challenge of figuring out what and when Moe would eat and just how to feed him in a way he would receive it and keep it down. Just two days before my visit, she had hit upon a system that seemed to work. It was all built around the idea of creating incentive for Moe—incentive to eat and be clean. Moody Moe was being fed, groomed, and cared for in spite of himself.

I had to laugh. This scenario seemed all too familiar—because I've met my share of Moody Moes on the high school and college campuses I visit. It's very possible you've met them too.

I'm not talking about ferrets, of course, but about students from Generation iY. After working with them from the time they were born, I've found you just can't assume you know how to "feed" them or when they'll be ready to "eat" the mental, emotional, and spiritual food you offer. Connecting with them and leading them can be a tricky proposition.

I hear adults say this all the time when talking about Generation iY: "They're a different animal." And they have reason to be. Consider these facts:

- *They never rode a bike without a helmet.*
- *They never rode in a car without a seatbelt.*
- *They never watched a TV without a remote.*
- *They've never known a world without the Internet.*
- *They've always cooked popcorn in a microwave.*
- *They've purchased one song at a time (not an album), for over a decade.*
- *They've been able to e-mail our U.S. president since they were six.*
- *They own a cell phone that doubles as a mini-computer.*
- *Iraq and Afghanistan have always been front-page stories.*
- *To them, George Foreman has always been a barbecue-grill salesman.*
- *They can't remember when* America's Funniest Home Videos *wasn't on TV.*
- *They think of hip hop as a "classic" music form.*
- *Bono and Madonna are aging singers.*
- *They don't remember when "cut and paste" involved scissors.*
- *The terms "roll down your window" and "you sound like a broken record" have to be explained.*

Because they've been catered to and their experience has been so different from yours, you might be tempted to dub your iY acquaintances "Moody Moe." Nevertheless, we must initiate the process of connecting with them if we're going to lead them. Lets face it. Adults must learn the "care, feeding, and grooming" of this new generation.

An EPIC Generation

So how do we do it? In this chapter, I'd like to guide you as you attempt to connect with this generation of young adults. I can only scratch the surface in a single chapter, but let me begin by suggesting a strategy for gaining an audience and becoming relevant with this batch of kids.

I mentioned in Chapter 3 that futurist Leonard Sweet calls Generation iY an EPIC generation.[1] He uses EPIC as an acronym to describe how this generation learns and receives information best. They respond best to input that is:

E—*Experiential*

Forget the lecture, unless it is accompanied by an experience that enables them to remember the point you are making. This means they want to *see* something, or *do* something, not just *hear* something. Communication, in other words, must be more than two-dimensional. It must include other senses.

Why are iY kids this way? They're accustomed to many messages competing for their attention. Their filters are strong, and only memorable experiences get through. Schools that understand this incorporate outside activities (such as field trips), artistic expressions, and creative projects to help students experience what they need to learn.

Educator Edgar Dale is famous for his "Cone of Experience," a visual representation demonstrating that people learn and retain information better when the learning moves from mere words to pictures, symbols, and experiences.[2] His research told us that retention and learning increases in this order:

1. Verbal symbols (i.e. text)
2. Visual symbols (drawings, etc.)
3. Recordings, radio, still pictures
4. Motion pictures/TV
5. Exhibits
6. Demonstrations
7. Contrived experiences
8. Dramatized experiences
9. Direct, purposeful (real world) experiences

I believe Dale's ideas have never been more relevant than they are today with Generation iY.

P—*Participatory*

Generation iY has been invited to upload their own thoughts all their lives. They expect to do it at school and work as well. They want to express themselves, to learn through dialogue, to participate fully in the outcomes of where a program is going.

Case in point: When *American Idol* shot to the top of TV ratings several years back, it quickly became clear that Generation iY watched *Idol* (and similar shows) differently than the adult generation. Adults would sit passively on the sofa hoping their favorite singer would win. But iY kids would actively text in fifty votes to make sure their favorite singer won. That's just the way Generation iY operates. They will support what they help create.

In June of 2009, MTV launched a program, *It's On with Alexa Chung*, that took participatory television to a new level. The stars not only invited viewers to follow them on Twitter and Facebook; they incorporated the interaction with viewers right on the screen, in effect, making the viewers stars as well. An audience member could tweet a question or a comment to a person on TV and get a response in real time. Viewer's homemade videos are part of the show, and some will even appear on the show.

Why do this? The short answer: because today's viewers are participatory.

The meteoric rise of social media, in fact, is convincing evidence of the power of the participatory in the life of the average person today—especially the average iYer. In January of 2010, Facebook passed four hundred million users. If it were a country, it would be the third largest country in the world behind China and India. In that same month, 1.2 million tweets were sent. That's just one month. It seems that Generation iY is teaching all of us to participate a little more.

I—*Image-rich*

Generation iY is definitely a visually oriented generation. They grew up with MTV, videos, digital cameras, the Internet, VH1, DVDs and cameras on their cell phones. They think in images, and they want their communication to be either image-based or image-enhanced. One professor recently told me that his students watch thirty-five movies for every one book they read. Leonard Sweet believes that images, not words, are the language of the twenty-first century. In fact, he suggests that companies create "image statements," not mere mission statements. The power of the images sticks in the minds of people so much better.

Growing Leaders developed our Habitudes® material for this very reason. Habitudes® are images that form leadership habits and attitudes. The books and videos convey timeless principles using the power of a picture and conversation. We at Growing Leaders have found that when we use only words to communicate with kids, we engage the left side of the brain only and may invite an argument. When we use images, however we engage the right side of the brain as well, and we invite story and conversation. In the words of Socrates, "The soul does not think without a picture."

Ellen Pate, a program director at the University of Alabama, was kind enough to do some research for me. As she dug further into history, she reported to me that images may be humankind's oldest form of values education. Pictures carved on the walls of caves or pyramids in ancient Phoenicia and Egypt tell stories that communicate values and record cultural history. Jesus taught using the power of images (parables), and those mental pictures have stuck for millennia. During the Middle Ages, stained glass windows shared stories with parishioners who couldn't read. Even during the American Revolution, images of snakes, stars, and trees were used to spark patriotism among citizens in our own country.

Today, because of our media-rich society, images may be the perfect stimulus to help students grasp and retain valuable information. Just as important, iY kids may have trouble even hearing us if we try to communicate without images. Now, more than ever before in history, a picture is worth a thousand words.

C—*Connected*

As I've mentioned throughout this book, Generation iY kids are constantly connected—socially and technologically. Most young people don't want to work, learn, study, or exercise alone. One NCAA coach told me recently he can't get his athletes to do their workouts unless they do them with a friend or a cell phone.

So how does this affect us as we lead them? Most students I have interviewed say that utilizing technology is vital if your message is to be perceived as relevant and current. In addition, I have found most of them would agree they need to connect with each other to truly engage in learning.

Not long ago, I put this reality into practice. Our team did an all-day assembly for middle-school students. We called it "A Habitudes® Experience." From nine in the morning until three that afternoon, we taught kids about character, discipline, focus, self-esteem and leadership—all with the power of images, conversations, and experiences.

We knew connection with peers would be a huge part of the kids' engagement, so we started each Habitude® segment with an activity. Next, I taught a bit using an image and a video. I had three students hop up on the platform for me to interview. Then I drew some diagrams on the white screen before allowing the students to gather in small groups for discussion and feedback. After that we had some music, then we pulled together a student panel to give feedback. All day, students were connected to technology and each other—and they definitely retained what was taught. At the end of the day, one by one, the students stood up and relayed the principles they had learned throughout the day.

So, here's my question for you: is your communication EPIC? I believe more and more parents, leaders, employers, teachers and coaches will need to revolutionize the way they communicate if they plan to stay relevant. The simple reality is this: EPIC communicators get through to the widest audience, and this is especially true for Generation iY.

What a Difference a Generation Makes...

- Baby Boomers asked: **Why?**
- Generation X asked: **Why ask why?**
- Generation iY asks: **Why not?**

Left-Brain Schools in a Right-Brain World

When we were elementary age, my sisters and I used to play school. We'd get out the chalkboard, the chairs, and the map, and one of us would be the teacher. Sometimes, we'd get the G.I. Joes or stuffed animals involved, just to enlarge the class size a bit. Even when we didn't know what we were doing, we never lost our passion. We just got creative and made something up. It was a blast.

And the thing is, I felt that way about my real school too. I liked the crayons, the games, and even arithmetic—when I was little, that is.

Over time, however, my whole perspective changed, and school became somewhat of a drudgery to me. I stopped playing it at home, and I stopped looking forward to going to school.

Sadly, I was like most kids. School was fun when we were young, but eventually school came to mean boredom and irrelevance—or worse.

For Generation iY, this dynamic has become critical. The disconnect between how schools "feed" and how kids "eat" has widened, and they're just not swallowing what the schools are dishing out. In many cases, they're not only bored; they've completely checked out. There are a number of reasons, but the biggest one is that traditional teaching methods just can't compete with their EPIC expectations. They would never "play school," because for them *school* and *fun* just can't coexist.

But education isn't meant to be fun, you may be thinking. That's not its purpose. Education is not entertainment.

Agreed.

The purpose of school is not pleasure and amusement. However, according to our research, education that sticks in the minds of students—especially iY students—is usually connected to three elements:

- *A healthy, trusting relationship with the teacher.*
- *An interactive learning community.*
- *A creative and innovative approach that stimulates the right brain.*

Daniel Pink has written some helpful insights about this last element in his book, *A Whole New Mind*. He convincingly argues that "a seismic...shift is now under way in much of the advanced world. We are moving from an economy and a society built on the logical, linear, computerlike capabilities of the Information Age to an economy and a society built on the inventive, empathic, big-picture capabilities of what's rising in its place, the Conceptual Age."[3]

In other words, the future will increasingly reward what we commonly think of as "right brain" thinking. And iY kids thrive on this kind of thinking. They are nonlinear. They prize relationships. They love to make connections between people and ideas and to get their hands on what they're learning about. They thrive on pictures and stories, and their eyes glaze over when requested to just sit still and read or listen.

So here's the problem I see with education as it's commonly practiced today. First, we are preparing students in left-brain schools to enter a right-brain world. In other words, the school does not resemble the world they will enter after graduation—if they graduate at all. And students, who are already tuned into that world, tend to tune out input that to them seems totally irrelevant to their needs.

The left brain is about *knowledge*. The right brain is about *creativity*. The left brain is calculated and definitive; it's about data. The right brain is innovative and dynamic; it's about art. Certainly both are necessary. But more and more, our world is driven by right-brain thought: imagination, story, music.

Now, consider what's happening today in schools. More and more, teachers are forced to teach in a left-brain manner. Students must memorize information. Faculty must teach for the test. Standards must be kept. No child is left behind. Schools become concerned with downloading the facts, stats, and dates.

What's more, with a struggling economy in recent years, budget cuts are being made all over the country. The first courses dropped by public schools are the "unnecessary" right brain courses: art, music, and drama. Sadly as the world shifts toward right-brain thinking, schools are focusing more and more on left-brain learning.

Albert Einstein once said, "Imagination is more important than knowledge." What he meant was that knowledge is finite, but imagination can take a person into the infinite. Knowledge includes only what has already been developed.

Imagination is about our dreams, which have no limits. Unfortunately, our educational institutions tend to revolve around self-contained "silos" of existing information. They're about lecture, drill, and test. Testing involves students regurgitating facts they have heard from instructors that semester. Not much more. Not much less.

Not long ago I had the privilege of conducting a leadership session with the Georgia Teachers of the Year. After our time together, I realized one of the chief reasons these faculty members were chosen as the best was that they included a balance of right-brain and left-brain methods. In conversations, several of them confirmed my suspicions:

- *Schools often teach and test for questions that aren't relevant to life.*
- *Schools drill for memory rather than critical thinking.*
- *School departments function independently and don't collaborate, communicate, or look at the big picture.*
- *Schools prepare kids in a twentieth-century style for a twenty-first century world.*

Increasingly, our schools are coming to resemble George Santayana's cynical statement, "A child educated only in school is an uneducated child." And this has to stop. Those of us who teach and train students must turn a corner and transform the way we deliver our content. Lesson plans cannot be taught the way we did in 1989 or even 1999.

The culture has changed. If we are to have any hope of leading the iY generation effectively, the way we teach them must change as well. How should it change? Let me suggest the following:

- *Teaching must supply not only information, but inspiration for students.*
- *Teaching must do more than measure a kid's memory; it must motivate a kid's imagination.*
- *Teaching must cover not just the facts of history but the feelings that history produced.*
- *Teaching should not just be about increasing intelligence, but also about increasing innovation.*
- *Teaching cannot only be about **what** to think, but **how** to think.*

Download Style with Upload Students

The disconnect between left-brain institutions and a right-brain future is not the only problem with the way we "feed" our students today. A second issue is a growing disconnect between the methods we employ to teach young people and what actually gets through to them. I already touched on this in other chapters.

For many adults, "download" is our default teaching method. We get impatient and want to pursue the shortest distance between two points. Our straight line to them is to simply download our information. We lecture. We direct. We preach. We give them books and articles to read, and we like to control the content we dish out to them.

In other words, we insist on teaching exactly the way that iY students have trouble learning.

Students today are more geared to learn through uploading. As I've mentioned repeatedly, they want to express themselves, and frequently they find out what they believe by hearing themselves talk. They grow through participation. And they're used to the free flow of information with multiple sources, so they expect to interact with those sources. "Just listening" to a single voice is not only boring to them; increasingly, it doesn't make sense.

My colleague, Holly Moore, and I just had lunch with Jennifer Martin, who heads up digital public relations at CNN. She candidly shared how much this emerging generation is affecting her work at CNN, the largest news broadcasting company in the world. A nineteen-year old blogger named Brian Stelter began blogging and tweeting the news he picked up on CNN—basically, uploading his comments to his followers like a reporter. There was no criminal involvement; he was just reaching out to his mushrooming network of people all over the world.

The legal department at CNN felt they should step in and stop the whole thing. But Jennifer (just beyond a twenty-something herself) saw a whole new opportunity. She got in touch with Brian and began to collaborate instead of compete. They decided it was a good thing to utilize his uploads. In fact, shortly thereafter, Jennifer launched a new division for CNN called iReport that took the idea to a whole new level. The Web site iReport.com provides the opportunity for ordinary people to upload their own eyewitness news and video to CNN in real time.

This is all difficult for the adult generation because control and centralization are evaporating quickly. If we want to influence our future leaders, wise adults need to steer the conversation. We must rethink what our message is and how we're transmitting it to Generation iY.

Mind the Gap

While visiting England, I have often traveled by train and subway. During my last trip, I found myself listening with fresh ears to a phrase that is used hundreds of times each day as passengers board: "Mind the gap." It's a reminder to travelers that there is a space between the platform and the train, and they need to be careful as they board to avoid falling.

This is my sentiment exactly when it comes to how we lead Generation iY—we must "mind the gap" between our world and the world our young people experience. The chart below shows this gap clearly and suggests why typical education methods often fail to engage Generation iY.

The Gap

Students today...	Schools today...
Typically are right-brained thinkers.	Typically use left-brained delivery.
Learn by uploading; expressing themselves.	Teach by downloading lectures.
Are experiential by inclination.	Are passive by nature.
Are helped by music and art to retain information.	Are having music and art programs cut back or eliminated.
Desire to learn what is relevant to life.	Teach for the next test.
Are driven by creativity.	Are driven by curriculum.

Keep in mind that schools are not the only culprits here. Companies, non-profit organizations, military bases, and other government agencies are also slow in keeping up with the shift to the Conceptual Age. We insist on communicating information the way it was communicated to us years ago. We stick with what's familiar, not what is most effective. This is part of the reason we experience such disparity between college graduates entering the marketplace and the Baby Boomers supervising them.

Once again, I'm not just saying we need to make everything "fun." I'm certainly not suggesting that we dumb down our curricula, adopt a touchy-feely approach that sacrifices content for "relevance" or employs technology for technology's sake. I'm just suggesting we put thought into how we can best bridge the gap between how we teach and how Generation iY learns.

No doubt, the young people who make up Generation iY need to grow up and become adults. They even need to get used to work that isn't always fun. Company executives and college professors remind me of this all the time. Generation iY's future success will be based on whether they can transition to a grownup world that's not always glitzy, glamorous, or entertaining.

I get it. However, all good communicators follow a rule we'd do well to remember: Begin where your audience lives. We must start with a method they are familiar with and build a bridge to a place they are not yet familiar with.

To do this, I think it might be helpful to pay attention to precisely how young people learn and how we can best teach them.

The Learning Journey

Have you ever wondered what happens inside of a young person when she really discovers something new? What enables a kid to be captured by an insight or remember an important truth?

These are questions that leaders, parents, and teachers must take seriously if we intend to connect with Generation iY. To help answer them, I'd like to describe the stages of the internal learning journey as I've come to understand it. Based on my research and my own experience, this description follows what happens in a student's brain when he or she is confronted with a new idea or input from somebody else.

I've also tried to show how adults can most effectively steer students through this journey—basically, how we can help them learn. If you're a leader, you can apply this to your next team meeting. If you're a teacher, you can apply this to your next lesson plan. If you're a parent, you can apply this to the wise counsel you plan to share this week.

Note that for each stage I pinpoint the internal status of the reader—the mental and emotional response to what is happening. Note also that while I've listed this as a measured, step-by-step process, it rarely works that way in real life. Some stages happen quickly, almost instantaneously, while others will take some time.

Stage 1: Incentive

Internal Status: Desire ("I Have a Need and Must Find a Solution.")

Youth have strong filters and screen out most messages coming at them. Leaders and teachers who want them to listen must first provide them a reason for tuning in—convince them that the information is relevant and nurture an internal desire to receive it. One way of doing this is to create a dilemma that your input will address.

Stage 2: Disequilibrium

Internal Status: Resistance ("This Is an Uncomfortable, Unfamiliar Situation.")

Once we've created an incentive to learn, leaders/teachers must welcome the idea that young people may experience a period of discomfort or awkwardness.

They may resist at first, especially if the new data opposes what they assume to be true. Most genuine learning happens after this period of resistance.

Stage 3: Schema

Internal Status: Urge for Connection ("I Must Relate the Unfamiliar Concept to a Familiar One.")

A schema is essentially a mental file, a way of organizing information in our minds. (If you were an education major in college you recognize this term.) We all make use of schemas when we learn something new and unfamiliar. Usually we compare it to the familiar we already embrace. An effective teacher helps the learner make these connections through the use of metaphors or analogies.

Stage 4: Emotion

Internal Status: Ignition ("My Neurotransmitters Spark Feelings and Emotions Inside.")

Once a young person grasps a concept and connects it with previous understandings, his neurotransmitters begin to fire. This process sparks emotions as well as thoughts. Leaders/teachers should acknowledge this reality and give encouragement. When both the mind and emotions are ignited, real learning takes place.

Stage 5: Social Integration

Internal Status: Processing ("I Need to Respond and Interact.")

Learning is enhanced when young people are permitted to process the data they've just received and integrate it socially with others. It may be their peers or with a mentor, but at this stage they both share with and listen to the responses of others. This stage occurs best when there is abundant interaction and debate and when many angles are examined.

Stage 6: Filters and Pushback

Internal Status: Conclusion ("My Filters Screen Out the Illogical and Produce Ideas.")

Young people hear and process others' responses to the data, then perhaps push back against many of them until they can figure out what fits their rationale or worldview. Then they draw their own conclusions. At this point they may agree and disagree with the viewpoints of others. (Educators commonly call this stage "dendrites," after the brain cells that grow and branch during the process of learning.)

Stage 7: Active Involvement

Internal Status: Action ("My Grasp Increases as My Experience Reinforces What I Have Learned.")

Learning is sealed when young people move beyond simply discussing information, and they get to experience firsthand what they have learned. This is commonly called experiential learning, and it's all about reflection and practice. Students learn best when they are allowed to act on what they've learned and confirm the information through application.

The Learning Journey in Practice

I recently watched a twenty-something experience each of these stages. Justin (not his real name) is sharp, but a little cocky and self-confident. Consequently, he's not always open to the idea that others may know more than he does. He tends to live in his own little world, and he's quite comfortable being "king" of that world.

In a mentoring meeting a few months ago, I shared some insights with Justin that I felt would be helpful to his budding career. He had taken a job with a growing company but wasn't enjoying the day-to-day grind, and he wanted to quit. I shared some steps he could take to test if that was the right decision. Unfortunately, my insights went against his assumptions. He felt I was asking him to compromise who he was and to "kiss up" to his supervisor.

Instead of getting defensive or impatient, I decided to ease into stage one by creating a dilemma in his mind. I convinced him that the issue we were talking about represented a principle he would face many times over the course of his career. He started to listen.

After that I shared a management principle and gave him the supervisor's point of view. Because he didn't see things that way, we entered stage two: disequilibrium. I allowed for some silent awkwardness as he considered his situation. In a few minutes, we were ready for stage three.

I suggested a schema and shared one of our Habitudes® with him. It made sense to Justin, but now he had to experience the next two stages—emotion and social integration. I told him to take some time and bounce his thoughts off of other people, but I suggested he do that with a variety of people of different ages.

He agreed. Over the next week, he experienced the next stage: pushback and filter. He had to determine what he agreed with and what he didn't. I gave him time to do this.

Finally, Justin tried out my advice. He entered stage seven and acted on it. The good news is, he gained a bigger perspective through the whole experience and stayed at his job.

I may have won the debate, but Justin was the real winner in that situation.

Are You Getting Through?

It's time that all of us who are involved with leading young people today take a good look at our leadership and teaching methods. Ask yourself:

- Am I primarily a left-brain or a right-brain communicator?
- How can I balance my approach to engage both sides of the brain?
- Am I preparing students in a relevant way for their entrance into the real world?
- Can I find more creative ways to deliver content?
- Do I allow enough time for my students to respond creatively?

A Reality Show for Adults Who Want to Communicate

We all want our young people to grow and achieve, to live both happily and responsibly. That means we should give serious attention to the way we lead, teach, coach, direct, inspire, and help Generation iY. And to do that, we need to face certain realities about what works with them and what doesn't. We must intentionally "feed" them in ways they can swallow.

To that end, I'd like to relay a set of realities that guide me whenever I prepare to lead or speak to young people. Based on the learning process I have previously described, these simple ideas help me connect with my own two kids as well as with the young people I teach worldwide. Perhaps they'll work for you as well.

1. **Generation iY learns on a "need to know" basis.** Don't just jump into your topic when you communicate. Take time to explain the relevance of what you're teaching. Why should they listen? We must create incentive for them to believe they need to know what we are communicating.

2. **Remember that schemas frame their world—so use them.** Don't forget— when students encounter new information, they attempt to relate it to something they already know. They process new data via their present experiences and understanding. An effective leader uses what is cultural to say what is timeless.

3. **The less predictable your words, the more memorable they will be.** Spend as much time on the "how" of your delivery as you do the "what" of your content. Will they miss what you're saying because it's old news shared in an old way? Find a fresh way to say it, with a new twist. Avoid clichés like the plague.

4. **The first four minutes must grab their head or their heart if you want to sustain their interest.** Be quick to get to some content or reveal your own heart. Provide a reason for them to listen by stimulating their minds or their emotions. Share your story. Be transparent. Take them on a journey— enlist them quickly to join you on this adventure of growth.

5. **The best learning occurs in a social context.** Russian psychologist Lev Vygotsky is famous for confirming this. A student's worldview emerges from interaction with others.

6. **The more "in your face" your words are, the more trust you will earn.** Generation iY students love to speak their minds and tend to trust communicators who are blunt in the same way. Don't be afraid to be forthright and truthful. You don't have to be rude, but be straightforward.

7. **If you challenge the status quo, they will hunger to take a journey with you.** They have high expectations of themselves and of anyone "up front." Challenge the norm. This doesn't mean you're a rebel or a renegade—but simply that you're re-thinking assumptions from the past. Demonstrate you are open to change.

8. **They grew up loving images, so give them a metaphor.** This is just another reminder. The iY generation's world is MTV, video games, photos, DVDs, VH1 and the Internet—you must have a picture too. This will help them retain your message. (I try to give them a point for their left brain and a picture for their right brain.)

9. **Accelerate learning by pairing students with a partner, peer, or mentor.** By learning together, they experience growth firsthand but can also learn through observing an advanced partner. So provide a guide when possible. Again, relationships are key. Students tend to learn better in circles than in rows.

10. **Once you prepare your message, you must find a way to twist it to exceed their expectations.** Movies and popular novels stand out when they add another layer of story. The story creates buzz because it includes unexpected elements and delivers more than was promised. Adjusting communication in this direction can really help you connect with students. Once you know your message, get creative on your delivery.

11. **For your message to be remembered, keep the pace of change high, and call students to change.** *Change* is the key word here. Students know their world is changing fast, and they don't sit still for very long. They also plan to change their world. Your communication must reflect this. Your talk should

be full of changes. Try to engage different learning styles in a single message.

12. **It's best to teach less for more.** Even while you're changing approaches, keep the central message simple and focused. Although this sounds contradictory, it isn't. To be remembered, don't attempt to deliver a large variety of topics. You need a strong, focused message to get through iY students' strong filters. Use creative elements, but stick to your point.

13. **Remember, students today are both high-performance and high maintenance.** Walk the delicate balance between nurture and challenge. Help them "own" your message via relationship. If you can earn their trust through feedback and support, they will perform in extraordinary ways.

14. **Include a challenge.** Generation iY students hunger to participate in projects that are very important and almost impossible to accomplish. They love moving toward a goal when it is significant and others may feel it cannot be done. Make use of this tendency whenever possible. Engage students by appealing to their love of challenge.

Teaching Kids to Change the World

Chris Hughes may just be a prime example of an iY response to adults who give young people the opportunity to participate in a cause.

You may have heard of Chris. He is the cofounder of Facebook, a Harvard student who changed the way the world connects through a Web site. Interestingly, that wasn't enough for him. During the 2008 presidential campaign, he attended a rally and heard Barak Obama. Like many twenty-somethings, he was intrigued by Obama's message.

If you stop and think about it, the Obama campaign was run much like a SGA campaign at a university. It was about a cause to buy into, and it was about hope and change. It felt very grassroots at the beginning, much like a college campus. So Chris felt right at home with the campaign and offered his services. The campaign leaders were receptive but reserved. They had no idea what a kid could do to transform a political campaign, but they did give Chris a cubicle and computer. That's when he set about changing everything about the way people got involved in politics.

Chris created multiple Web sites to register voters, enlist volunteers, set up local town-hall meetings, ask for ideas, and put people to work. People were given the opportunity to weigh in and express their opinions on the issues as well as on how they felt the campaign could work in their community.

The online community Chris created made a difference. The young adults who responded to Chris's innovations helped determine the way the Obama campaign reached its goal. (Remember—young people support what they help create.) In a sense, Chris mobilized a generation to elect his candidate. *Fast Company* magazine called him "The Kid Who Made Obama President."[4]

You may not agree with what Chris did or what he stands for. You don't have to agree. I am only asking you to look at what happened when someone in the adult world paid serious attention to what an iYer could do. Chris's accomplishment is a picture of the vast potential of the iY generation.

They can do so much if we let them. And we can learn so much if we just pay attention to how they think and how they learn. Once we learn to "feed" them appropriately, we might be surprised at how they grow.

LINKING UP

For more ideas on teaching and leading Generation iY, see **www.SaveTheir FutureNow.com/Habitudes**.

12 Save The Future
Unleashing Their Leadership Potential

PERHAPS YOU IDENTIFY WITH A POLICE RECRUIT who entered the police academy with incredible enthusiasm and a determination to make a difference. Over the weeks of training, however, the academy sobered his passion. He began to see the difficult work ahead of him as an officer—the challenges of enforcing the law, arresting criminals, and serving the community 24/7. On the final day of classes, the instructor stood in front of his young recruits. He felt compelled to give the cadets a challenge they'd never forget. He would test their wit and courage with an impossible scenario.

"Imagine you're on duty downtown," he said, "and you suddenly realize the First National Bank is being robbed. Thieves begin pouring out onto the street to make their getaway. Before you can respond, a woman across the street gets mugged and begins running after the mugger who stole her purse, screaming for help at the top of her lungs. Within seconds, a building just one block down catches fire, bursting into flames before the wide eyes of pedestrians and traffic. This causes a speeding driver to smash into a parked car in front of you, which then hits a fire hydrant. Water begins spewing out onto the streets, sending everyone running in pandemonium."

The police instructor looked at the class: "How would you respond to this crisis?"

One by one, each recruit stood and verbalized his or her course of action. But the entire class unanimously voted one young man's answer as the best and most authentic response. He simply said, "Remove uniform, mingle with crowd."

If I were honest, I identify with that police recruit from time to time. It's likely you can too. After watching the news, or catching the latest tweet on current events, any of us can become overwhelmed. What can we possibly do about all that trouble? More to the point, what can we do to equip the upcoming generation—with its distinct gifts and challenges—for the world they will inherit?

It is very possible that in the election of 2032, someone from this generation will become the U.S. president. Doubtless, Generation iY will be leading companies, military bases, governments, nonprofits, schools, and churches. We must begin now to train the hearts and minds of Generation iY if we're to prevent crisis later. The strategy is like planting trees; you work now for the future. It has been wisely noted: "The best time to plant a tree is...twenty years ago. The second best time is...now."

But what exactly do we need to "plant" in the hearts and minds of Generation iY? My brief answer is this: we must instill in them the *habits* and *attitudes* they will need to be effective leaders.

In 2000, The Kellogg Foundation sponsored a study of both private and state universities by the Higher Education Research Institute. The objective was to find out whether schools really were developing tomorrow's leaders, as they claim to do. In the end, they drew some interesting conclusions that confirm what I have just proposed. Allow me to list just a handful:

- *Every student has some leadership potential.*
- *Leadership virtues can no longer be the property of an exclusive group.*
- *We cannot separate leadership from values.*
- *Leaders are made, not born.*
- *In today's complex world, every student will need leadership skills.*[1]

Can Everyone Be a Leader?

That raises a question I am often asked: can every young person be a leader? *Should* everyone aspire to fulfill a leadership role?

It all depends on how you define the word *leader*.

If you define it in the traditional fashion—that a leader is someone in a position of authority or in charge of a group of people in an organization—then the answer is no. Not everyone and certainly not every student is gifted to become the president, the chairman, the CEO, or the supervisor of a team of people. If leadership means possessing a gift to organize groups of people to accomplish a task, then it's obviously not for everyone.

If we define leadership differently however, we open up an entirely new perspective. What if we think of leadership more in terms of influence? What if, instead of focusing on positions, we focused on leveraging our influence to benefit others? What if the point was serving others and watching our influence increase as we serve in our areas of strength?

Focusing on that kind of leadership changes the whole picture. Being an influencer is an available option to anyone regardless of gifting, background, or personality. So I'd like to propose a new and different definition for the kind of positive leadership we must instill in Generation iY: *Leadership is leveraging my influence for a worthwhile cause.*

We all exercise some influence, some kind of power over others—and this is a good thing. Granted, power can be perverted. History is full of leaders who tried to dominate others by force, such as Nero, Stalin, Hitler and Saddam Hussein. But we cannot let counterfeits of good leadership convince us that leadership should be avoided. In fact, if there is a counterfeit, it means there is something genuine that's valuable.

I believe healthy leadership is intended to be about serving others in the area of our giftedness. It's more about connection than control. As people mature, we should naturally uncover our primary gifts, and by serving those gifts up to the world, we'll naturally influence a sum of people. Becoming a leader is about moving from merely being influenced by the world around you to being an influencer in that world.

I meet such influencers all the time, on every campus I speak. Many are introverts. Some are downright shy. They may not have a clue as to what profession they should choose, and the thought of "being in charge" may be foreign to them. But they often have a calling they want to fulfill, and they are choosing to have a positive influence on their world. As far as I'm concerned, they are growing leaders.

But what about those men and women who are natural take-charge types—the ones who do end up running organizations and even countries? Aren't those leaders at all? Of course they are. They're just a specific *kind* of leader. I think of them as "Leaders" with a capital *L*—or *habitual leaders*. They are the born chiefs who tend to be good at organizing or inspiring others. They feel comfortable running point on just about any project. And they make up only about 10 to15 percent of the population.

The remaining 85 to 90 percent, however, are potentially "leaders" with a lowercase *l*—or *situational leaders*. They often don't feel like leaders, but they bloom when they find a situation that fits their identity—their passions and their strengths. It's their sweet spot, their zone—the particular combination of place, time, and role where they can leverage their best influence and fulfill their purpose. When they get there, they come alive and actually come into their own as leaders.

Our goal, as we work with Generation iY, should be to help young people find their "situation"—the sweet spot where they are most...

- *Confident. (They are excited and optimistic.)*
- *Intuitive. (They naturally know what to do.)*
- *Productive. (Their activity gets results.)*
- *Comfortable. (They feel at home and natural.)*
- *Magnetic. (They are appealing and exhibit charisma.)*
- *Satisfied. (They are fulfilled and rewarded.)*
- *Influential. (They exercise their best influence.)*

There will always be folks who have a natural bent for organizing large teams of people or inspiring large groups of people to follow a particular vision. But if leadership is only for this small minority, we'll never accomplish the good that needs to happen in our lifetime. We need a new generation of leaders who want to solve problems and serve people. Let's use our own leadership skills to help all iYers find their sweet spot and take their place in history as leaders with influence.

No Excuses!

Leadership is...
- more about disposition than position.
- more about service than superiority.
- more about perspective than behavior.
- leveraging my influence for a worthwhile cause.

I hear loads of excuses as to why people (young or old) just can't be a leader. They are varied, but I've found one common thread. All of the excuses fail to embrace what I consider to be an authentic definition for leadership. Here are some of the most common excuses:

Excuse #1: "I Can't Lead. I Don't Have a Position of Authority."

This excuse stems from equating leadership with a power position instead of defining it in terms of influence. Note that influence and authority are not synonymous (though one person can have both). Authority comes from a title or position or role that enables one person to require other people to do what he or she tells them to do. This is not influence, but obligation or manipulation or intimidation. A title can give you authority, but it cannot give you influence or make you a leader. Healthy influence is earned by the credibility you bring to a relationship or an organization. Some of the greatest leaders in history never had a title or position. In fact, I would say that if you need a title to accomplish a task, something is not working right.

Excuse #2: "If Everyone Is a Leader, Then Who Is Following?"

I hear this question all the time, but I believe it displays poor logic and an outdated understanding of leadership. If we define healthy leadership the way I have in this chapter, it's easy to see that we are *all* leading and we are *all* following. If I am leveraging my influence, using it to have a positive impact on my world, and you are doing the same, then we are all leading in some way. It isn't about one person being in charge and everyone else following orders.

To ask, "If everyone is leading, then who's following?" is like asking folks at a shopping mall, "If everyone is selling, then who is buying?" The answer is simple: Everyone is selling and everyone is buying. The people who sell sandwiches at the food court are selling to the clothing-store employees during lunchtime, and vice versa—the clothing-store employees are selling new outfits to the food court employees.

So it is with healthy leadership. Everyone leads from his or her area of strength. We are all leading and influencing in certain areas. Everyone is involved in an economy of influence.

Excuse #3: "I'm Just Not the Leadership Type."

Many people believe that people are either natural-born leaders or they are not and that we should not try to force someone to lead who isn't a "natural." They assume certain personality types are more suited to leadership roles than others. But as we have seen, anyone can be a leader when they find a situation that fits them, when the problem matches the problem solver. When that happens, they become the right one to lead in that particular situation.

I teach that every student who is willing has the potential to lead and influence others—no matter the temperament, personality, natural gifts or what some call "cognitive type."[2] That means all kinds of kids can be leaders if we let them do it in their own style, including:

- *Drivers. These are the strong-willed kids who tend to want to be in charge. They naturally pursue goals but may need to learn people skills, patience, and planning. In a group setting, they should be in charge of setting goals.*
- *Diplomats. These kids are peacemakers. They want harmony and cooperation. They are naturally good with people but may need to learn to cultivate their own values, vision, and convictions. They should be in charge of building teams.*

- **Dreamers.** *These are often-misunderstood kids with boundless creativity, imagination, and energy. They offer out-of-the-box thinking but may need to learn to focus on one target at a time. They should be the visionaries of a team.*

For years I have reminded people that the most introverted of people will influence ten thousand others in an average lifetime. What if all of us who don't feel like great leaders didn't try to influence at all? What if we just left leadership up to those who like to take charge? That would be like saying you don't have to pay taxes if you don't have lot of money, or you don't have to interact with people if you don't have the "gift of gab," or you don't have to wait at stoplights if you have no patience. That's ludicrous. We all have the responsibility to do what we can, but to go about it based upon our strengths.

Excuse #4: But No One Is Asking Me to Lead. I Don't Have the Opportunity.

Throughout history, the finest leaders didn't wait to step forward until someone asked them to do so. They emerged when they spotted a need and wanted to do something about it. They were simply individuals who became dissatisfied with their current reality and, instead of complaining, became problem solvers.

There will be times, in other words, when an opportunity or a crisis will surface, and someone must respond. No one will ask directly, but someone will simply know it is time to take action. I believe leaders step forward for a handful of reasons:

- *Some are gifted to lead—they are enabled by their ability.*
- *Some are positioned to lead—they are enabled by some authority.*

These are the people we traditionally think of as leaders. But this isn't the only way people become leaders.

- *Some are situated to lead—they are enabled by an opportunity.*
- *Some are summoned to lead—they are enabled by a crisis.*

These people draw on their gifts and perspective and begin handling the situation...and a brand-new leader will be born.

Excuse #5: Leadership Is Only for a Select Few in a Top Role of Authority.

More and more researchers agree that leadership is a 360-degree proposition. We influence all around us. In fact, most of the people who influence their team, their corporation, their nonprofit organization, and even their nation are not the top office-holders of those organizations. Our leadership doesn't have to be limited to managing those below us. We can also "lead up" (to our bosses); we can "lead out" (to our peers); we can "lead down" (to those under us). Most important, we can—and must—lead ourselves. Dee Hock, founder and former CEO of Visa International, was the first person I heard propose this notion, and I believe he's right on. Influence happens everywhere—and often from the middle of the pack.

When we define leadership this way, it puts the cookies on the bottom shelf. Every one of us can do it. And every one of us can help someone else to do it. Every one of us has the potential to be an effective mentor to a potential leader of the iY generation.

The Least Likely Leader

I am convinced that Mother Teresa never tried to be a great leader. She left Albania at age nineteen and made her way to Calcutta, India, to teach at a Catholic girls' school. But even as she fulfilled her teaching duties, she found herself called to something else. She would peer outside her classroom windows to see beggars, she would walk past sick and dying people on the way to the market, and her heart broke for them. She eventually became principal of the school, but she could never shake the haunting sight of the homeless, the destitute, and the dying on the streets of Calcutta. She felt she had to do something to help.

She ventured out alone at first, seeking ways to provide some compassion and dignity for the poor and dying. Her influence in the city deepened when she treated a dying Hindu leader and restored him to health. Eventually others joined her effort and her work became known throughout the world. By 1979, she had won a Nobel Peace Prize by doing things that most people try to avoid. She founded and led what is now the largest order of its kind, the Sisters of Charity, and started eleven more organizations before she died in August of 1997. She was invited to speak to the Harvard faculty and students as well as to U.S. presidents. More than once, she was voted the most influential woman in the world.

Mother Teresa never pursued fame. Her goal was never to be in charge and make people do what she said. But she was a phenomenal leader because she found her calling. She discovered her gift and served it up to the world. Her story is a beautiful embodiment of a basic reality: Leadership and influence are byproducts of using our gifts in an area we have a passion for and offering them in the service of others.

You're Never Too Young to Be a Leader

- Wolfgang Amadeus Mozart composed his first symphony at age 8.
- Bill Gates started Microsoft at age 19.
- Trevor Ferrell began Trevor's Place to feed the homeless at age 12.
- John Wesley launched the beginnings of the Methodist movement at age 17.
- Albert Einstein wrote his first scientific paper at age 16.
- Stephen Spielberg directed his first indie film at age 16.
- Mark Zuckerberg launched Facebook at age 19.
- Louis Braille designed his system of reading for the blind at age 15.
- Josiah became king of Israel at age 8 and began reforming the country at age 16.
- Joan of Ark led three thousand French knights into battle at age 17.
- Sagen Woolrey started a free-lunch program for the poor at age 12.
- Steve Jobs launched Apple Computers at age 21.
- Pioneer missionaries of the Student Volunteer Movement in the late 1800s set out to sea when they were 18 to 24.
- Teresa of Calcutta started her work in India at age 19.
- Cassie Burnall stood for her faith at gunpoint at age 17.
- DesMonte Love led kids to safety in Hurricane Katrina at age 6.
- George Williams started the YMCA at age 23.
- Zach Hunter launched a modern initiative to set slaves free at age 15.[3]

One of the important lessons of history is that we should never underestimate a person's potential. That was true of Mother Teresa, and it's true of every single member of the iY generation. With the proper guidance, every one of them can be a leader, a person of influence. After all, some of history's most significant leaders got their start at a very young age, and they didn't fit a predictable profile.

Look at the list above and reflect for a moment on how the gifts of young leaders have changed the lives of others. If we are up to the challenge, if we have the patience and foresight, if we have faith in their potential, I believe there are untold numbers of new young leaders to be discovered and developed. All these young people need is someone to come along beside them and guide them, to challenge them to be the leaders they can be. And I believe there's no time to wait.

Growing Leaders Are Made, Not Born

I've referenced the Growing Leaders organization frequently in this book because I'm passionate about what we do. Growing Leaders was launched in 2003 because we wanted to redefine what it means to lead and to unleash a generation of young people to transform the world. Our goal is to turn ordinary students into growing leaders who stand in countercultural contrast to their peers around the world. (See the chart below.) How will this happen? We believe growing leaders are made, not born. Even the natural take-charge person may need to learn patience, teamwork, and people skills. Shyer people might need some encouragement to step up. All need some guidance to grow into the best version of themselves.

And this is where you come in. Whether you're a parent, a teacher, a coach, a youth worker, or even a boss, you have the opportunity to serve as a mentor to a young person. You can be one who leads the leaders of tomorrow.

For the remainder of the chapter, I want to suggest some guidelines for how you can make a difference.

What Is a Growing Leader?

Ordinary Students	Growing Leaders
Self-absorbed	Sacrificial
Imitate others	Authentic
Apathetic	Committed
Consuming/greedy	Generous
Presumptuous	Grateful
Controlling	Empowering
Status quo	Hungry mind
"What can I get?"	"What can I give?"
"It's about the money."	"It's about a mission."
Blend in	Stand out

www.GrowingLeaders.com

Healthy Habitudes® for Growing Leaders

I have now entered my fourth decade working with high-school and college students. During that time, I have made it my goal to determine what they most need to succeed in life and how adults can best meet those needs.

I've determined that "what" and "how" are both vital questions to answer if we plan to equip Generation iY to be effective leaders. Let's summarize those two issues first.

The "what" of leading Generation iY has to do with the content they must master if they are going to be effective leaders in the future. What are the issues they are in desperate need of wrestling with? What do they need to learn and embrace?

The list could be endless. But I believe the top items ought to be those *habits* and *attitudes* that will open the door widely for them and enable them to lead no matter what kind of challenges they encounter.

As I have studied young people and leadership, I've come to believe there are at least four essential qualities that are intrinsic to healthy leadership—the qualities that enable a person to leverage his or her influence positively. It's crucial to note that though some kids display them naturally, they can also be learned. In fact, I believe we must deliberately nurture these four qualities in our young people because they're foundational for future success. In essence, they are "what" we must help Generation iY to develop.

Leadership Quality #1: Perception

The first leadership signal has to do with the way a person thinks. Leaders perceive the world differently than the majority of their peers; they're able to see a bigger picture. While they remain most concerned with their own needs (like most youth), their perspective extends beyond those needs. They see how situations impact others around them, and they can look beyond the immediate moment.

Perception can show itself in a number of ways. For instance, a twelve-year-old may arrive at a restaurant with her parents knowing the family will be meeting friends for a meal. Without instruction, she enters the restaurant and figures out how big the table must be and how many chairs they'll need to request of the hostess.

Leadership Quality #2: Responsibility

Leaders are motivated to cover bases and make things right even without being told to do so. Young people with this quality feel responsible for outcomes. They assume it is up to them to help solve problems or correct false statements or even help someone who cannot do something for themselves. They "own" the tasks they're given. Their sense of responsibility may take the form of attention to detail and concern about matters that their peers might find trivial. Other times, it manifests itself as an extra effort to reach a desired goal or fulfill a task as thoroughly as possible. Young people who display this trait are often an establishment's best workers.

Leadership Quality #3: Gratitude

Research on what gratitude does for a person has shown results that are nothing short of amazing. Not long ago, I listened to Dr. Jean Twenge confirm the positive power of gratitude in youth. In a speech to educators, she stressed that a grateful attitude subdues self-absorption, depression, and anger. (It is difficult to be grateful and angry at the same time.) What's more, gratitude fosters hope and humility.

Reflect on this for a moment. People who have an "attitude of gratitude" naturally express humility as they acknowledge thanks for the people and experiences they've encountered. Gratitude also lends hope as the grateful person focuses on the positive input in their life instead of the things they never received.

I no longer hire team members who don't express gratitude about their past. This quality may seem disconnected from their leadership but I've come to believe the two walk hand in hand. Gratitude enables people to see holistically and to recognize that life is about something bigger than them.

Leadership Quality #4: Initiative

This is the internal drive to act. When leaders perceive something could be done to improve a situation, they believe it *should* be done, and they step out first to do it. They don't necessarily wait for peers to approve. At times, they don't even wait to see if their behavior is the norm or if it is safe. They go first.

This quality can lead young people to do some very stupid things—things they might even get punished for. Immaturity might color their judgment, but that urge to act is a clear sign of a leader's desire to take initiative. The young person's perception is clear and his dissatisfaction is compelling. I've known kids to get involved with recycling bottles or raising money for a friend who has cancer or even collecting clothes and food for Haiti because they have a strong sense of initiative.

The "How"—Delivering the "What"

Perception, responsibility, gratitude, and initiative—those are what we must help Generation iY master so that they can effectively lead us into the future. How we do that has to do with delivery. It's about communicating in ways that this EPIC generation can receive them. I've already suggested some of these in chapter 11, but in the following pages I'd like to get a little more practical and specific by sharing some ideas and methods that have worked for me.

When I began creating the Habitudes® curriculum in 2004, my goal was to communicate timeless principles in a relevant, right-brain fashion. Designed to help students develop leadership habits and attitudes, the four-book Habitudes® set employs images, questions, stories, and exercises. The books are short. They do not feel like textbooks. They're also available electronically via podcasts, DVDs, video streams, and PDF downloads. (To preview these resources, visit www.Habitudes.org.)

The Habitudes® curriculum is deliberately designed to deliver what Generation iY needs to learn in the way they learn it best—to allow teachers, coaches, parents, employers, and youth workers to "put their training on ICE" by using:

Images, which lead to...
Conversations, which lead to...
Experiences...which change lives.

As we have seen, this is how Generation iY learns. To them, a picture is worth a thousand words. When they talk about the images, they get to upload their own thoughts through conversation instead of enduring the usual "download" teaching style they often experience in school or church. Finally, the conversation leads to a shared experience that fosters better retention. The combination of pictures (images), response (conversation), and action (experiences) increases the chance of actually getting through to the iY generation. I am convinced if we ever hope to connect long-term with Generation iY, we'll fare better engaging their right brain with an image instead of approaching the left brain with information. (For a step by step plan on teaching with images, visit www.SaveTheirFuture.com/Habitudes.)

Cultivating Three Kinds of Intelligence

Helping young people grow isn't just a matter of delivering content, of course. It's about developing men and women who leverage their influence in positive ways—which is another way of saying we must cultivate three vital qualities in Generation iY:

- *Emotional intelligence. We need to help them develop their EQ— self-awareness, self-management, social awareness, and relationship management.*
- *Moral intelligence. We need to coach them toward robust character—personal discipline, secure sense of self, strong positive values. (Perhaps we could call this MQ.)*
- *Leadership intelligence. Finally, we need to encourage clear vision, courage, priorities, big-picture perspective, and planning skills (LQ).*

Perhaps more than traditional targets like GPA, SAT or ACT scores, or even IQ rankings, we should aim toward helping young people increase their EQ, MQ, and LQ. All three of these "intelligences" will significantly nurture healthy leaders in this emerging generation.

Here's an example that hits me close to home. I've mentioned already that my daughter Bethany is a diplomat. She is not a Leader, but a leader—a situational leader rather than a habitual one. Her nature is to be laid-back and casual. However, because she has developed the three important areas above, she has naturally stepped up to lead in a variety of contexts at her college. She has been a resident advisor (RA) in the dorms. She has been a student trustee. She has also served on the executive team for the annual leadership conference and as a teacher's assistant.

Not long ago, Bethany called me and told me how inadequate she felt when she was asked to serve in another leadership role. She knew she could handle the duties, but she confided that there were so many other smarter students on campus who could fill that role as well.

I simply reminded her that good leaders aren't necessarily the ones with the highest IQ, but the ones with the highest EQ, MQ, and LQ. Faculty and staff had noticed she was savvy in relationships, that she had strong character and thought like a leader. She was exactly the kind of person they were looking for.

Mentoring Strategies for Generation iY

To produce young leaders who possess these qualities, I believe we must engage in five specific mentoring strategies. Each year I select a community of emerging leaders, choose one of the needs listed above, and then pursue these strategies, all targeted on helping the young person develop in that one need area.

Mentoring Strategy #1: Expose.

One important activity to build young leaders is to connect them to people who possess the quality you're focusing on. Expose them to great leaders, people with high EQs and robust character. Raise their awareness of extraordinary people and different cultures.

For years, Growing Leaders, has included interns on our team. I have enjoyed taking those interns all over our home city of Atlanta and exposing them to great ideas and leaders. I've taken them to Chick-fil-A corporate headquarters to meet executives who model "second mile service," to the Martin Luther King, Jr. Memorial to allow them to reflect on a man with vision, to the World of Coca-Cola to talk about how ideas grow and strategy unfolds. I help those student interns learn to interview leaders and grasp what is important and reproducible.

This kind of exposure is always the highlight of the students' internship. Countless former interns contact me saying these experiences were priceless and helped to direct them as they later made decisions about their life and career.

Mentoring Strategy #2: Explain

Young people need mentors not for information, but for interpretation. They need help in understanding what they're learning and how to respond to it wisely. And mentors can be invaluable in translating what they've seen and heard into life application, helping them glean what will be most relevant for their own strengths and style. I'm not talking about imparting great wisdom—just spending time over coffee, talking about life.

In my work with interns, after a visit with an executive leader or other potential role model, I often schedule time to talk about the visit. I'll point out strengths in the leader that I feel the young person may share. I want them to gain some transferable concepts from the person, not necessarily become a clone. I often find that time spent discussing what they're picking up is the most rewarding part of my week.

As a kid, Michael Dell frustrated his parents with his curious mind. When he was fifteen years old, he begged his mom and dad for an Apple II computer, but when they gave him one, he promptly took it apart. Over the years, Michael and his dad had many conversations about where he best fit. Based on these discussions, Dell eventually figured it out. He dropped his pre-med major in college to do something he was more suited for: launching Dell Computers.

Mentoring Strategy #3: Exemplify

Young leaders in the making need role models, and that's part of the mentor's role—to let them see a model of healthy leadership, a healthy EQ, and strong ethics and character. Nothing beats a sermon they can see.

My wife did this beautifully as our two children grew up. A woman of strong character and rigorous honesty, she's been known to drive back to the grocery store, kids in tow, to pay for an item that slipped past the cashier. It would have been easy to ignore the mistake; a can of beans or loaf of bread didn't cost much. But she knew the importance of letting our children see us living out our values.

People do what people see. This is why some of my favorite mentors have been men and women of very few words. They didn't have to talk a lot because their actions made the message clear. It's cliché but true: after one week, people remember very little of what they heard, but much more of what they've seen.

Mentoring Strategy #4: Evaluate

The fourth task for a mentor is one that is often omitted or ignored—possibly because it can be uncomfortable. In fact, it is conspicuously absent between adults and youth today. Young people need someone to give them honest feedback, to help them evaluate and assess their progress and shortcomings.

As we have seen, Generation iY kids tend to think well of themselves. Many were showered with ribbons, trophies, and praise all through their K–12 school years. As a result, they have huge blind spots. They need honest feedback. While it may be difficult at first, this is what turns potential into performance. It can be a priceless missing piece that turns them into true leaders. Honest feedback will be instrumental in building emotional, moral, and leadership intelligence in an iY young person.

Mentoring Strategy #5: Encourage

Mentors can encourage young people to develop leadership potential by encouraging them and supporting them as they:

- *Explore their possibilities*—*to hone in on their gifts and passions.*
- *Experiment with roles and tasks*—*through volunteer work, part-time jobs, even school courses. Nothing beats firsthand experience.*
- *Examine how they felt as they explored and experimented. Did the tasks feel natural? Did their work add value to anyone's life? Did anything make them feel uncomfortable?*
- *Expect feedback from others about where their gifts most fit. Confirmation from people further along than they are can be invaluable. So can honest criticism— but learning to listen can be a challenge.*

Time to Act: A Plan for Launching Leaders

Generation iY has enormous potential to build a positive future if parents, teachers, coaches, youth leaders, and other adults can help them leverage their influence and take their place as leaders. In the final pages of this book, I'd like to suggest some ideas for doing that.

1. **Let them be different from previous generations.** Generation iY is motivated to create new realities. They have boundless energy and creative spirits. It's important to encourage these qualities while helping iYers be themselves and define their own identity. (It may be far different from their older siblings).

2. **Work with them to develop strong personal values.** They live in an eclectic and pluralistic world. If they are not value-driven, they will shift as they encounter pressure from the culture. They must come to see themselves as individuals who possess a solid set of values and can collaborate with each other and with other generations to create something new.

3. **Help them learn to make and keep short-term commitments.** Young men and woman accustomed to "instant everything" may well need some specific training in deferring gratification and keeping commitments. Help them put legitimate wins under their belt—not contrived "everyone wins" accolades! Succeeding at such short-term commitments could lead them into attempting longer, deeper commitments. If they commit to a team or a project, for instance, and later want to quit because they didn't get a lot of playing time or the project got boring, challenge them to stick to it until the end of the season. (Remind them they don't need to recommit, but they must follow through with what they started.)

4. **Work with them to simplify their lives and deal with stress.** As we have seen, Generation iY students feel a lot of pressure...and they can put pressure on themselves. They have a passion to make a difference and get all they can out of life, and many have perfectionist tendencies. They must learn to simplify, to figure out what really matters, to set realistic goals and organize their time. They may need help turning their lofty dreams into bite-sized objectives with doable deadlines. In the process, they will learn to set short-term, achievable goals and maintain momentum toward their long-term goals. At the same time, it's important to realize that for an iYer, multitasking isn't necessarily stressful, and simplifying life doesn't necessarily mean "one thing at a time." In fact, forcing an iYer to stop multitasking by forbidding cell phones, music, and so forth may actually add to his or her stress. If a kid is doing well in school, relating well to others, and getting enough sleep to be healthy, having lots of "i" input may not be a problem.

5. **Communicate that there is meaning even in the small, mundane tasks.** Give them a sense of the big picture and how all the little things they do fit into the big picture of history, or at least into the big picture of the organization. Provide a macro view in their present micro world. (As an educator, for instance, I have asked students to set up chairs—a quite menial task—but I've taken time first to share how that simple job helps us achieve the strategic objective for the student body.) As much as possible, provide consistent feedback, at least at the beginning of a task. Help young people determine

personal achievement goals, and stick by them in a mentoring role while they work to achieve them. And don't forget to celebrate even small wins.

6. **Help them to focus.** As we have seen, Generation Y tends to spread themselves too thin and go wide instead of deep. Work with them to focus on one meaningful objective at a time. You might sit down with a kid and list all the goals she has for the week, then help her prioritize, challenging her to do first things first and not proceed to a new item until she has completed the item before it.

7. **Work with them to appreciate strengths in others.** Generation iY already embraces diversity. In fact, they may be able to teach adults a thing or two about that. But they might need a little encouragement to recognize other people's strengths. Highlight individual differences and point out how each person's gifts and skills adds value to a team. In addition, help them become willing to function independently of their friends. Work to build interdependence rather than codependence.

8. **Create opportunities for face-to-face interaction so they can learn to interact in the nonvirtual world (other than school).** For instance, my wife, and I have had our kids host parties where they learn how to initiate face-to-face relationships. We worked to position them in social settings where they interacted with people outside of their peer group, both younger and older. By the time they turned twelve, we also worked with other parents to prepare them to resolve conflict with friends (peers), on their own when possible. We felt it was important for them to learn to communicate and work out differences as well as enjoy being together.

9. **Provide opportunities for kids to participate in a cause that's bigger than they are.** Challenge them to expand their horizons and give their time and money sacrificially for a cause that speaks to them. Give them the chance to invest their lives in something truly worthwhile. I have done this with teens and college students for years, and more recently I have done it with my own kids. Trips to a local rescue mission or to a developing nation can give young people a chance to serve and see how most of the world lives with less. (One in six people in the world live on a dollar a day.) Even work days at local social service agencies can offer kids the chance to be involved. Encourage them to bring their friends if it makes the experience easier. Their lives will be richer when they learn that fulfillment comes not from personal pleasure, but from global purpose.

10. **Enable them to take control of their lives, to boss their calendars.** Young people tend to be reactive, not proactive, when it comes to their time. They don't have a plan; they just let things happen. Work with them to set their priorities and require them (within limits) to live with the consequences of their decisions. Let them see that failure isn't final and poor judgment does not necessarily reflect poor character. Help them slow down and make sense of what goals they really want to pursue. Balance schedules and allow kids to ease into challenges that are beyond a parent's ability to shelter them.

11. **Resource them with your network.** Their dreams will require your assets. In other words, you can accelerate their growth by exposing them to the social networks you've established. Help them pursue internships at organizations you're a part of and invite them to gatherings where they can meet potential mentors. For the last few years, I've taken my kids to meet adults who do what they've dreamed of doing in their careers. Over dinner, they can ask questions they've prepared to learn more about the people and their professions. If nothing else, such outings give kids practice in interacting outside of their limited world of peers.

12. **Challenge them to take their place in history.** Do what you can to give them a sense of destiny and a desire to make a long-term contribution. Talk to them about heroes from history (historical mentors) and give special focus to ones from their grandparents' generation. In my experience, Millennial young people long for mentors who are genuine and accessible. In fact, assessments we've done at Growing Leaders indicate that mentoring communities are their preferred method of learning. They don't want a sage on the stage, remember, but a guide on the side. Know anyone who could fill this role?

Transforming the Future

I wish you could meet Taylor. He just wrote me an e-mail to say thanks for helping him launch into his adult life after college. These kinds of e-mails are always encouraging, but Taylor's was the epitome of what I am talking about in this chapter.

I met Taylor four years ago. He had begun his college years as a shy, cautious, self-absorbed freshman. He had come from a small town and had no real goals except to survive college. The last thing he expected to do was to make an impact on the world around him.

During his first year, Taylor attended an event that we hosted in Atlanta and caught a vision for being a leader. Although it didn't fit his self-image, he decided to join a mentoring community that met on a weekly basis. And week by week, as he did this, his perspective was transformed.

In his sophomore year, Taylor joined a city outreach program and began serving underprivileged children. His vision grew. He wanted to get other students involved, so he took over the leadership of the city outreach during his junior year. By the time he was a senior, he was so convinced of his calling to make an impact on his world that he decided to run for student body president. Believe it or not, this shy young man won the election.

When he wrote me later, he actually said that our organization had "saved his life." He also said that during the spring semester of his final year, he was busy training his successor, so that the leadership virus he had caught would remain contagious. Taylor is now in Los Angeles, serving underprivileged kids.

The good news is—if Taylor can do it, anyone can do it. I believe there is a Taylor somewhere near you. This may be your chance to transform his future—and our future. Remember, "If you want happiness for a lifetime, help the next generation."

LINKING UP

For ongoing ideas on how to develop leadership qualities in Generation iY, go to **www.SaveTheirFutureNow.com/LeadershipIdeas**.

Acknowledgments

It sounds cliché, but no book is ever written solely by one author. This one is no exception.

I have to thank my team at Growing Leaders, who constantly serve the students, staff, and schools we work with each year. They inspire me and provide ideas for the work we do each week. I want to add a special thanks to Sarah Johnson, who helped with research and worked diligently to locate documentation for the notes section. Sarah, you are amazing. I need to especially thank Holly Moore, our Vice President and my great partner, who read these pages over and over to make sure they said what must be said. Thanks for who you are and what you mean to me.

I want to thank our board of directors at Growing Leaders who insisted three years ago that this book had to be written. They were right and they've stood by me as we undertook the project together.

I want to thank Anne Christian Buchanan, who edited this book. She put in far more hours than she bargained for, mixing and matching, cutting and pasting, trimming it down from its original size of three hundred fifty pages. Thanks, Anne, for your patience and sleepless nights.

I want to thank Anne Alexander, who did the copy editing, making sure we didn't miss a thing, from grammar to punctuation. You saved us a few times. Thanks, Anne for your years of friendship and belief in our cause.

I want to thank The A Group, who believed in this project enough to say you wanted to market it and insure the word got out to parents, teachers, coaches, retailers, pastors, youth workers, and employers across America. A special thanks goes to Tami Heim and Shannon Litton for your intuition and support.

Finally, I want to thank my family for the years of belief and support you've shown me. My wife, Pam, and my two children, Bethany and Jonathan, who are consistent sounding boards about Generation iY because you live in that world. I love you.

Notes

Chapter 2

1. American College Health Association, *National College Health Assessment Spring 2007*, reference group data report 55, no. 4 (January-February 2007):195–206.

2. Neil Howe and William Strauss, *Millennials and the Pop Culture: Strategies for a New Generation of Consumers* (McLean, VA: LifeCourse Associates, 2006).

3. Neil Howe, "Excerpt from Who Is the Millennial Generation," PowerPoint presentation, Council of Independent Colleges (full presentation originally given at the Presidents Institute, January 4–7, 2003, Naples, Florida), www.cic.org/conferences_events/presidents/previouspres/pi2003millennial-generation.pdf.

4. Neil Howe and William Strauss, *Millennials and K–12 Schools: Educational Strategies for a New Generation* (McLean, VA: LifeCourse Associates, 2008), 3.

5. Jean M. Twenge, *Generation Me: Why Today's Young Americans Are More Confident, Assertive, Entitled—and More Miserable Than Ever Before* (New York: Free Press, 2007), 69.

6. Jean M. Twenge and W. Keith Campbell, *The Narcissism Epidemic: Living in the Age of Entitlement* (Free Press: New York, 2009).

7. Twenge, *Generation Me*, 53.

8. Neil Howe and William Strauss, *Millennials and K–12 Schools.*

9. Twenge, *Generation Me*, 69.

10. Ibid.

Chapter 3

1. Neil Howe and William Strauss, *Millennials Rising*, 198, 204, 207.

2. Lev Grossman, "Grow Up? Not So Fast," *Time*, January 16, 2005, http://www.time.com/time/magazine/article/0,9171,1018089-4,00.html.

3. Stephanie Steinberg, "A Change of Heart for College Students," reported in *USA Today*, June 8, 2010, 7D

4. Jon Swartz, "Purveyors of Porn Scramble to Keep Up with Internet," *USA Today*, June 6, 2007, 4B.

5. Quoted in Cole Kazdin and Imaeyen Iganga, "The Truth About Teens Sexting," Good Morning America page of CBSNews.com, April 15, 2009, http://abcnews.go.com/GMA/story?id=7337547&page=1.

6. NielsonWire, "In U.S., SMS Text Messaging Tops Mobile Phone Calling," September 22, 2008, http://blog.nielsen.com/nielsenwire/online _mobile/in-us-text-messaging-tops-mobile-phone-calling/.

7. *The Economist*, "The Net Generation: The Kids Are Alright," November 13, 2008, accessed online at http://www.economist.com/culture/ displaystory.cfm?story_id=12591038. (Note: This article is only available to magazine subscribers)

8. Don Tapscott, *Grown Up Digital: How the Net Generation Is Changing Your World* (New York: McGraw Hill, 2008), 6.

9. Ibid., 3–5.

10. *Economist*, "Net Generation."

11. Alexandra Robbins and Abby Wilner, *Quarterlife Crisis: The Unique Challenges of Life in Your Twenties* (New York: Tarcher, 2001).

12. Howe and Strauss, *Millennials Rising*.

13. Mark Bauerlein, *The Dumbest Generation: How the Digital Age Stupefies Young Americans and Jeopardizes Our Future* (New York: Penguin, 2008), 77.

14. CTIA—The Wireless Association and Harris Interactive, "Teenagers: A Generation Unplugged," September 12, 2008, PDF report downloaded from files.ctia.org/pdf/HI_TeenMobileStudy_ResearchReport.pdf.

15. Greg Hearn, quoted in Samantha Healy, "Reality of an Online World," *Sunday Mail*, May 11, 2008, http://www.couriermail.com.au/news/ sunday-mail/reality-of-an[online-world/story-e6frep20-1111116301398.

16. Howe and Strauss, *Millennials Rising*.

17. Mel Levine, *Ready or Not, Here Life Comes* (New York: Simon and Schuster, 2005), 217–218.

18. Bauerlein, *Dumbest Generation*, 3.

19. Howe and Strauss, *Millennials and K–12 Schools*, 4.

20. Ron Alsop, *The Trophy Kids Grow Up: How the Millennial Generation Is Shaking Up the Workplace* (San Francisco: Jossey-Bass, 2008), 27. The

book referenced is David Walsh, *No: Why Kids—of All Ages—Need to Hear It and Ways Parents Can Say It* (New York: Free Press, 2007).

21. Robert D. Putnam, *Bowling Alone: The Collapse and Revival of American Community* (New York: Simon and Schuster, 2001).

22. Alsop, *Trophy Kids Grow Up.*

23. George Barna, *Real Teens: A Contemporary Snapshot of Youth Culture,* (Ventura, CA: Regal Books, 2001).

24. Levine, *Ready or Not,* 27.

25. Ibid., 27.

26. Bauerlein, *Dumbest Generation,* 10.

27. Habitudes® are image-based presentations designed to teach leadership habits and attitudes. For more about the Habitudes® curriculum, see chapters 11 and 12 or visit www.Habitudes.org.

28. Bauerlein, *Dumbest Generation,* 63.

29. *World Watch,* "Matters of Scale," January/February 2000, http://www .worldwatch.org/node/755. Article credits David W. Orr, "Verbicide," *Conservation Biology,* August 1999.

30. Howe and Strauss, *Millennials and K–12 Schools.*

31. Bea Fields, Scott Wilder, Jim Bunch, and Rob Newbold, *Millennial Leaders: Success Stories from Today's Most Brilliant Generation Y Leaders* (Buffalo, IL: Writers of the Round Table Press, 2008), 11. See also Sharon Jayson, "Generation Y's goal? Wealth and fame," *USA Today,* October 1, 2007, http://www.usatoday.com/news/nation/2007-01-09-gen-y -cover_x.htm.

32. Leonard Sweet, *Post-Modern Pilgrims: First Century Passion for the 21st Century World* (Nashville: Broadman and Holman, 2000).

33. Quoted in Fields, Wilder, Bunch, and Newbold, *Millennial Leaders,* 12.

Chapter 4

1. Michael Kimmel, *Guyland: The Perilous World Where Boys Become Men* (New York: Harper Collins, 2008), 11. Quote in the middle of the paragraph is from *Publishers Weekly* review of this book excerpted on the Amazon.com page, accessed at http://www.amazon.com/Guyland -Perilous-World-Where-Become/dp/0060831340.

2. Lev Grossman, "Grow Up? Not So Fast." Time, January 16, 2005. http:// www.time.com/time/magazine/article/0,9171,1018089-1,00.html

3. U. S. Census Bureau, "Back to School: 2009–2010," Facts for Features news release, June 15, 2009, http://www.census.gov/newsroom/

releases/archives/facts_for_features_special_editions/cb09-ff14.html.

4. Deirdre van Dyk, "Parlez Vous Twixter," *Time,* January 24, 2005, http://www.time.com/time/covers/1101050124/sotwixter_chart.html.

5. Grossman, "Grow Up? Not So Fast," 9.

6. Mel Levine, *Ready or Not, Here Life Comes,* 5.

7. Newt Gingrich, "Let's End Adolescence," *Bloomberg Businessweek,* October 30, 2008, http://www.businessweek.com/magazine/content/08_45/b4107085289974.htm.

8. Ibid.

9. *Dictionary of American History*, s. v. "Adolescence" (by Howard Chudacoff), Encyclopedia.com, 2003, http://www.encyclopedia.com/doc/1G2-3401800042.html (accessed May 23, 2010).

10. Ibid.

11. Quoted in Alex and Brett Harris, "Addicted to Adultescence," Pure Intimacy, 2006, http://www.pureintimacy.org/piArticles/A000000423.cfm.

12. Daniel Goleman, *Primal Leadership,* (Boston: Harvard Business School Press, 2002), 4–9.

13. Alison Gopnik, quoted in Robert Boyd, "Teenagers Can't Think Straight, Scientists Say" *Orlando Sentinel,* December 21, 2006, http://articles.orlandosentinel.com/2006-12-21/news/TEENBRAINS21_1_brain-pruning-cells.

14. Ian G. Campbell, "EEG Recording and Analysis for Sleep Research," Current Protocols in Neuroscience, October, 2009, accessed online at http://www.currentprotocols.com/protocol/ns1002.

15. Diana Baumrind, "The Influence of Parenting Style on Adolescent Competence and Substance Use," *The Journal of Early Adolesence*, Vol. 11 No. 1, February 1991 61-62. The online version of the article can be found at: http://jea.sagepub.com/cgi/content/abstract/11/1/56

Chapter 5

1. Peg Tyre, "The Trouble with Boys," *Newsweek,* January 30, 2006, http://www.newsweek.com/id/47522.

2. Ibid.

3. Tom Mortenson, "The State of American Manhood," *Postsecondary Education Opportunity,* September 2006, quoted in Leonard Sax, *Boys Adrift: The Five Factors Driving the Growing Epidemic of Unmotivated Boys and Underachieving Men* (New York: Basic Books, 2007), 8–9.

4. Leonard Sax, "What's Happened to Boys? Young Women These Days Are Driven—But Guys Lack Direction," *Washington Post*, March 31, 2006, http://www.washingtonpost.com/wp-dyn/content/article/2006/03/30/AR2006033001341.html.

5. Samms-Vaughn, "Impact of Family Structure."

6. Jamaica Ministry of Education and Youth, "Absentee Fathers a Major Problem—Henry Wilson," Jamaica Information Service, March 9, 2007, http://www.jis.gov.jm/edcation/html/20070308t100000-0500_11412_jis_absentee_fathers_a_major_problem_henry_wilson.asp.

7. Kazi Jahid Hossain, *Male Involvement in Family Planning in Bangladesh: Factors Constraining Low Use and the Potential for Augmenting the CPR*, CPD-UNFPA Paper 27 (Dhaka, Bangladesh: Centre for Policy Dialogue/United Nations Population Fund, 2003), 1, http://www.cpd.org.bd/pub_attach/unfpa27.pdf.

8. Christina Hoff Sommers, *The War Against Boys: How Misguided Feminism Is Harming Our Young Men* (New York: Simon and Schuster, 2000).

9. Dan Kiley, *The Peter Pan Syndrome: Men Who Have Never Grown Up* (New York: Avon, 1995).

10. Leonard Sax, *Boys Adrift: The Five Factors Driving the Growing Epidemic of Unmotivated Boys and Underachieving Men* (New York: Basic Books, 2007).

11. Ibid., 58.

12. Ibid., 64–65.

13. Quoted in David Schneider, "Smart As We Can Get?" *American Scientist* 94, no. 4 (July-August 2006), http://www.americanscientist.org/issues/pub/2006/7/smart-as-we-can-get.

14. Frank Wilson, *The Hand*, quoted in Richard Louv, *Last Child in the Woods: Saving Our Children from Nature-Deficit Disorder* (Chapel Hill, NC: 2005, 2008), 67.

15. The Center for Successful Parenting, "Can Violent Media Affect Reasoning and Logical Thinking," http://www.sosparents.org/brain%20study.htm. See also "Playing with Kids' Minds," *Indiana University Medicine*, spring 2003, http://www.medicine.indiana.edu/iu_medicine/03_spring/articles/kidsMinds.html.

16. "Study Links Violent Video Games to Violent Thought, Action," *Washington Post*, March 1, 2010, http://voices.washingtonpost.com/checkup/2010/03/study_shows_violent_video_game.html.

17. Tamar Lewin, "At College Women are Leaving Men in the Dust," *New York Times,* July 9, 2006, A-1, 18–19.

18. Sax, Leonard, *Boys Adrift,* 89–90.

19. Linda Johnson, "Adult Use of Drugs for ADHD Doubles," Associated Press, September 5, 2005, quoted in Sax, *Boys Adrift,* 85.

20. David Derbyshire, "Ban Gender-bender Used in Baby Products," *Mail Online,* April 8, 2010, http://dailymail.co.uk/news/article-1264400/ Leading-scientists-urge-Government-ban-gender-bending-chemicals-baby-products.html.

21. Derbyshire, "Ban Gender-bender."

22. Sax, *Boys Adrift,* 107.

23. Ibid., 106–107.

24. National Center for Health Statistics, "Data on Child Health" updated February, 2005. quoted in Sax, *Boys Adrift,* 108–109.

25. Sax, *Boys Adrift,* 104.

26. Ibid., 104–107.

27. Lenore Skenazy, *Free-Range Kids: Giving Our Children the Freedom We Had Without Going Nuts* (San Francisco: Jossey-Bass, 2009).

28. Lance Morrow, John F. Dickerson, John D. Hull, Martha Smilgis, "Men—Are They Really That Bad?" *Time,* February 14, 1994, http://www.time.com/time/magazine/article/0,9171,980115,00.html.

29. "Depression," in *Men and Depression* (Bethesda, MD: National Institute of Mental Health Public Information and Communications Branch), http://www.nimh.nih.gov/health/publications/men-and-depression/complete-index.shtml.

30. Gordon Daulbey, *Healing the Masculine Soul* (Waco, TX: Word), 1988.

Chapter 6

1. Howe and Strauss, *Millennials and K–12 Schools,* 3.

2. Neil Howe and William Strauss, *Helicopter Parents in the Workplace,* nGenera Insight Talent 2.0 Big Idea (Austin, TX: nGenera Insight, November 2007), 4, http://www.wikinomics.com/blog/uploads/helicopter-parents-in-the-workplace.pdf.

3. Ibid.

4. Ibid.

5. *USA Today,* "Snapshots," Pew Charitable Trust Survey, February 2009.

6. Frank A. Clark wrote the text for a one-panel cartoon called "The Coun-

try Parson" for nearly forty years, first for the *Des Moines Register* and later in national syndication. This aphorism, which is widely quoted, was probably one of the Country Parson's offerings.

7. Dave Boehi, "Where Do We Draw the Line?" *Moody Monthly,* June 1989.
8. Nancy Gibbs, "Parents Behaving Badly," *Time,* February 21, 2005, 38.
9. Quoted in Harris H. Simmons, "America's Financial Literacy Crisis," ABA Banking Journal, January 1, 2006, AllBusiness, http://www .allbusiness.com/finance/858065-1.html.

Chapter 7

1. Laura Fraser, "My So-Called Genius," *More,* March 20, 2009, 1, http:// www.more.com/2051/3068-my-so-called-genius/1.
2. Ibid.
3. Ibid.
4. Ibid., 2.
5. Edward E. Gordon, "Help Wanted: Creating Tomorrow's Workforce," *The Futurist* 34, no. 4 (July-August 2000), accessed at Highbeam Research, http://www.highbeam.com/doc/1G1-63173340.html.
6. W. J. Reeves, "College Isn't for Everyone," *USA Today,* May 2003, accessed on BNET, http://www.findarticles.com/p/articles/mi_m1272/ is_2696_131/ai_101497549/.
7. Thomas Reeves, "Some Heretical Thoughts for a New Academic Year," NAS Forums, National Association of Scholars, August 25, 2003, http://www.nas.org/forum_blogger/forum_archives/2003_08_24 _nasof_arch.cfm.
8. Quoted in William Harris, "Heckman's research shows non-cognitive skills promote achievement," *University of Chicago Chronicle* 23, no. 7 (January 8, 2004), http://chronicle.uchicago.edu/040108/heckman.shtml.
9. Lynn Austin, *The Christian Reader,* 2000.
10. Chris Thurman, *The Lies We Believe* (Nashville, TN: Thomas Nelson, 1990).
11. Ibid., 105–106.

Chapter 8

1. United States Department of Labor, Bureau of Labor Statistics, "Employment Situation News Release," December 2009, http://www.bls .gov/news.release/archives/empsit_01082010.htm; see also Richard Wilner, "The Dead End Kids," New York Post, September 27, 2009, http://www.nypost.com/p/news/business/item_AnwaWNOGqsXMuIl GONNXIK#ixzz00f90Pk6p.

2. *USA Today,* "Ready for College, Not for Life," ACT Report, August 8, 1999.

3. Ginger Murphy, "Women in Their 20s Stressed About Life," *Arizona Republic,* May 13, 2008, accessed on *Arizona Living* online print edition, http://www.azcentral.com/arizonarepublic/arizonaliving/ articles/0513dove0513.html.

4. Robbins and Wilner, *Quarterlife Crisis.*

5. Neil Howe and William Strauss, *Millennials Rising,* 186.

6. *Time,* "Time Poll: Over Half (52%) of Young Adults in Debt When They Finish College," January 16, 2005, http://www.time.com/time/press _releases/article/0.8599.1018036.00.html.

7. Penelope Trunk, "What Gen Y Really Wants," *Time,* July 5, 2007, http:// www.time.com/time/magazine/article/0.9171.1640395.00.html.

8. Howe and Strauss, *Millennials Rising.*

9. Sharon Jayson, "Generation Y gets involved," *USA Today,* October 14, 2006, http://www.usatoday.com/news/nation/2006-10-23-gen-next -cover_x.htm.

10. Trunk, "What Gen Y Really Wants."

11. Northwestern Mutual, "New Research on America's Millennials Find Their Mood `Eager but Anxious,'" news release, July 21, 2004, http:// www.northwesternmutualnews.com/article_display.cfm?article_id=1111.

12. W. P. Carey School of Business, Arizona State University, "Millennials in the Workplace: R U Ready?" Knowledge @ W.P. Carey, March 26, 2008, http://knowledge.wpcarey.asu.edu/article.cfm?articleid=1580.

13. Neil Howe, quoted in Kevin Neidermier, "Millennials in the Market- place: Money and the Millennial Generation Marketing to Today's More Practical and Savvy Teen," Teenagers: The Millennial Generation, WKSU.org (Kent State University radio station), December 14, 2004, http://www.wksu.org/news/features/adolescence/story/14.

14. Max DePree, *Leadership Is an Art* (New York: Dell, 1989), 11.

Chapter 9

1. François de Waziéres, *Trophy Kids Grow Up.*

2. Van Dyk, "Parlez Vous Twixter."

3. Ibid.

4. US Dept. of Labor, quoted in Business and Legal Resources, "Improve Engagement and Performance Through Generational Total Awards," HR.BLR.com, May 22, 2008, http://hr.blr.com/HR-news/Staffing- Training/Recruiting/Improve-Engagement-and

-Performance-through-Generat/.

5. Most of these figures were taken from "All in Their Lifetime," a sidebar accompanying Sharon Jayson and Maria Puente, "Gen Y shaped, not stopped, by tragedy," *USA Today*, April 20, 2007, http://www.usatoday .com/news/nation/2007-04-17-millenials_N.htm. I have added a few additional figures from general sources.

6. Sharon Jayson and Maria Puente, "Gen Y Shaped, Not Stopped, by Tragedy," *USA Today*, April 20, 2007, http://www.usatoday.com/news/ nation/2007-04-17-millenials_N.htm.

7. I ask that question in my book, *Nurturing the Leader Within Your Child: What Every Parent Needs to Know* (Nashville: Thomas Nelson, 2004).

8. Gunnar Heinsohn, *Söhne und Weltmacht: Terror Im Aufstieg und Fall de Nationen* (*Sons and World Power: Terror in the Rise and Fall of Nations*), (Zurich: Orell Füssli, 2003).

9. Christian Caryl, "Iraq's Young Blood," *Newsweek*, January 22, 2007.

10. Ibid.

11. Gunnar Heinsohn, "Exploding Population," *New York Times*, January 7, 2008, http://www.nytimes.com/2008/01/17/opinion/17iht-edheinsohn.1.9292632.html?scp=1&sq=exploding%20population%20 gunnar%20heinsohn&st=cse.

12. Caryl, "Iraq's Young Blood."

13. Christopher Caldwell, "Youth and War, a Deadly Duo," *Financial Times*, January 5, 2007, http://www.ft.com/cms/ s/1eb43b70-9cf3-11db-8ec6-0000779e2340,Authorised=false. html?_i_location=http%3A%2F%2Fwww. ft.com%2Fcms%2Fs%2F1%2F1eb43b70-9cf3-11db-8ec6-0000779e2340.html&_i_referer=http%3A%2F%2Fsearch.ft.com%2Fs earch%3FqueryText%3D%2522youth%2Band%2Bwar%252C%2Ba%2B deadly%2Bduo%2522%26ftsearchType%3Dtype_news.

Chapter 10

1. See Daniel H. Pink, *Drive: The Surprising Truth About What Motivates Us* (New York: Riverhead Books, 2009), 18.

2. Liz Worth, "Career Crisis Hits Overachieving Generation Y," *The Star*, May 1, 2008, http://www.thestar.com/living/article/419999.

3. Northwestern Mutual, "New Research on America's Millennials."

4. Marcus Buckingham and Donald O. Clifton, *Now, Discover Your Strengths* (New York: Free Press, 2001), 5–7, 25–27.

5. Ibid., 6, 213.

6. Tim Elmore, *Nurturing the Leader Within Your Child: What Every Parent Needs to Know* (Nashville: Thomas Nelson, 2004).

7. *Time,* "Time Poll."

Chapter 11

1. Sweet introduced this acronym in the book, *Post-Modern Pilgrims: First Century Passion for the 21st Century World* (Nashville: Broadman & Holman, 2000). Growing Leaders has expanded on this idea over the years and applied it directly to leadership training.

2. The Cone of Experience was first published in Edgar Dale's book, *Audio-Visual Methods in Teaching* (New York: Dryden, 1948) and revised slightly in the 1969 edition. Since then, many others have adapted his ideas. My list here is based on Dale's revised list, with my own parenthetical explanations.

3. Daniel H. Pink, *A Whole New Mind: Why Right-Brainers Will Rule the Future* (New York: Riverhead, 2005), 2.

4. Ellen McGirt, "How Chris Hughes Helped Launch Facebook and the Barack Obama Campaign," *Fast Company,* April 1, 2009, http://www.fastcompany.com/magazine/134/boy-wonder.html.

Chapter 12

1. Helen Astin and Alexander Astin, *The Status of Leadership on University Campuses in America* (Los Angeles: Higher Education Research Institute: 2000).

2. The descriptions of the three "cognitive types" is taken from Dana Scott Spears and Ron L. Braund, *Strong Willed Child or Dreamer: Understanding the Crucial Differences between a Strong-Willed Child and a Creative-Sensitive Child* (Nashville: Thomas Nelson, 1996). Spears and Braund's book is aimed specifically at parents of Dreamers, but I find the description of the three types helpful in understanding how people who think and act very differently can still grow into healthy leaders.

3. Growing Leaders, *Onefluence Manifesto,* 2006, PDF file downloaded from www.onefluence.org.

A Word About Growing Leaders

Do you want to learn more about how to mentor and train the next generation in your school, home, athletic team, workplace, or faith community?

Founded by Dr. Tim Elmore, Growing Leaders is an Atlanta-based nonprofit organization providing public schools, state universities, civic organizations, and corporations with the tools they need to help develop young leaders who can impact and transform society.

Growing Leaders offers a variety of resources to help you equip the Generation iY students in your life to live and lead well. These tools include:

- *Student leadership training curriculum for educators*
- *Leadership resources for mentoring communities*
- *An annual National Leadership Forum*
- *Conferences held at your organization or campus*

Some of the organizations that use our training resources include:

- *The U.S. Department of Justice*
- *Boys and Girls Clubs of America*
- *National Future Farmers of America organization*
- *The Kansas City Royals Baseball Club (minor league affiliates)*
- *University of Texas*
- *University of Alabama*
- *Stanford University*
- *University of North Carolina*
- *Baylor University*
- *Pepperdine University*
- *Georgia Institute of Technology*
- *University of Oklahoma*
- *Duke University*
- *University of South Carolina*
- *Florida State University*
- *Auburn University*

Tim Elmore and the Growing Leaders team are available to help you invest wisely in the next generation. For more information, please visit www.GrowingLeaders.com.

About the Author

DR. TIM ELMORE is the founder and president of Growing Leaders (www.Growing Leaders.com), an Atlanta-based nonprofit organization created to develop emerging leaders. Since founding Growing Leaders, Elmore has spoken to more than 300,000 students, faculty, and staff on hundreds of campuses across the country, including the University of Oklahoma, Stanford University, Duke University, Rutgers University, the University of South Carolina, and Louisiana State University. Elmore has also provided leadership training and resources for multiple athletic programs, including the University of Texas football team, the University of Miami football team, the University of Alabama athletic department, and the Kansas City Royals Baseball Club. In addition, a number of government offices in Washington, D.C. have utilized Dr. Elmore's curriculum.

From the classroom to the boardroom, Elmore is a dynamic communicator who uses principles, images, and stories to strengthen leaders. He has taught leadership to Chick-fil-A, Inc., The Home Depot, HomeBanc, and Gold Kist, Inc., among others. He has also taught courses on leadership and mentoring at nine universities and graduate schools across the U.S. Committed to developing young leaders on every continent of the world, Elmore also has shared his insights in more than thirty countries—including India, Russia, China, and Australia.

Other Books by Tim Elmore

Habitudes®: Images That Form Leadership Habits and Attitudes (four volumes)

Nurturing the Leader Within Your Child: What Every Parent Needs to Know

LifeGiving Mentors: A Guide to Investing Your Life in Others

Authentic Influence: Leading Without Titles

Wired for Influence: Skills to Lead Others

Intentional Influence: Investing Your Life in Others

A Life of Influence: Exploring Your Identity, Sharpening Your Focus

Leveraging Your Influence: Impacting College Students for the Kingdom

Leaders Everywhere: Creating a Leadership Culture

Portrait of a Leader (three volumes)

Pivotal Praying: Connecting with God in Times of Great Need

Soul Provider: Becoming a Confident Spiritual Leader

What's Gotten Into You?

52 Leadership Ideas You Can Use with Students

HABITUDES®

IMAGES THAT FORM LEADERSHIP HABITS & ATTITUDES

We've all heard it before:
a picture is worth a thousand words.

Habitudes is a "sticky" way to learn what it means to be a healthy, effective leader. They teach leadership with the power of an image, a conversation and an experience. *Specifically designed for Gen iY,* they are a fun, creative and engaging way for students to learn and practice leadership.

VALUES-BASED HABITUDES | FAITH-BASED HABITUDES | ATHLETIC HABITUDES

"Tim Elmore's masterful usage of visual, cognitive and experiential learning tools makes Habitudes one of the best teaching tools available."
—Dr. L. Keith Whitney/Chairperson of the Business Division, Pepperdine University

Join the conversation at

www.SaveTheirFutureNow.com.

- ■ **Sign our Commitment Wall.**

- ■ **Download additional study materials**

- ■ **Explore free resources for Parents, Educators, Employers, Pastors and others.**

- ■ **Connect with others who want to Save Generation iY.**

- ■ **Discover opportunities to really make a difference.**

Share *Generation iY* with your faculty, church, parenting group, staff and others who can help us save their future.

to **www.SaveTheirFutureNow.com/Bulk** for special pricing on orders of 24 copies or more.